LIFE AND WORK IN BENARES AND KUMAON 1839-1877

LIFE AND WORK
IN
BENARES AND KUMAON
1839-1877

JAMES KENNEDY

WITH AN INTRODUCTORY NOTE
SIR WILLIAM MUIR

ILLUSTRATED

GYAN

Published by

Gyan Publishing House
5, Ansari Road
Daryaganj, New Delhi-110002
Phone: 011-47034999, 9811692060
E-mail: books@gyanbooks.com

Distribution Network
gyanbooks.com
India, USA, Canada, UK, Australia, France

ISBN : 978-81-212-3711-6 (PB)
First Published, London, 1884

2nd Impression 2020

Printed at: Gyan Press, Delhi.

Life and Work
in
Benares and Kumaon
Author: James Kennedy

LIFE AND WORK

IN

BENARES AND KUMAON

1839—1877

BY

JAMES KENNEDY, M.A.

Late Missionary of the London Missionary Society, Author of "Christianity and the Religions of India," &c.

WITH AN INTRODUCTORY NOTE

BY

SIR WILLIAM MUIR, K.C.S.I., LL.D., D.C.L.

Late Lieutenant-Governor North-Western Provinces of India

ILLUSTRATED

London

T FISHER UNWIN

26 PATERNOSTER SQUARE E.C.

1884

UNION CHURCH, RANEE KHET.

PREFACE.

THE history of this volume can be given in a few words. Months ago I said to a beloved relative that during the greater part of my life I had more to do than I could well accomplish, and that now, with health and strength in a measure restored, I sometimes thought I had not enough to do. He said: "Why not write the reminiscences of your Indian life?" The counsel struck me as good, and I have acted on it.

My theme has not the advantage of novelty: I cannot tell of a new country explored, and a new people brought within the knowledge of the world; but it has the advantage of greatness and variety. I am not aware that any book on Indian Missions has achieved signal success. I do not think, however, a single one has been written in vain. That must have been a singularly poor book on so great a subject which has not had something in it fitted to interest and inform readers. That must have been a very solitary, lonely missionary, who has had no friends ready to listen to what he has had to say. These books may have received little general attention; but here and there, as the result of their perusal, there has been a more intelligent apprehension of our work, deeper sympathy with us, and heartier support rendered to us. I have ventured to add a volume to those already published in the hope that it may do some good before it passes into the oblivion which necessarily awaits most of the productions of the press.

A glance at the contents of this volume will show it takes up a number of subjects, some of which are merely touched in most books on Missions, and others not at all. Reminiscences, especially when they spread over many years, and embrace great events, admit of very discursive treatment. They leave the writer unfettered to take up any subject within his wide scope which he may deem fitted to interest his readers. I have allowed myself the freedom thus afforded me. My aim has been to take my readers with me to our Indian home, to see us at our work, to hear us conversing with the people, to accompany us on our journeys, to surround them in thought with our surroundings, so that they may realize our position, trials, difficulties, and joys. I have throughout maintained the standpoint of one whose Indian life has been devoted to Mission work. My two spheres of labour—Benares during the greater part of my course, and Ranee Khet, in the Hill Province of Kumaon, in later years—have come in for extended remark.

My attention has not, however, been confined to Missions. I have endeavoured to write as one interested in everything which ought to interest a resident in the land. I have given some account of the climate, aspect of the country, condition and character of the people, changes which have taken place, modes of travelling, and the British Government. I have again and again travelled in the North-West, and some account of these journeys has been given. On one occasion I spent the greater part of two months in Ceylon, and to that beautiful island a chapter is devoted.

I have recorded at some length my experiences of the Indian Mutiny of 1857. No one who was in that terrible storm can ever forget it; and the European inhabitants of Benares at that time have special reason for thankfulness for their marvellous escape.

I have found it convenient to follow, as a rule, the chronological order, but I have not kept closely to it. When recording the more remote past, the nearer past has been continually coming into view, and the contrast has found expression.

Indian names are written as ordinary English readers would pronounce them, in preference to using the diacritical marks with which I have been long familiar in the writing of Hindustanee in the Roman character. The term "Hindu" is so established that I have used it in preference to "Hindoo."

At the end of this book the reader will find statistics fraught with interest to all who wish to understand the great Indian problem in its many aspects.

It is impossible to keep one's self out of view in a work like this; but I hope the candid reader will give me credit for saying as little of myself, family, and doings as is compatible with the conditions under which I have written.

I beg to dedicate this book to the friends of Christian Missions, in the hope it may increase the interest of some in that great Continent, with its teeming population, which has in God's providence come under the rule of our land, and has special claims on our prayers, sympathy, and efforts. I cannot doubt that my Indian friends, both those who have come back to England and those who are still in India, will give a kindly reception to the volume. They will, I believe, confirm the general accuracy of my statements, and to a large extent acquiesce in my views. With them so long as my heart beats it will go forth in heartiest wishes and fervent prayer for the land with which our past has so inseparably bound us.

J K.

ACTON, *August*, 1884.

CONTENTS.

CHAPTER VI.

First Year in Benares (continued).

CHAPTER VII.

The City of Benares.

CHAPTER VIII.

Benares as a Mission Sphere.

CHAPTER IX.

Second Year in Benares.

CHAPTER X.

The Religious Gatherings of the Hindus.

CHAPTER XI.

The Object of Christian Missions.

CHAPTER XII.

Mission Schools.

CHAPTER XIII.

Orphanages.

CHAPTER XIV.

Mission Tours.

CHAPTER XV.

From 1847 to 1857.

CHAPTER XVI.

The Mutiny, 1857 *and* 1858.

CHAPTER XVII.

The Mutiny (continued).

CHAPTER XVIII.

*Visit to Ceylon—*1858 *and* 1859.

CHAPTER XIX.

From 1859 *to* 1868.

CHAPTER XX.

From 1868 *to* 1877. *Kumaon.*

CHAPTER XXIX.

Hindus.

CHAPTER XXX.

Europeans in India.

CHAPTER XXXI.

The Government of India.

LIST OF ILLUSTRATIONS.

PREFATORY NOTE.

NEITHER the author nor his book stands in need of any introduction to the public. But having been asked for such, I cheerfully respond. During his long residence in the North-Western Provinces of India, where I myself happened to reside, ample opportunities were afforded me of knowing and observing the Rev. Jas. Kennedy and his work. And I am therefore able, and glad, to say that no man was ever better placed than he was for gaining a thorough acquaintance with Hindustan and the various races inhabiting it, during the four decades of which he treats. I have met with none whose calm and sagacious judgment might more surely enable him to form correct conclusions, nor whose high and scrupulous principle should impart to the reader greater confidence in the fair and truthful statement of them.

I regard this book as possessing a rare interest, not only for the missionary student, but equally so for the general reader. The amount of information it contains, descriptive, social, evangelistic, and even political, is astonishing; and the discursive and, in part, autobiographical form in which it is written, renders it so easy, that he who runs may read. The contrast is drawn graphically, and with a light and lively pen, between the state of things fifty years ago and that which now prevails: the exchange of slow and cumbrous means of conveyance for those which enable you in these days to perform the journey of weeks in, you might say, as many hours; and the not less marked advance in education and intelligence. The retrospect, material as well as moral, social, and religious, is useful in many ways.

But that which lends its chief value to this work is the faithful picture of missionary labour—its trials and difficulties, its results, rewards, and prospects. During the considerable period brought under review, standing by, as I did, and looking carefully on, I can unhesitatingly attest, as a whole, the correctness of my friend's statements, and the reasonableness of the lessons he would draw therefrom. This book should be read by every one who wishes to acquaint himself with the attitude of Christian agencies towards the people of India, and of these towards the Gospel. There is here a fertile field of facts and materials for thought. The author resorts to no roseate colouring, nor any kind of varnish. Nothing is unduly sanguine. All is tempered by sound judgment and wise discretion.

If I may add a word from my own experience, it is this—Let my fellow-countrymen and countrywomen in India give their countenance to the Missionaries labouring around them. They well deserve it, but too often are allowed to stand alone. The loss is theirs who keep aloof, and neglect the man and his work. While our people are running to and fro in the busy whirl of Indian life—some hasting to be rich, others engrossed in the labours of administration—higher things are too frequently forgotten. The spiritual life is prone to fade and droop. Many men —and women as well as men—who would at home be cultivating some corner of the Master's vineyard, begin to forget that similar obligations follow after them in their private walk and life abroad. Against these deteriorating tendencies, to mingle with the missionary band affords a wholesome antidote. For myself, I can never be thankful enough that in my early Indian life I found valued friends in the missionary circle, not only of the highest mental culture, but of a devoted Christian heart; and was privileged with their intimacy to the end. Among them I cannot refrain from naming such noble Missionaries as Perkins, Smith, and Leupolt, French, Stuart, Welland, and Shackell, Owen, Humphrey, Budden and Watt, Hoernle, and Pfander—that grand apologist to the Mahometans—all of whose friendship I enjoyed, as well as that of the Author himself. If some of these were men the like of whom we may not soon look upon again—a galaxy of rare appearance—yet, as we may learn from these pages, the field is in the present day stocked even more plentifully than ever it was before. Opportunities of cultivating in this field Christian friendship—and may I not add Christian work, and that for Ladies also—are happily multiplying all around; and I can promise an ample reward to such as make a faithful use of them.

In conclusion, I will only say that I am much mistaken if this work fails to take its place as a standard book of reference in every library of missionary labour and Christian work abroad.

W. MUIR.

16th September, 1884.

CHAPTER I.

VOYAGE TO INDIA.

IN 1837 I was accepted by the London Missionary Society as one of its agents. On September 15, 1838, I embarked at Portsmouth with thirty other passengers on the *Duke of Buccleugh*, a vessel of 650 tons burthen, and landed in Calcutta on January 19, 1839, *en route* to Benares, to which I had been appointed. The only land we sighted from Portsmouth to Saugar Island was a rock in the Indian Ocean. The time we thus spent at sea was four months and five days. Every now and then speedier voyages were made, but a few years previously this voyage would have been deemed rapid. The *Duke of Buccleugh*, on her next voyage to India, went to pieces on a sandbank at the mouth of the Hoogly, but happily the weather was moderate, and passengers and crew were saved.

The route by the Cape of Good Hope has been abandoned for passengers for many years, and now Bombay is reached by the Straits of Gibraltar and the Suez Canal in a month, sometimes in less, while another week is required for the voyage to Calcutta. Those who travel with the Indian mails across the Continent of Europe can reach their port in less than three weeks, and distant parts of India by rail in four weeks or less.

All on board—officials returning to their posts, and persons going out for the first time—were delighted to find the voyage coming to an end; but new-comers like myself were under the spell of novelty, which gave new interest to everything we saw. At Kedgeree, near the mouth of the Hoogly, the Post Office boat came to our ship with welcome letters from friends, who were looking out for our arrival. The level land on each side of the river, with its rich tropical vegetation; the numerous villages on the banks, with their beehive-like huts; the craft on the river, large and small, many of them so heavily laden as to bring them down almost to the water's edge; the little boats, with plantains and other fruits, which tried to attach themselves to our ship in the hope of getting purchasers; the strange appearance of the people, with their only covering of cloth round the middle—all gave us a thrill of excitement which can be known only in similar circumstances. Then, we were about to set foot on the great land, of which we had read much, to which we had looked with the deepest interest, and where we purposed to spend our days in the service of Christ. Though so many years have since elapsed, we can yet vividly remember the peculiar feeling of that time.

The day before we landed, the Native agent of the mercantile house to which our ship was consigned made his appearance with letters and fresh supplies. To the surprise of us new-comers, roast beef was on our dinner-table that day. We thought it strange that in the land where the cow was worshipped, beef should be one of the first things brought to us.

Our missionary friends in Calcutta had heard of the arrival of our ship, and arranged for our accommodation. Some of them came on board when we anchored in the

Hoogly, off Fort William, and gave us a hearty welcome. We were right glad to find ourselves on land again.

Calcutta is a hundred miles from the sea, but the country is so level that the tide runs up in great strength many miles beyond, and the tidal wave, which comes in at certain times, is very dangerous to small craft, and requires care on the part of large ships. The great trade of the city is shown by the vast number of ships at anchor in the river, many of them stately vessels of large tonnage, of which in our day many are steamers.

On landing, a stranger gets the impression that Calcutta is rightly called the city of palaces. On the great plain adjoining the river, at some distance from each other, are two notable objects—Fort William and Government House. Beyond the plain lies Chowringhee, a range of lofty houses extending for more than a mile, with balconies and flat roofs, giving one an impression of grandeur, which is scarcely sustained when more nearly seen, as that which looked at a distance like marble is found to be stucco and plaster. Behind Chowringhee are a number of wide streets with similar, but generally smaller houses, each apart, with offices and servants' houses in the enclosure. When entering the city one sees that strange combination of meanness and dirt with grandeur with which travellers in Eastern lands are so familiar. In the neighbourhood of Government House there are a number of shops in the European fashion, but a very large proportion of the business of Calcutta, we suppose the most of it, is carried on in bazaars, in which there are no showy shops, but where there is abundance of goods of every description. When we went to India, and for many years afterwards, in front of these shops were open sewers, over which customers had to pass on slabs of stone. Amidst houses for Europeans, even in the most aristocratic part of the city, were native houses of every description, many of them miserable grass huts.

Since the time of which I speak, some forty-five years ago, Calcutta has been greatly improved. It has been drained, supplied with good water, instead of being dependent on great open tanks, to which all had access, which no arrangement could keep tolerably pure, and is lit with gas. Open sewers are no longer to be seen, and from the best parts of the city many native houses have disappeared. The changes effected must conduce immensely to the health and comfort of the inhabitants. There is no part of India, we suppose, free from the plague of the musquito, but in all my Indian life I have not been so much tormented in any place by it as I have been in Calcutta. It adds insult to injury. If it would only bite, sharp though its bite be, one could put up with it; but before it bites, and after, it goes on buzzing, as if mocking you, and evades every attempt to catch it. The last time we were there musquitoes were comparatively few, and they seemed to have lost much of their former mischievous vigour. We suppose the improved sanitary arrangements have not agreed with them.

When in Calcutta everything reminded us that we had left our own country behind, though not all our own people. We saw them on every side, but they were a mere handful in the midst of a strange people in a strange land, where man and nature presented entirely new aspects. The look of the people, the exceedingly scanty dress of the labouring class, and the long flowing robes of those in better circumstances, the marks on the foreheads and arms of the Hindus, showing the gods whose worshippers they were, their processions with noisy, unmusical music, the public buildings of the people, the mosques of the Muhammadans, and the temples of the Hindus, with a church here and there to show that Christianity had also its shrines—all brought to our view characteristics of the great land on which we had entered. Bombay, since the opening of the Suez Canal, has made progress which somewhat affects the pre-eminence of Calcutta among the cities of India, but it still remains the capital of British India—I ought rather to say of India—and its position will continue to make it, what it has been in the past, a vast emporium of commerce, the abode of a great population, and a place of most stirring activity. It continues to be the resort of persons of every civilized, and almost every semi-civilized, nation on the face of the earth.

My stay in Calcutta of six weeks was longer than I had anticipated, but my time was very pleasantly and profitably spent. A few days after arrival a united prayer-meeting was held : missionaries of all societies were present, the attendance was large, the spirit was earnest and devout, and I then began to realize, what it was my happiness to realize more fully afterwards, the uniting power of the missionary enterprise. I had the happiness of attending services with Native Christians, and of joining them in spirit, though not with understanding. I was especially interested in the noble Missionary Institution of the Church of Scotland, and in the smaller, but promising, school of our own Society. I felt as if the sight of such a number of boys and young men, many of them with most pleasing and intelligent countenances, all learning our language, and, what is vastly better, all taught from the Word of God, was enough in itself to repay one for the long voyage to India. I heard them examined, and was surprised at the knowledge of English possessed by some of them, at the extent of their Biblical knowledge, and at the Christian tone with which they gave replies to questions. I asked a tall, slightly built young man, with a most intelligent face, dressed in the flowing white robe of his people, who had spoken with what struck me as the accent of conviction, "Are you a Christian?" to which he replied, "Yes, in heart; but I fear persecution." To this subject of schools I shall have often occasion to revert in the course of my reminiscences.

During my stay in Calcutta I had much pleasant intercourse with missionaries of different Societies. I was the guest of Mr. Boaz, afterwards Dr. Boaz, of Union Chapel, by whom I was treated with much kindness. Mr. Gogerly had been my fellow-passenger to India. Mr. Lacroix and Mr. Piffard were, at that time, the senior missionaries of our Society in Calcutta. Both were admirable men. Mr. Piffard was a gentleman of property, who devoted himself to missionary work, and laboured for many years most faithfully, without requiring to take, and without taking, any salary from the Society. A short time afterwards he was suddenly carried off by cholera. Mr. Lacroix lived for many years. I had the pleasure of meeting him in my visits to Calcutta, and in his visits to the North-west, and also of frequent correspondence with him. He was esteemed and loved as few have been. He was a man with a commanding presence, tall and well-built, and had a geniality of manner which won all hearts. He spoke and wrote English remarkably well, with a slight foreign accent and sprightliness, an *elan*, as our French friends call it, which told of his French birth and upbringing. He had a thorough knowledge of the Bengalee language, and used it with a commanding eloquence, to which his voice, look, and gesture greatly contributed. His last illness, the result of his long residence in the enervating climate of Bengal, was borne with Christian patience, and drew forth the sympathy and kindly inquiry of all classes. At his funeral such tokens of respect and love were rendered to him by every class of the community, Native and European, as have been seldom witnessed in Calcutta.

Like all newly-arrived missionaries in Calcutta, I made a pilgrimage to Serampore. The illustrious trio—Carey, Marshman, and Ward—whose names are indissolubly connected with that place, as first their refuge and, for many years afterwards, the scene of their plans and labours for the evangelization of India, had passed away by that time (January, 1839), but the Rev. John Mack, who had been long associated with them, and Mr. John Marshman, Dr. Marshman's eldest son, remained. I was taken by Mr. Mack to the college, the printing-office, the type manufactory, the paper manufactory, the mission chapel, the station church, Dr. Carey's garden, and the native Christian village, indeed, to every object of interest about the place. I remember seeing an elderly man engaged in type-making, and observing a little image in a niche above him. I was told this man had been many years in this department of work, and had remained so strict a Hindu that he would work only under the protection of his god. The teaching of the missionaries had had no effect in weaning him from his ancestral idolatry. Yet many were won to Christ by the Scriptures and books, for the preparation of which the work of this man, and of others of his class, was indispensable.

When visiting Serampore, and hearing from Mr. Mack

of the doings and achievements of the great men whose residence at Serampore has given it a sacredness it will ever retain in the annals of Indian Missions, I felt as a young Greek would feel on being taken to Marathon and Thermopylæ. I felt I was entering on a war, where there had been heroes before me, which demanded courage and endurance of a far higher order than had ever been enlisted in the cause of patriotism.

CHAPTER II.

VOYAGE TO BENARES.

March, 1839.

I LEFT myself in the hands of friends in Calcutta as to the best mode of proceeding to my destination. There were at that time three modes of travelling to the North-Western Provinces. One was being carried in a palanquin on men's shoulders, arrangements being made to have fresh bearers every few miles. For a long journey of more than four hundred miles to Benares this was at once a very tedious and fatiguing mode of travelling. To one who knew not a word of the language of the people in whose hands one was to be for days it was additionally trying. Yet not a few persons newly arrived, some of them delicate ladies, did travel in that mode to far more distant places than Benares, and very seldom any mishap befell them. In this mode little more could be taken in the way of luggage than necessary clothing.

Another mode was by the river in a native boat, with a crew engaged to take the party to their destination. Not a few travelled in this way, even to Delhi. Weeks, often months, were spent on the voyage; great inconveniences were endured, and not infrequently great perils encountered from the sudden storms to which voyagers on the Ganges are exposed, from the strong and eddying currents in some parts of the river, and perhaps most of all from the treacherous character of the boatmen. In 1841 and 1842 a severe storm fell on a large fleet of boats taking a European regiment to the north-west. Many of the boats were wrecked, and, if I remember rightly, about three hundred men lost their lives.

There was a third mode of proceeding to the north-west. A few years previously a River Steam Company had been formed for the transmission of passengers and goods. Passengers were accommodated in flats drawn by steamers. As the Ganges enters Bengal it breaks into a number of streams, by which it makes its way to the ocean. The Hoogly, on which Calcutta stands, is one of these streams. Some of them are so shallow at certain seasons that native boats of considerable size cannot find sufficient water, and they are at that time impassable for steamers, though so constructed as to have the least possible draught. The result is that the steamers for the north-west (we believe none ply now) had to make a great detour, to go down the Hoogly to Saugor Island, and then to proceed by one of the channels there found to the main stream. This greatly increased the distance to the north-west. Except in the rainy season, steamers for Benares had to go about eight hundred miles.

Of these three routes this one of the river steamers was in many respects the most convenient and pleasant, especially for persons new in the country, and my Calcutta friends kindly arranged that I should be sent on in this way. I accordingly embarked for Benares on a flat, tugged by a steamer, in the first week of March. After going down the Hoogly to Saugor Island, we made our way into the district called the Sunderbuns by one of the channels of the Ganges. We got into a labyrinth of streams, every here and there opening up into a wide reach of water, giving one the impression we were entering a lake; and shortly afterwards we found ourselves in a channel so narrow that we almost touched the banks on both sides, and which barely allowed a passage where there was a sharp turn in the stream. We had native pilots who knew the region thoroughly, and were in no danger of going astray. The land down to the water's edge was covered with the densest tropical vegetation, so that the banks often bounded our view, except when the trees on it were lower than those beyond. In the waters and out, wild beasts abound. Alligators were seen dropping from the banks into the stream on hearing the approach of the steamer. We saw no tigers, but we heard much about them as we were threading our way through that region. The previous year, early one morning, the watch on the deck of the flat was startled by a tiger leaping on board, and, evidently bewildered by its new circumstances, leaping off on the other side. Messrs. Lacroix and Gogerly, when on a native boat in the Sunderbuns, were witnesses of a desperate fight between a tiger and an alligator. The story has been often told.

Less than two centuries ago there was a large population in what may be called that amphibious region, the soil when cleared being very rich; but owing to the incursions of Mug pirates from the coast of Burmah, and the oppression of Muhammadan rulers of Bengal, the most of the inhabitants perished, others fled, and so complete was the ruin that the exact site of once prosperous cities is unknown. In a region like the Sunderbuns, when man's restraining and improving hand is withdrawn every trace of his presence disappears under the rank vegetation, which speedily covers the sphere of his labours. The country, under British protection, was in 1839 beginning to be reoccupied. Patches of ground were reclaimed from the jungle, and since that time cultivation has been greatly extended. We occasionally met native boats, and were thus reminded we were not the only human begins in that district. Nearly a week elapsed before we emerged from the Sunderbuns.

Our passengers were a motley band. Between twenty and thirty were Europeans, two or three were Eurasians, and there was a company of Sepoys under a native officer in charge of treasure. Most of the Sepoys were Hindus, and as they cannot cook on the water, which is forbidden by caste-law, they were obliged to subsist as they best could on dry grain. The Muhammadans had no convenience for cooking on the flat, but they were allowed partial use of the steamer. All were delighted when they got into the open country, and could get on shore at night to prepare their meals.

The steamer and flat were brought to anchor at all the important towns on the river, for lading and unlading goods and for landing passengers, of whom very few left us, as most were bound for Benares and Allahabad. When evening came on we always anchored, wherever we might be. We saw a little of Bhagulpore, Monghyr, Dinapore, Patna, Ghazeepore, and some other places. At Monghyr I spent a very pleasant evening with Mr. Leslie of the Baptist Mission, even then of considerable standing, and years afterwards a highly esteemed veteran in the missionary host.

Our progress was slow. In some places the stream was too strong for our steamer tugging the flat, and in other places the water was too shallow. Sometimes we got for hours, in one case for a whole day, on sandbanks, from which we got off with great difficulty. The most memorable incident of the voyage was a storm, which came on us one evening as we were nearing Dinapore. There was so little warning of its approach that we, who knew not the climate, were quite unprepared for its coming. Before breaking on us we were brought to a standstill, the flat was separated from the steamer, and both flat and steamer were brought to anchor. The sky suddenly became dark, we heard puffs of wind, and then the storm burst on us in all its fury. The dust was so raised that we could see only a few feet from the flat, and the flat so rolled that every now and then a splash of water came in at the windows. A scene of great confusion ensued. Some Indo-Portuguese servants were on their knees, imploring Mary—"Mariam, Mariam!"—to save them. The Hindus were loud in their appeals to "Ram, Ram!" while the Muhammadans shouted "Allah, Allah!" A newly arrived English lady almost fainted from fright, and her husband tried to calm and assure her. Every face indicated anxiety. In less than an hour all was over, and we were thankful to find ourselves once more in safety.

Before leaving England I had possessed myself of a Hindustanee Grammar, and in Calcutta of a Hindustanee Dictionary. On the voyage to India I did not make much of the grammar, but on the way to Benares I gave myself resolutely to learning the language. I found a young native officer on the flat who knew a little English, and who professed to be a good Hindustanee scholar. I got the consent of the native officer in command to his coming to my cabin when off duty, and I spent hours daily with him, trying to get my tongue about the strange sounds, with which I knew I must be familiar if I was to do the work for which I had come to India. I received great help from this young Muhammadan, and felt as if I was beginning to get my foot into the language before reaching my destination.

On the three Sabbaths I was on the river I had the pleasure of preaching to the Europeans on board.

A voyage on the Ganges does not enable one to see much of the country. The banks are often very high; in many places there is a great extent of sand; the country, with the exception of the district where the main stream is entered, is very level, and the country is therefore very imperfectly seen. The native craft, so unlike the vessels of our own country, with their lofty prows and sterns, and great ragged square sails, many laden with wood and grass, which made them like moving stacks, were constant objects of interest.

At length, after more than three weeks on board, we were delighted one Sunday forenoon to see in the distance the domes and minarets of Benares.

CHAPTER III.

ARRIVAL AT BENARES.

ON Sabbath, March 31, 1839, we came to anchor at the northern end of Benares, at a place called Raj Ghat, the ferry connecting the city on the left bank of the river with the Trunk road on the right, leading to Behar and Bengal. Near this place the most of the native craft employed in the city traffic is moored. Many of the vessels are of considerable size.

For hours Benares had been in sight, but owing to the strength of the stream our progress had been slow. It was early afternoon by the time of our arrival. In so public a place as Raj Ghat there are always a number of people, but the early afternoon is a time when few bathe, and there is a lull in the stir of the community. As the afternoon comes on, and the evening advances, there is fresh activity. We therefore, on landing, saw little of the scene with which we were afterwards to become familiar.

Word of the approach of our steamer and flat had reached Secrole, the European suburb of Benares, three miles inland, and no sooner had we come to anchor than the agent of the Steam Company and the friends of expected passengers came on board. Among these was the Rev. William Smith of the Baptist Mission, whose house was on the high bank immediately above Raj Ghat, and who had been requested by my brethren of the London Missionary Society to be on the look-out for me. This good man gave me a kindly welcome, and took me with him to his house, built very much in the native fashion, with flat roof, with small, low rooms entering from one into another, and a verandah extending along its front, from which a commanding view was obtained of the river and craft below, the country on the other side of the river, and a part of the front of the city. Immediately behind the house was the chapel, in which daily worship was conducted.

The first thing I saw on getting to Mr. Smith's house was the chapel crowded with very poor-looking people, of whom a number were blind and lame. I was told these were beggars, who came every Lord's-day to receive a dole, either pice or dry grain, from the missionary and his wife, and who listened very patiently to an address before the dole was given. This service was kept up for many years, and there was no falling off in the attendance. Those who have read the life of Henry Martyn, and others of the early missionary period in India, know that they ministered to this class. Here were persons whose destitution appealed directly to the Christian heart, and who were content to be present when the gospel message was delivered, while little access to others could be obtained. How far these poor people heard it would be difficult to say. I am afraid few heard with any desire to understand and consider what was said, but there is every reason to believe some did obtain lasting spiritual good. We have heard of instances of genuine conversion, though it must be admitted these were rare; and it must be also acknowledged there were instances of pretended conversion, when the life soon proved that the motive for seeking baptism was entirely sordid. Still the work in itself was worthy of the followers of Christ, and could not fail to make a favourable impression, not only on the persons helped, but on the community around. Almsgiving stands high among virtues in the estimation of both Hindus and Muhammadans; it is considered sufficient to atone for many sins, and it is practised so indiscriminately as to pauperize many who could provide for themselves. It is unfit that Christianity should seem less careful of those who are really poor and helpless than Hinduism and Muhammadanism are. Work such as I saw in Mr. Smith's chapel is carried on in some places down to the present time.

A short time after our arrival at Raj Ghat my dear friend the Rev. W. P. Lyon appeared, and took me in his conveyance by a road skirting the city to the Mission House in Secrole, which he then occupied. From Mr. and Mrs. Lyon, both of whom I had known intimately for years in our own land, I received a hearty welcome.

At the corner of the mission compound, facing the public road, was the humble chapel, built of sun-dried bricks, in which service was conducted in the native language. I arrived half an hour before the time for the afternoon service. Before its commencement I had the pleasure of meeting Messrs. Buyers and Shurman, with whom I was to be for years associated in mission work. With them I went to the service, which was conducted by Mr. Shurman. There were at that time only two or three native Christians connected with the mission, and these, with their families, the missionaries and their wives, and a few orphan children, constituted the congregation. I had just enough of the language to catch an expression here and there, and from my ignorance of what was said my mind was left at greater freedom for realizing my new and strange position.

I had just had a glance of the sacred city of the Hindus. I had seen at a short distance the domes of some of the principal temples, and the minarets of some of the principal mosques, especially those of the mosque built by Aurungzeb, soaring far above every other object in the city. I had dimly seen the bathing-places of the people stretching away for miles, and the houses on the high bank of the river. As I landed I had seen a few bathing, and a number moving about.

And now, in this poor chapel, with its low roof and earthen floor, I found a few assembled for the worship of the living God through the Lord Jesus Christ. I realized, as I had not done before, that I had left my native land behind, and had come among a people the vast majority of whom were wholly given to idolatry, and the rest followers of Muhammad, the bitter enemies of my Lord and Saviour. The greatness and difficulty of the missionary enterprise presented themselves to me with a painful vividness, and but for the conviction that the work was of God, and that my long-cherished desire to enter on it and the gratification of my desire in my appointment to Benares had come from Him, I should have been ready to retrace my steps. Yet here I was, worshipping with a few persons who had been idolaters, and one of whom at least had made great sacrifices when he had avowed his faith in Jesus. Why should we despise the day of small things? Forty-four years have elapsed since that, to me, memorable 31st of March, 1839, and I can now realize myself sittting with Messrs. Buyers and Lyon in front of that humble pulpit, while Mr.

Shurman preached, and remember, as if it were yesterday, the strange feelings that thrilled me that afternoon.

I had to make no arrangement for my accommodation on reaching Benares. Previous to my arrival it had been arranged that I was to take up my abode with my dear friends, Mr. and Mrs. Lyon. I was at once at home with them, for Mr. Lyon had been my fellow-student at Glasgow, and Mrs. Lyon was the member of a family with whom I had been intimately acquainted while studying at Edinburgh. Within a few days of my arrival I was introduced to the missionaries of the Church Missionary Society, and to a few European residents who took an interest in missionary work.

CHAPTER IV.

CHRISTIAN MISSIONS IN BENARES.

FROM 1816 TO 1839.

IT may be well to give, before proceeding further, a brief account of what had been done for the evangelization of Benares up to that time.

Our Baptist brethren were first in the field. All who have read the biography of the illustrious trio of Serampore are aware that they formed, and with ardent zeal and untiring energy prosecuted, great schemes for the evangelization of the millions to whose spiritual good they had consecrated their lives. The translation of the Scriptures into the languages of India was their special service, but it was far from standing alone. They were fully alive to the importance of preparing and sending out men of God to go among the people, and make known to them Jesus as the Saviour of the world. They gladly availed themselves of Europeans, Eurasians, and natives, who seemed qualified for the work by Christian character, zeal for the conversion of the people, and aptness to teach, though, with few exceptions, destitute of any considerable measure of mental culture. Some of these agents had force of character and native talent, and much good and useful work was accomplished by them. One of their number was Mr. Bowley, who afterwards joined the Church Mission, and was for many years located at Chunar. He translated the entire Scriptures into Hindee, and did beside much excellent literary work in the translation and composition of books and tracts. As he had no knowledge of Greek and Hebrew, his translation of the Bible has marked defects, though from his knowledge of Hindee and his good judgment it has also marked excellences. His translation of the New Testament is now largely superseded, but his translation of the Old Testament is the only one yet possessed. The style of his smaller works in Hindustanee, or Urdu, as it is commonly called, is remarkably idiomatic and pleasing.

Missionary work was commenced in Benares by Mr. William Smith, who was sent to it by the Serampore missionaries in 1816. I have already mentioned him as having welcomed me on my arrival. He secured a house for himself at Raj Ghat, the northern boundary of the city, with a crowded population around him, and there till his death he lived with his family, during all the period diligently prosecuting his missionary work. He had been a drummer in the native army, spoke the Hindustanee as his mother tongue, and belonged to the large class who, having European blood in their veins, are professing Christians, but as to their ordinary habits of life are more native than European. Mr. Smith was a man of limited education and of little talent, but of sterling excellence, and secured the respect and love of all classes of the native community by his kindly and consistent life. For years before his death there was in his house the strange spectacle of five generations, and his great-great-grandmother was heard by a friend of mine murmuring, "It looks as if God had forgotten to take me away." Mrs. Smith, who was, I believe, a pure native, was a woman of remarkable energy, and exercised a powerful influence for good on all connected with her. Owing to the unhappy controversy between the Serampore missionaries and the Baptist Missionary Society, and the separation in which it ended, Mr. Smith was left for a time without any salary; but by the establishment of a Eurasian boarding-school his wants were fully supplied. On to old age he moved about among the people, conversing with them, going to their great religious gatherings and distributing tracts and portions of the Scriptures in a very quiet, unostentatious manner, and succeeded, by God's blessing, in bringing a few into the fold of Christ.

Among the pioneers of modern missionary work in India the late Bishop Corrie, of Madras, has a high and honoured name. He was one of the small band of Government chaplains who gave themselves heart and soul to the work of diffusing the gospel among the native population. Henry Martyn is the best known of this band, and with him men like Brown, Thomason, and Corrie deserve to be held in everlasting remembrance. Mr. Corrie was, in 1817, the chaplain of the European community in Benares. Previous to that time a rich native, Rajah Jay Narayan, had established and endowed a school in the part of the city inhabited chiefly by Bengalees. This Rajah formed so high an opinion of Mr. Corrie, and of his ability to carry on the school efficiently, that he asked him to undertake its management. Mr. Corrie accepted the offer in the name of the Church Missionary Society, whose sanction to the measure he had obtained, and to it the school was made over by formal deed of gift in 1818. Under the name of Jay Narayan's School, and afterwards of Jay Narayan's

College, it has continued down to our day; and it has done much for the education, on Christian principles, of successive generations of Benares youth. A Mr. Adlington was the first head-master, and a short time afterwards a missionary was sent. He was succeeded by others, but owing to their failure of health little was done on to the fourth decade of the century, except the securing of suitable ground and the erection of mission-houses at Segra, in the immediate suburbs of the city on its south-western side. This place had formerly been noted for the thieves and thugs that infested it. In 1839 the two missionaries at Segra were the Rev. William Smith and the Rev. C. B. Leupolt. Mr. Smith reached India in 1830, and after spending fifteen months in Goruckpore, on the borders of Nepal, was transferred to Benares in 1832. He was joined by Messrs. Knorpp and Leupolt in 1833. The two Church missionaries in Benares in 1839, Messrs. Smith and Leupolt, laboured for many years afterwards with singular devotedness for the spiritual good of the people. As it is invidious to make comparisons, I will not say that they were foremost in the first rank; but all who knew them will bear me out in saying they they attained a high place in the first rank of the missionary band..

The Rev. Matthew Thomson Adam was appointed by the London Missionary Society to Benares in October 1819, and reached his destination in August, 1820. He remained at his post till 1830, when he returned to England, and resigned his connection with the Society. He afterwards went to the United States, where he undertook a pastorate. Mr. Adam was a scholarly and diligent man. He prepared and published a Hindee Grammar, an English and Hindee Dictionary, and some tracts. He secured a site for a mission-house on the border of cantonment towards the city, and erected on it a commodious and substantial structure; and since his day a church, a school-house for girls, and houses for native Christians, have been erected in the mission compound. He also secured a very central site in cantonments for a place of worship for holding English services, and by the liberal help of the English military and civil residents erected on it a building which was called Union Chapel. His services among our country-men seem to have been greatly valued, but owing to a change in the *personnel* of the station, a change which is going on incessantly in India, the congregation fell off, Union Chapel was sold, and the money realized by the sale was spent on the erection of a chapel in the city, on a site obtained with great difficulty. Mr. Adam left Benares before this building, erected with a view to native services, could be turned to account. In a brief record of his labours drawn up by himself, he says that he deemed it a high honour to live near such a city, and to testify to his Master by pressing His claims on individuals with whom he had an opportunity of conversing; but he did not think it advisable to attempt the preaching of the gospel in places of public resort. He was at times encouraged by the prospect of persons becoming the followers of Christ, but in every case his hopes were disappointed. No native was baptized by him.

The London Mission of Benares was reinforced in 1826 by the arrival of the Rev. James Robertson. He was a man of linguistic talent, and was full of plans for setting up the standard of the Cross and assailing the idolatry around him. He opened a number of schools in various parts of the city, and organized a system of

Bible-reading in the streets. Seven men, chosen from among Hindus, whose sole qualification was ability to read, were appointed to read daily in different parts of the city our Scriptures without note or comment. We have no doubt they took care to tell their hearers that they did their work to please the sahib, and get his pay, but had no intention of accepting the new teaching, and had no wish that others should do so. No other missionary has followed this plan. Mr. Robertson left behind him in MS. translations into Urdu of a part of the Old Testament, which were carefully examined and partly used by Mr. Shurman; but the style was too difficult for any except those who were well acquainted with the Persian language.

The Rev. William Buyers joined the Mission at the beginning of 1832, and Mr. Robertson was carried off by cholera fifteen months afterwards, in his thirty-fourth year. Mr. Buyers was thus left alone, but early in 1834 he was joined by the Rev. J. A. Shurman and the Rev. Robert C. Mather. In 1838 the Rev. W. P. Lyon arrived at Benares, and that year Mr. Mather went to the great commercial Mirzapore, where he established, and for many years afterwards conducted with great efficiency, a very important mission. When I reached Benares I was thus the fourth on its staff, and the seventh from its commencement.

Much good work had been done by the brethren with whom I was to be associated. They had established schools for primary education, but owing to the want of funds all but one had been given up by 1839. They had taken part in preparing tracts and revising the translation of the New Testament in Urdu. A place of worship had been erected, and a few orphans had been gathered. Evangelistic work was being actively prosecuted in the city.

A short time previous to 1839 the Church Mission had undertaken a very benevolent and a very difficult work. In 1837 the North-Western Provinces were desolated by famine. Many thousands perished, everywhere miserable boys and girls were to be seen who had become orphans, or who had been abandoned by their parents. At this terrible crisis missions came forward with the offer of adopting these forsaken children. Fifty were made over to the Church Mission at Benares, and afterwards many more were added to this number. Suitable buildings were speedily erected for their accommodation, and arrangements were made for their education and support. These children were so emaciated that many died within a few days of their being brought to the mission. At the close of 1838 an excellent missionary and his wife, Mr. and Mrs. Knorpp, were carried off by a low fever which attacked them while attending to their charge. By the hot weather of 1839 the health of the orphans had greatly improved, and everything was being done which could be done for their temporal and spiritual welfare.

By the time of my arrival, the missionaries of the Church and London Missionary Societies—Mr. Lyon excepted, who had arrived only the preceding year—had fully entered on their work. They had been from seven to five years at their posts, had acquired a good knowledge of the native languages, had all the vigour and hopefulness of early middle life, and were giving themselves zealously to the prosecution of the great work for which they had gone to India.

CHAPTER V.

MY FIRST YEAR IN BENARES.

A STRANGER passing hurriedly through a country may carry away impressions about its climate, products, and people, which residence for a considerable time would not merely modify but reverse. There are some things of which he can speak with some confidence. The great natural features of a country, its mountains and plains and rivers, do not undergo any marked change, and these may be truly described by the casual visitor. The general aspect of a people, their houses, dress, and look, remain much the same, and of these an accurate observer may give a trustworthy account; but if from what he himself has seen and heard he attempts to give a general estimate of the character of the people and of the state of the country, he is almost sure to fall into great mistakes.

Within the last few years India has become a favourite field for travellers who can without inconvenience spend a few hundred pounds, and be absent from home three or four months. Swift steamers take them quickly to and from Bombay, and railways carry them in a short time from one end of India to the other. They travel at the season when travelling is delightful, and thus see the different countries of that great region in their most attractive form. If they infer what they do not see from what they see, they are sure to make statements utterly discordant with fact. Mr. Wilson, who was sent out to India to put its finances into order after the Mutiny, travelled through the North-Western Provinces in the cold weather, when the country was covered with abundant crops, and was delighted with all he saw. He declared it was the finest country he had ever seen. He returned to Calcutta as the hot weather was setting in, and died in the succeeding rainy season. It is said that some time before his death he pronounced the climate to be the most detestable on the face of the globe. Dr. Norman McLeod was our guest for a very short time in Benares, as he was prosecuting his Indian journey. When driving about on a fine balmy morning, he said, in his genial fashion, "You missionaries often complain of your climate; I only wish we in Scotland had a climate like this." To which I replied, "Ah, doctor, kindly stop with us through our coming seasons; prolong your stay till next November, and then you will be able to speak with authority." The worthy doctor did not take my counsel. His death some time afterwards was attributed to his Indian tour; but if it left in him the seed of disease, the blame rests not on the climate, but on the excessive fatigue caused by overmuch travelling and work.

The case of a person who has lived through a whole year in a country, and has during that period moved among the people, is very different from that of the passing stranger. He knows the climate as a traveller for a few weeks or even months cannot. The seasons during that year may have been more or less abnormal, and yet the resident cannot fail to have obtained that knowledge which enables him to form a notion of what he has in the main to expect every year. He gets a glimpse into the character and peculiarities of the different classes of the population, both native and foreign. He may know little of the language of the country; but if he has an observing mind, and moves freely about, he is constantly receiving information about the people in a degree which he himself does not always realize. If his residence be prolonged for many years, as he looks back to his first year, and remembers its experience, he finds that his views have been greatly enlarged, on many points greatly modified; he is sure that his knowledge is much more accurate and mature; but there is scarcely any subject on which he finds his views entirely reversed.

This, at least, has been my experience. I have a vivid remembrance of my first year in Benares—a much more vivid remembrance than I have of subsequent years, and it would be strange if I did not find that my views on many Indian subjects have been greatly modified, and on all much enlarged; but I do not discover that on any subject there has been a complete reversal.

I have already mentioned that on my voyage from Calcutta to Benares I spent much of my time in the study of the Hindustanee language, commonly called Urdu. Within a week of my arrival I gave myself to it with all the application of which I was capable. I had as my teacher a munshee, who had been long employed by the missionaries of our Society, but who could not speak a sentence in English, though he knew the Roman character well. I was told that his ignorance of English would prove an advantage, as I should on this account be obliged to speak to him, in however broken and limping a fashion, in the language which it was indispensable for me to acquire. We had before us an English and

Hindustanee Dictionary, a Hindustanee and English Dictionary, a Hindustanee Grammar, and a book of easy sentences in both languages in the Roman character. At first my teacher and myself had to put things into many forms before reaching mutual intelligibility; but gradually our work became easier, and when two or three months had passed we fairly understood each other—I trying to express myself in Hindustanee, and he performing the much-needed work of correcting my words and idiom. I commenced with a portion of the New Testament, and soon got into some of the classics of the language. The use of the Roman character in the writing of Indian languages had been strongly advocated by Sir Charles Trevelyan, by Dr. Duff, and other men of mark, and was accepted by the majority of the missionaries. Portions of the Scriptures and other books were printed in it. Like all young missionaries, I learned the Persian and Nagree characters, in which the languages of Northern India had always previously been written; but the Roman character was very convenient, and I regretted afterwards I used it so much.

This study of the language was felt to be a foremost duty, and was prosecuted from day to day. This went on for months with little interruption, except what was caused by the serious and continued illness of Mrs. Lyon, which, to the great regret of all their friends, led before the end of the year to the departure of Mr. and Mrs. L. for Europe.

In the seventh or eighth month of my residence at Benares I wrote a short sermon in Hindustanee on John i. 29, and read it at the native service. Within a year I took my part regularly at that service, first using my manuscript, and then extemporizing as I best could.

I must confess I regarded my new linguistic acquisition with much more complacency at the end of my first year than at the end of my fifth or sixth. On my way to Benares, as I have already mentioned, I spent a few hours very pleasantly with Mr. Leslie, the Baptist missionary at Monghyr. I mentioned to him that my friend Mr. Lyon had learned the language, and was preaching in it. Looking me full in the face, he said, to my surprise and chagrin, "Depend on it, Mr. Lyon may use the words of the language, but no one can be said to acquire it in a year." I thought this a hard saying, but years afterwards I was forced to feel its truth. I had in a year got such a glimpse into the Hindustanee and Hindee languages as to have some conceptions of their nature, to know their tone, and to bring them into partial use; but I had a very limited notion of their nice distinctions, their peculiar idioms, and their vast vocabulary. I cannot say that the opinion on this subject I formed in my first year was entirely reversed by my after experience, but it was largely modified.

While studying the native language, I felt myself studying the native character as well. My teacher was very patient, correcting my mistakes—mistakes, I must confess, often repeated—without allowing even the slightest surprise to appear in his countenance. He did not smile at blunders at which, when I knew better, I myself heartily laughed. When I showed the slightest impatience at being checked he at once allowed me to go on as I liked, though, as I afterwards knew, I needed to be corrected. He was loud in praise of my progress, declaring that I would soon surpass all my predecessors. In my intercourse with him I had illustrations of the patience, the courtesy, and also the flattering, cozening character of the people, when dealing with those by whom they think they can be benefited. The impressions of native character thus obtained were amply affirmed by the experience of after years.

This munshee was well acquainted with our Scriptures. He belonged to the Writer caste, and had from his early years been in contact with Europeans. He was ready for conversation on religious subjects, and had much to say in favour of the philosophical notions which underlie Hinduism. Three or four years afterwards he seemed to awake all at once to the claims of Christ as the Saviour of the world, and under this impulse he openly appeared in a native newspaper as the assailant of Hinduism and the advocate of Christianity, which led to the hope that he was to avow himself, by baptism, a follower of the Lord. But he became alarmed at what he had done; he could not bear the reproaches of his friends, and he fell back into the ranks of his people. Though he had ceased to be my teacher I had opportunities of seeing him, and I tried to speak to his conscience, to his conviction of the Divine origin of the gospel. The last time I spoke to him he said, with marked emphasis, "There is no use in speaking to me. Let Hinduism be false or true, I am determined to live and die in it as my fathers have done!" His case was that of many with whom every Indian missionary is brought into contact.

During this year I was introduced into the methods in which evangelistic work was conducted. In addition to attending the services of the Lord's Day, I went now and then with my brethren to the city. We had at that time two little chapels in good positions, at the doors of which the people were first addressed, and were then invited to enter that they might hear the new teaching more fully expounded. There was, of course, nothing of the staidness or quietness of a Christian congregation. The speaker was often interrupted; questions, sometimes very irrelevant questions, were asked; and the people came and went, so that those who were present at the commencement were seldom present at the close. During the year I saw the principal places in Benares—its main streets and markets, its temples and mosques; and thus formed some idea of the great city, where for many years afterwards it was my privilege to labour in the gospel of Christ.

The work of the missionary in Northern India would be greatly simplified if he had to learn only one language. He has to learn the two I have named, the Hindustanee and the Hindee. The Hindustanee arose from intercourse between the Muhammadan invaders and the people they had subdued. It is written in the Persian or Arabic character, and draws its vocabulary mainly from the Persian and Arabic languages. It is the language of law, of commerce, and of ordinary life to many millions. The Hindee in its various dialects, some of which almost rise to the dignity of languages, is the vernacular of the vast Hindu population of North-Western India. It rests mainly on the Sanscrit, and is written in the Sanscrit or Deonagree character. In some of the most popular books the languages are so strangely combined that it is impossible to give any definite name to the language used. An acquaintance with these languages is indispensable to missionary efficiency in Northern India, but it is very difficult to attain marked excellence in both.

CHAPTER VI.

THE FIRST YEAR—SOCIETY AND CLIMATE.

A VERY brief residence at Benares led me to see the great difference between the society to which I had come and that which I had left. The European community formed a mere handful of the population, and was almost exclusively formed of officials, with all the peculiarities of a class privileged by office. We had some two hundred European artillerymen with their officers, of a regiment paid and controlled by the East India Company; three native regiments officered by Europeans; three or four members of the Civil Service, charged with the administration of the city and district; one English merchant, and two or three English shopkeepers. I now learned for the first time the difference in rank between Queen's and Company's military officers. The Queen's officer regarded himself as of a higher grade. Members of the Civil Service and Company's officers met on terms of social equality; but the Civilians looked on themselves as of a higher order, as the aristocracy of the land, and the assumed superiority put a strain to some degree on social intercourse. The persons sent out from this country for the administration of India are called Covenanted Civilians, as they bear a commission from the Queen; while those engaged for administrative work by the

Indian Government are called Uncovenanted. The former class continue to have a great official advantage over the latter; but forty years ago there was a great social inequality which has in a measure ceased, where these uncovenanted servants are English gentlemen, as they often are. English merchants were regarded as in society; but shopkeepers, however large their establishment, were deemed entirely outside the pale, except for strictly business purposes. This was partly accounted for by European shopkeepers having been previously stewards of ships, or soldiers who had received their discharge. Missionaries were looked on as sufficiently in society to be admissible everywhere, and were treated courteously by their European brethren when they met, though only a few desired their intercourse.

As to the people of the land, both Hindu and Muhammadan, I discerned at once, what I might have fully anticipated, that between them and us there was a national, social, and religious gulf. Some were in our houses as servants. We had to do with them in various ways; we could not go out without seeing them on every side. There was on the part of many a courteous bearing towards each other; there was in many cases a kindly feeling; but the barriers which separated us could not be for any length of time forgotten. I speedily saw that some Europeans looked with contempt on the natives, as essentially of a lower order in creation; but the better class of Europeans, the higher in position and education, as a rule, regarded them with respect, and treated them not only with justice but with kindness. Native servants received as kind treatment as servants do in well-conducted families in our own country, and in many cases repaid this kindness by devoted attachment and the efficient discharge of the work entrusted to them. When native gentlemen came in contact with Europeans of the higher class, all the honour was accorded to them to which by their position they were entitled. Even in this case there were national and religious differences, which effectually prevented the intimacy which is often maintained where such differences do not exist.

Within the first year I got an insight into a large and growing class, who were connected with both Europeans and natives, and yet did not belong to either. I refer to persons of mixed blood; some almost as dark, in many cases altogether as dark, as ordinary natives—many of these being descendants of Portuguese; others, again, so fair that their Indian blood is scarcely observed; some in the lowest grade of society, very poor and very ignorant; and others, with many intermediate links, most respectable members of the community in character, knowledge, position, and means. All these, whatever may be their rank, are Christians by profession, and they dress so far as they can after the European fashion; but the poorer class, in food and accommodation live very much as natives do, and mainly speak the native language. The people of mixed blood are called by different names—Eurasians, East Indians, and not infrequently by a name to which they most rightly object, Half-caste.

I was surprised and sorry to observe the feeling with which many Europeans regarded this class. They were looked down upon as of an inferior grade, who, whatever might be their character or position, were not entitled to rank with Europeans. In the dislike of natives shown by some Europeans there was something to remind one of the American feeling in regard to colour, though of a much milder type; but I was not prepared for the degree in which the feeling prevailed in reference to Eurasians, though I might have been had I remembered that the slightest tinge of African blood, a tinge to many eyes not perceptible, had been considered in America a fatal taint. I speedily observed the effect the feeling had on Eurasians in producing an unpleasant sensitiveness, and impairing the confidence and respect indispensable to social intercourse.

Since that time I have understood the causes of this feeling much better than I could have then done. The most candid and thoughtful of the class will allow that as a community they labour under great disadvantages. Though they have native blood in their veins they are entirely separate from natives in those things to which natives attach the highest value; and though by the profession of Christianity, by the adoption of European habits so far as circumstances allow, and by the use of the English language, they draw to Europeans, yet they are forced to feel they do not belong to them. They occupy an awkward middle position, and the knowledge that they do leads to unpleasant grating. Then they have not had the bracing which comes from residence in a Christian land. Though proud of their Christian name and profession, they have been injuriously affected by the moral atmosphere of their surroundings. The lower their social position, the closer has been their connection with the lower class of natives, and the more hurtful have been the influences under which they have come. Eurasians are noted for their excellent penmanship, and a great number from generation to generation have found employment in Government offices, the greater number as mere copyists, but a few as confidential clerks and accountants, whose services have been highly appreciated by their official superiors. A considerable number have risen to important offices in the administration of the country. An increasing number are able to take their place in every respect abreast of their European brethren. Individuals have gone to England, and have succeeded in getting by competition into the Covenanted Civil Service. The class has been steadily growing for years in intelligence and character; and as the members of their families are enjoying educational advantages to a greater extent than at any previous period, there is every reason to hope progress in the future will be still more rapid than in the past. The distinction between them and persons of pure European blood will thus become less and less a barrier to social intercourse; they will be delivered from the unpleasantness the barrier has often caused, their character will grow in strength, and they will become increasingly fitted for exerting a happy influence on the native community. In the case of individuals the distinction is now practically ignored. There are no more honoured and honourable persons in India than some who belong to this class. There have always been devoted Christians among them, and of late years an increasing number have come under the power of Divine grace.

It has been often remarked that one of the most pleasing traits of native society is reproduced among Eurasians—the tie of kinship prompting those who are in better circumstances to help their needy relatives, often to the giving of large pecuniary aid, not unfrequently to the taking of them into their houses. In the humbler portions of the community there is often seen a patriarchal household like that so often seen in native society.

The new-comer's experience of climate prepares him for what he has to expect during his future residence. We have three marked seasons in the North-Western Provinces, the one melting gradually into the other—the hot season beginning in March and ending in June, the rainy season beginning with July and ending in October, and the cold weather beginning with November and ending in February. The seasons may thus be described in a general way, but in fact every year differs somewhat from others, as they do in our own country. The hot weather is sensibly felt before March begins, and the heat of March is far less than that of the succeeding months. The first burst of the rains is often before the middle of June, but after that burst, called the "little rainy season," it is not uncommon to have a spell of very hot sunny weather. In some years, indeed, there is so much weather of this kind during what is called the rainy season, that the heat is most intense, and the crops are burnt up. Towards the end of September there is commonly the last great outpour of rain, and as October advances there is the cooling freshness of the approaching cold weather, with enough of heat in the day-time to tell us it has not quite let go its grasp. December and January are our coldest months. In England, after an unpropitious summer, the remark is often made, "We have had no summer!" and in the same manner in India, when the temperature has been high in the cold season, and we have not had the expected bracing, we say, "We have had no winter!" Yet as in our own country, so in India; we have our marked seasons, though we cannot be sure of the weather at any particular period.

As India is an immense region, a great continent, with every variety of scenery, with plains extending hundreds of miles, and vast stretches of forests, with table-lands and lofty mountains, with land of every description from barren sand to the richest alluvial soil, the climate and products of its different countries are so different, that the statements made about one region, however correct, when applied to the whole are utterly misleading. I have been describing the seasons of the North-Western Provinces; and yet, as Benares is in the lower part of these provinces, its climate is considerably different from that of the country farther north and west. The farther north we travel the longer and colder is the cold season, and as a rule the hotter and briefer is the hot season. On one occasion the heat was so great in Benares in March that we found the night punkah pleasant; but on reaching Delhi, nearly six hundred miles distant, a few days afterwards, instead of seeking a night punkah we were thankful to have blankets to keep ourselves warm.

I have a vivid recollection of my experiences of the climate during my first year. During our voyage on the Ganges the heat during the day was like that of a cloudless July in England, and at night it was pleasantly cool, the wood of the flat speedily giving off the heat it had taken in during the day, and the flow of the river contributing to our comfort. Reaching Benares as April was setting in, I speedily felt I was getting into the experience of an Indian hot season. The doors were opened before dawn to let in whatever coolness might come with the morning, and before eight they were shut to keep out the heat of the day. The lower part of the door was of wood, and the upper part of glass. Outside the doors were heavy wooden blinds, made after the fashion of Venetian blinds, the upper part of which were opened to let in from the verandah the degree of light absolutely necessary with the least possible degree of heat. No prisoner in his cell is more excluded from an outside view than we were in our rooms during the day in the hot season. There was a remarkable contrast between the outside glare and the inside dimness, so that a person coming from without could not on entering see anything. The prevailing wind is from the west. There is enough in the morning to show the direction from which it is coming. It rises as the day advances; by two or three it blows with great strength, raising clouds of dust, and lulls towards evening. This wind is cool and bracing in the cold weather, but as the season advances it becomes warm, and by May its heat resembles the blast of a furnace. It every now and then gives place to the east wind, which is not nearly so hot, but is so enervating that the hot wind is greatly preferred. During the day we sit under the punkah, a great wooden fan suspended from the roof with great flapping fringes. This is pulled by a coolie, sometimes in the adjoining room, but when it can be arranged in the verandah outside, who has in his hand a rope attached to the punkah, which is brought to him by a small aperture in the wall, through which a piece of thin bamboo is inserted to make the friction as little as possible. When the west wind is blowing freshly, it is brought with most pleasant coolness into the house through platted screens of scented grass, on which water is continually thrown outside. For years machines resembling the fanners so much used by farmers in former days, with scented grass on each side and a hut of scented grass over them, on which water is continually thrown, with wheels turned round by hand labour, have been brought largely into use. These machines are appropriately called "Thermantidotes."

The night in the hot season is much more trying than the day. There is not a breath stirring, and the heat of the day, taken in by the walls, is radiated all the night long. I found the night punkah in almost universal use but I thought I would get on without it, and used it very seldom. When the next hot season came I was glad to conform to the custom of the country, for I found when I had not the punkah I got up in the morning so tired and weary that I was unfit for the work of the day.

The aspect of the country at that season is very dreary. Some trees retain their freshness in the hottest weather; but not a blade of green grass is to be seen, and the ground is scorched, scarred, and baked, as if it had been turned into a desert.

A marvellous change is produced by the first heavy fall of rain. After stifling heat for some days, the rays of the sun beating with a fierceness which threatens to burn up all nature, and which drives the birds for shelter to the thickest foliage of the trees, the clouds gather, the thunder rolls, peal quickly succeeding peal, the lightning flashes incessantly, and then, after some heavy showers, there comes down for two or three days, with very little intermission, such torrents that it looks as if we were to be visited with a deluge. Within a week all nature is transformed. The parched earth gives way to the richest green. We in our country say in very propitious weather that we see things grow; but in India vegetation takes such a bound as it never does in our temperate climate. Immediately after the downpour of rain, the sun comes out in all its strength; and, under the action of heat and moisture, vegetation progresses marvellously. The fields are quickly ploughed, the seed, for which moisture and great heat is required, is sown, and in the course of three or four weeks they are far above the ground. Within three months the harvest of the rainy season, furnishing the people with rice, maize, and other grains, which furnish the principal food of the people, is gathered in.

The rainy season is productive in another and less pleasant manner. It is as favourable to insect life as it is to vegetable life. Flying white ants, flying bugs, and other unwelcome visitors of the same order, come out in thousands. At night, if the doors be open the white ants make for the lamps in such numbers that they are extinguished by them, and the room is in the morning found strewed with their dead. It requires a torpid temperament to remain calm under this visitation. All dislike it, and some find it a grievous trial. As the rainy season advances, the trouble abates, and by the time the cold weather sets in the ordinary house-fly by day and the mosquito by night alone remain to buzz about us. The mosquito has rightly got the first place among insect tormentors. The house-fly is at all seasons, in some more than in others, and gives not a little annoyance by its pertinacity.

The change at the commencement of the rainy season is delightful. The doors are thrown open, and the dry, parching wind gives place to a refreshing coolness. When the rain ceases, the heat returns; the weather is very muggy, the skin is irritated by the excessive perspiration, and many suffer more than during the hot season. When the rain is abundant and frequent, the suffering is much less than when there is little rain and much sun. There is one comfort at that time: we know we are going on to the cold weather, which will make amends for all that went before.

I can hardly conceive any country to have a finer

climate than that of the North-West Provinces of India in the cold months. Rain does sometimes fall during that season; it may fall at any time of the year. I remember a heavy fall on the first of May, and about Christmas and the New Year it is eagerly desired for the crops, but ordinarily from week to week there is an unclouded sky. There is a cool, pleasant breeze from the west. In the house it is not only cool but cold, so that a little sunning is pleasant, and at night in December and January, especially far up the country, fires are welcome. Then Europeans, so far as circumstances permit, get into the open air and move freely about, with everything in the climate to favour their travelling.

The beginning of the cold weather is a very busy season with the agricultural class, to which the great body of the people belong. If the rainy season has been favourable, especially if heavy rain has fallen towards its close, the wells are full, and from these, after the land has been ploughed, and the seed sown for the rabee crop, the most valuable crop of the year, the fields are irrigated. Whatever grows in our land in summer grows in North-Western India at that season: wheat, oats, barley, potatoes, carrots, are grown in abundance. About March the harvest is reaped.

As I proceed with these reminiscences, I shall have frequent occasion to refer to our North Indian winter, its scenes, and employments, and I have thought it well to enter at some length into a description of its peculiarities.

One thing I observed my first year which I had abundant opportunity to observe afterwards. The weather so welcomed by Europeans is very trying to most natives, especially to those of the humbler classes, whose clothing is very scanty. They never try to get warm by taking exercise.

They cower in the morning and evening round a fire, which has commonly for its fuel dried cow-manure, with a coarse blanket over their head and shoulders. As the sun gets above the horizon, they plant themselves against a wall to bask in its rays, and if they can, do not stir till they are well heated. As might be expected, many of them suffer from chronic rheumatism. The extreme heat is not liked by them, but from it they suffer far less than from cold.

While most Europeans get new life in the cold weather, the little ones showing by their rosy cheeks how much they are benefited, a few are in better health when the weather is warm, as then they are less subject to aguish attacks. The remark is often made by those who have much sedentary work that they like the cold season for enjoyment, but find it unfavourable for work, as they cannot keep so steadily at it as they can when the heat keeps them within doors.

While giving the reminiscences of my first year, my mind has been continually carried forward to the experience of after-years in reference to the vernacular languages, the various classes with whom residence in India brings one into contact, and the seasons of the country. In giving partial expression to this experience under the heading of my first year, I have gone far beyond it. Those who favour me with the perusal of my narrative may perhaps find it more intelligible by my having anticipated myself.

I must confess months of the first year passed before I ceased to feel myself an exile. The scenes around were so unlike those of my own country, the prevailing idolatry so repulsive, the society, associations, and climate so different, that I turned from them to my native land with many a fond longing look. This feeling of exile was no doubt deepened by the illness in the family with whom I was residing. We had an English service every Thursday evening, conducted by the missionaries in the hall of the mission-house, but I greatly missed the services on the Lord's-day to which I had been accustomed.

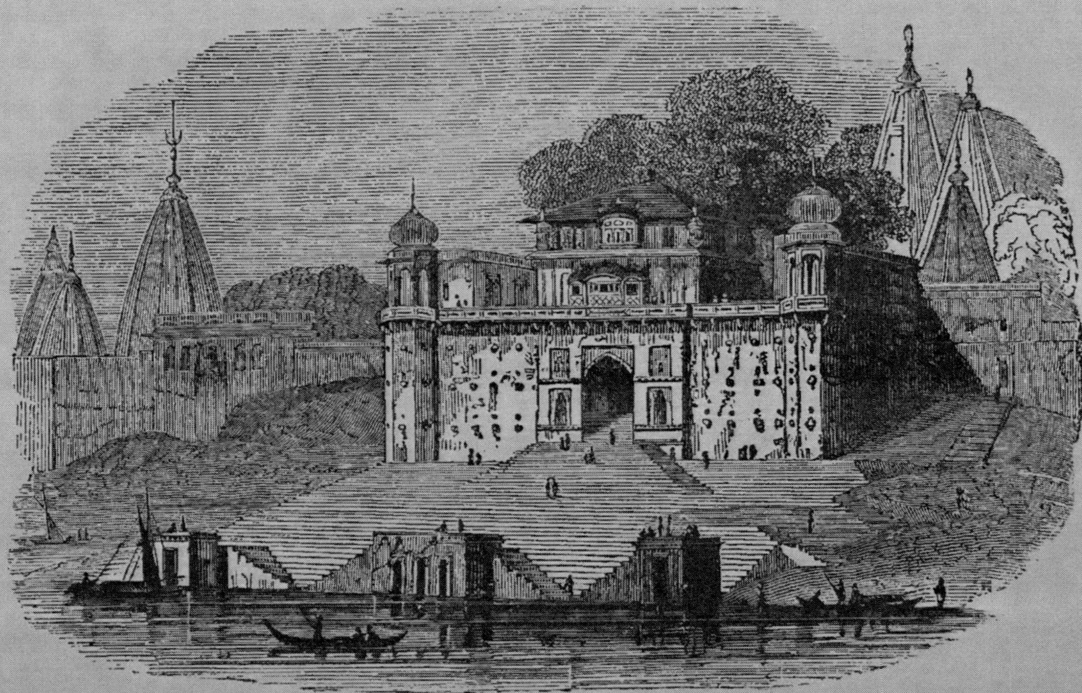

BATHING GHAT, BENARES.

CHAPTER VII.

THE CITY OF BENARES.

MY greatly beloved and much esteemed friend, the late Rev. M. A. Sherring, years ago published a handsome volume under the title of *The Sacred City of the Hindus*, in which he gave ample information about its history, temples, castes, festivals, commerce, and religious pre-eminence in Hindu estimation. To that work I must refer readers who are desirous to be furnished with details. My aim is to describe as concisely and vividly as I can the marked peculiarities of the place.

Benares is the largest city in the North-Western Provinces, though it is approached in population by some others, as Delhi, Agra, and Allahabad. It is among the largest purely native cities in India, but it is greatly surpassed in population and wealth by Calcutta, Bombay, and Madras, the great seats of British rule, and the great emporia of Indian as well as of European commerce in the East. These cities under our rule have risen to be among the greatest in Eastern Asia. For many a day the population of Benares was said to be above 500,000, but this has turned out a very exaggerated conjecture.[1]

[1] Bishop Heber visited Benares in 1824. He says in his journal, "The population, according to a census made in 1803, amounted to above 582,000—an enormous amount, and which one should think must have been exaggerated." The census which gives such a return must have been taken in a very singular manner.

When the first careful census was taken, the resident population was found to be under 200,000, and every succeeding census has confirmed its substantial accuracy. In the last census the number given is 207,570. When the first census was taken great surprise was expressed at the result, and some asserted no dependence could be placed on it. The ground of this assertion was that in the houses of some of the wealthier classes there are many females, who live, in native phrase, behind the curtain, who are never seen by outsiders, to whom the officials of the Government have no access; and on this account the accuracy of the return made to the enumerators entirely depends on the faithfulness of the head of the household. It has been said that when the first census was taken the general impression was a capitation tax was to be imposed, and that in consequence the inmates reported were far below the actual number. If there was error on this account it was to a very limited extent, as every subsequent census has agreed with the first, although the notion of a capitation tax has entirely died out. One going through Benares, from street to street, from one end of it to the other, does not get the impression its resident population exceeds the estimate found in official statements. The city has a great floating population, as it is the resort of strangers from all parts of India. It is reckoned that on the occasion of the great festivals there may be 100,000 visitors, some say 200,000, but we are not aware any attempt has been made to number them.

In commerce, as in population, Benares holds a high, but not the highest, place among Indian cities. The district of Benares is not so large as some others in the North-West; but it is very productive, is densely peopled, and the city has on this account a large local business.

Besides, the merchants and bankers of Benares have dealings with the other districts of the province, and indeed with all parts of India. The city has many artificers. It has workers in stone, wood, iron, brass, silver and gold. They produce articles which command a large and profitable sale. God-making and toy-making are among the staple businesses of the place. The making of idols in different materials to suit the taste and means of purchasers, gives employment to many. The images while being made are only stone, brass, or gold, as it may be, and no reverence is then due to them. It is when certain sacred words are uttered over them, and the god is supposed to take possession of them, they become objects ot worship. Benares is well known for its toys made of very light wood, and lacquered over. Of late years the enchased brass vessels made in Benares have been much admired, and have secured a large and profitable sale. Perhaps the most important manufacture of the place is *kimkhwab—kinkob* as it is called by Europeans—cloth made of silver and gold tissue, in which the princes and grandees of India array themselves on state occasions. I believe this business has fallen off, as with the incoming of European influence the love of barbaric pearl and gold has declined, if not among the rajahs of the land, among a class beneath them, who formerly thought they could not retain their rank in society if they did not appear on special occasions in gorgeous robes.

While in population and commerce there are cities in India which surpass Benares, in Hindu estimation it stands above them all in religious pre-eminence. Perhaps at the present time more eyes are turned reverently towards it than to any city on the face of the earth.

I must attempt a brief sketch of the history of Benares,

We are sure it was not among the first cities erected by the Aryans after leaving their home in Central Asia and crossing the Indus. They first took possession of the land in the far north-west of the great country they had entered, and gradually made their way to the south and east. Wonderfully acute and painstaking though the Pundit mind be, it has so dwelt in the regions of speculation and imagination that it has paid no attention to historical research. Its laborious productions have left us ignorant of recent times, and we need not therefore wonder that, except by incidental allusions, it throws no light on the early settlements of the Aryans in India. We know that they brought with them a considerable measure of civilization, and soon erected cities. Indraprastha, built near the site of the present city of Delhi, and Hastinapore, some thirty miles from it, figure largely in the Mahabharut, the giant Hindu epic. Kunauj, lying east and south of Delhi, became some time afterwards the capital of a widely extended empire, which lasted, with vicissitudes, down to Muhammadan times. Benares is seen in the dim light of antiquity as a favourite abode of Brahmans, and as sacred on that account, but it does not appear that it ever was the seat of extended rule. For many a day it was subject to Kunauj, and it afterwards came under the sway of the Muhammadans, to whom it was subject for six hundred years.

A clear proof of the influential position of Benares centuries before the Christian era, is furnished by the fact that Gautama, the founder of Buddhism, deemed it well to commence his public ministry there in the sixth century B.C.[1] The spot where he first unfolded his

[1] The names and titles of this famous teacher are perplexing to those who do not know the meaning. His father was chief or king

A JEWELLER AT WORK.

doctrine was a grove at a place now called Sarnath, about four miles from the present city. At this place there is a large Buddhist tower, which is seen from a great distance, and around it are extensive remains, which have been excavated under the direction of Major-General Cunningham, and have been found to be of Buddhist origin. The success which Buddhism had achieved and maintained for centuries in the country where it arose, is strikingly confirmed by the testimony of two Chinese Buddhists who went on pilgrimage to India, the one in the fifth century A.D., and the other towards the middle of the seventh. Their narratives have been preserved, and furnish us with most interesting details. From them we learn that down to the time of their visits Buddhism had temples, monasteries, and thousands of adherents; but it had not the field to itself, for these strangers tell us, especially the later of the two, that a large and increasing number of the people were warmly attached to Hinduism. We have no historical account of the overthrow of Buddhism, but we have reason to believe that towards the close of the eleventh century, or earlier, the devotees of Hinduism rose against it, and so stamped it out that not a temple was left standing and not a monastery remained. Major-General Cunningham says that about that period "the last votaries of Buddha were expelled from the continent of India. Numbers of images, concealed by the departing monks, are found buried near Sarnath; and heaps of ashes still lie scattered amidst the ruins, to show that the monasteries were destroyed by fire." This is con-

of a tribe called Sakyas, and therefore Gautama received the name of Sakya-Muni, or Sakya-Saint. When he announced himself as the inspired teacher of the nations he took the name of Buddha—the wise man, the enlightener, the inspired prophet.

firmed by excavations made at a later period by Major Kittoe, who says, "All has been sacked and burned—priests, temples, idols, all together; for, in some places, bones, iron, wood and stone, are found in huge masses: and this has happened more than once." From Benares having been the scene of Gautama's early ministry, and the place where his first disciples were called, it stands high in the reverence of the millions who compose his followers, although their only living representatives there now are a few Jains, whom orthodox Buddhists regard as heretics.

Long before the time of Gautama Hinduism prevailed at Benares, and we have observed its rites were practised side by side with those of Buddhism when the city was visited by two Chinese pilgrims. Some time afterwards it obtained full sway under the form of fanatical devotion to Shiva the Destroyer, and that sway it has maintained down to our day. What Jerusalem is to the Jews; what Mecca is to the Muhammadans; what Rome is to the Roman Catholics—that, and more than that, Benares is to the Hindus. They form by far the largest portion of the population of India, and to them Benares—or as they delight to call it, Kasee the Splendid, the Glorious City—is the most sacred spot on earth. They say, indeed, it is not built on the earth, but on a point of Shiva's trident. They assert that at one time it was of gold, but in this degenerate age it has been turned into stone and clay. In their belief the Ganges is sacred through its entire course, but as it flows past the sacred city its cleansing efficacy is supposed to be vastly increased. The rites performed at Kasee have double merit, and its very soil and air are so fraught with blessing that all who die there go to heaven, whatever their character may be. With this belief diffused among the millions who, differing widely from each other in nationality and language, are devoted to Hinduism, it may be supposed how many eyes are reverently turned towards Kasee, and with what eager steps and high expectations vast numbers resort to it. I have frequently seen persons entering the city, not on foot—that they did not deem sufficiently respectful—but prostrating themselves on the ground, measuring the ground with their bodies, and approaching the sacred shrines. And then, especially on the occasion of great festivals, bands may be seen entering the city, often composed of women—hand-in-hand lest they should lose each other in the crowd—singing the praises of Shiva and the glories of his city. Many aged people come from distant parts of India—the greater number, I believe, from Bengal—to reside and end their days in it, that by becoming Kasseebas (dwellers in Kasee) they may when they die become Baikuntbas (dwellers in heaven).

Though Benares be *par excellence* the sacred city of the Hindus, strange to say they are proportionately fewer than in ten cities of the North-West. According to the census of 1872, there were 133,549 Hindus and 44,374 Mussulmans: that is, a little more than three Hindus to one Mussulman. In the great commercial city of Mirzapore, about thirty miles distant from Benares, there were five Hindus to one Mussulman. The fact thus certified is entirely at variance with the conjecture made by those who look at the crowds bathing at the riverside, and frequenting the temples, and contrast them with the small number seen in the mosques, even on Friday, the Muhammadan weekly day of worship. In the district the Hindus vastly out-number the Muhammadans.

Benares is built on the left bank of the Ganges, and extends in a crescent shape three miles and a half along the bank, and a little more than a mile inward. The most imposing view is from a boat slowly dropping down the stream in the early morning—the earlier the better, especially if it be the hot season, as then the people betake themselves to the river in greater numbers than at any other time. Travellers in many lands who have seen this view, have declared it to be one of the most remarkable sights of the kind which the world presents.

Photographic and pencil pictures of Benares have appeared in illustrated newspapers, in periodicals and books, and give a more vivid and correct impression than can be conveyed by a verbal description. These pictures can, however, be better understood when those who look at them are furnished with information which no picture can afford.

The right bank of the Ganges at Benares is very low, and is always flooded when the river rises; but the left bank, on which the city stands, is in many parts more than a hundred feet high. The river sweeps round this high bank. The city is connected with the river by flights of stone steps, called "ghats." This word ghat often meets the reader of books on India. It has various meanings. It means a mountain-pass, a ferry, a place on the riverside where people meet, and, as is the case at Benares, the steps which lead down to the river. Two small streams enter the Ganges at Benares—on the southern side the Assi, on the northern side the Burna. Some have supposed that the city has received its name from lying between these two rivulets—Burna, Assi, making the word Burunassi, Benares; but this derivation is more than doubtful. Others maintain the word comes from a famous rajah called Bunar; but this, too, is a mere conjecture.

Let me take my readers with me on a trip down the river. We embark at early dawn on a native boat at Assi Sungam, which means the confluence of the Assi with the Ganges, at the southern extremity. Towards that end of the city some of the houses seen on the high bank are poor, some are falling into decay; but as you advance, lofty buildings, some of them of a size and grandeur which entitle them to the name of palaces, come into view. Their numerous small windows, their rich and varied carving, their balconies and flat roofs, give them a very Eastern look. Perhaps the most notable of the buildings are an observatory, built by a famous Rajput prince, Jae Singh, and a massy and extensive structure, with its buttresses and high walls looking as if recently erected, which was built in the last half of the eighteenth century by Cheit-Singh, the Rajah of Benares at that time, who was deposed by Warren Hastings on account of his refusal to comply with the demands of the British Government. In Macaulay's famous Essay on Warren Hastings there is a long narrative of this contest, which is amusingly at variance with the narrative given by Warren Hastings himself. This building is still called Cheit-Singh's Palace, but since his day it has been the property of the British Government, and has been for many years the residence of princes of the old imperial family of Delhi, who on account of family troubles had come to reside in Benares, and were, happily for themselves, far from Delhi during the mutiny of 1857. Some of the mansions facing the river belong to Indian princes, who occupy them on the rare occasion of visits to the city, and leave them in charge of servants, of whom a number are Brahmans performing sacred rites on their behalf.

There is one spot on the riverside from which most visitors avert their eyes with horror—the place where the dead of Benares and the surrounding country are being burnt, and the ashes thrown into the stream. The fire at that place never goes out. Cremation, not burial, it is well known, is the Indian mode of disposing of the dead.

The peculiarity of Benares as the sacred city of the country is strikingly attested by the temples, which crowd the high bank of the river, and arrest the special attention of the visitor. Some of these are much larger and more expensive than others, but there is little variety in their form; and all of them, even the largest and most frequented, are small compared with Christian and Muhammadan places of worship. They are circular, with heavy domes narrowing towards the top, and, as a rule, with a narrow doorway alone admitting light and air. Some domes are of respectable height, but none approach that of many of our church towers and steeples. Most of the temples are sacred to Shiva, Mahadeo, the Great God, as his devotees delight to call him, and are surmounted by his trident. Many have a pole at their side with a flag attached to it. One sees at a glance they must, though small, have cost large sums, as they are most solidly built of hewn stone, and have all more or less of ornamentation. A few temples are built close to the water's edge. One has got off its equilibrium, and looks as if it were about to fall into the stream; but for many years it has remained in this tottering position.

While the houses and temples on the riverside are viewed with interest, the visitor, as he looks from his boat, is still more interested in the living mass before him. It is the early morning. The sun has just risen above the horizon, and is shedding its bright rays on the river and the city. It looks as if all the inhabitants were astir and had made their way to the river. Crowds are seen on the steps, some even then making their way back after having bathed, and others going down to the stream. Thousands are in the water. Men and women, boys and girls, are there—the men and women at a short distance from each other. Immediately above the water are platforms with huge stationary umbrellas over them, and on these men are squatted, whose portly appearance betokens ease and plenty. These are Gungaputrs—sons of the Ganges—a class of Brahmans, whose duty it is to take care of the clothes of the people as they bathe, to put a mark on their forehead to show they have bathed, and who receive a small offering from them as they retire. All bring with them their bathing-dress, and they most deftly take off and put on their scanty clothing. When the bathing is over they wring out the clothes in which they have bathed, fill with Ganges water a small brazen vessel, which each person carries with him, and make their way into the city to pay their homage to their favourite gods before proceeding to their homes. I have been told that the very devout among them visit some thirty temples of a morning.

You watch the people as they bathe. It is evident they are not engaged in mere ablution, so important for health and comfort in that hot climate. They are engaged in worship. You see them taking up the water of the Ganges in the palm of their hands, and offering it up to the sun as they mutter certain prescribed words. You observe them making a circular motion, and if sufficiently near you see them breathing heavily, which you are told is their way of driving away demons, who even in that sacred spot are said to haunt them. There is no united worship: each worshipper apart performs his and her devotion. There is incessant movement among the crowd. As the words of worship—I might rather say the spells—they have been instructed to use are not whispered but uttered, and by many with a loud voice, a stream of sound falls on the ear. If, at some spot where bathers are not inconvenienced, the boat be moored, and the visitor ascends the steps, he may find on certain days, in two or three places, pundits reading and explaining the Ramayan, or the Mahabharut, the great Hindu Epic Poems, to a crowd of people, mainly composed of women. Sentence by sentence is read from poetical translations made long ago, which require to be re-translated into the ordinary language of the people to be generally intelligible. We have occasionally stopped to hear these pundits, and, judging by what we heard, we concluded they satisfied themselves with a loose paraphrase of what they were reading. These men are rewarded with a respectful and attentive hearing, and with something more substantial when the work is over.

If the visitor is bent on obtaining a full impression of the work continually carried on in Benares, he will make his way into the city from one of the principal bathing-places. He will speedily find himself in long narrow streets, with lofty stone houses on either side. The buildings are of hewn stone, and of the most substantial description. They have for the most part a narrow doorway, opening into a quadrangle, around which are the apartments of the inmates. The streets are so narrow that through some of them a vehicle cannot be taken, and in others conveyances pass each other with difficulty. There are parts of the narrower streets and lanes on which the sun never shines. In the few cases where houses on both sides of the street opposite each other belong to one proprietor, there is at the top a bridge by which the inmates pass from one to the other.

Not the houses, however, but the temples, secure the chief attention of the visitor. They are seen on every side. Numerous though they be, they are not sufficient to meet the demands of the people. At every few steps objects of worship meet your view. In niches of the walls are little images, so worn by the weather and by the water poured on them by worshippers that it is difficult to determine what they are intended to represent. At your feet, close to the walls, you see misshapen stones which are regarded as sacred. As you proceed you find yourself accompanied by a crowd who have bathed, and who are going to complete their morning worship by acts of obeisance to their gods. They are seen, as they walk, bowing their heads and folding their hands before the sacred objects that line their way. Every now and then one of a party will raise the shout "*Mahadeo jee kee jae!*" —("Victory to the Great God"), that is to Shiva, to whom this title is given; and the shout is taken up and repeated by others till the street resounds. It has occurred to me that this is done with peculiar force when Europeans are within hearing.

You speedily find yourself at the principal temple of Benares—the temple of Bisheshwar, sacred to Shiva under this name, which means *Lord of All.* This temple is in the midst of a quadrangle, covered in with a roof; over it are a tower, a dome, and a spire. The tower and dome glitter in the sun like masses of burnished gold, and on this account it is called the Golden Temple. Natives will tell you that it is covered with plates of solid gold, but in fact it is merely gilded with gold leaf, spread over plates of copper overlaying the stones beneath. Under the dome is a belfry in which nine bells are suspended, and these are so low that they can be tolled by the hand of those who frequent the temple. We are told that the temple, including the tower, is fifty-one feet in height. "Outside the enclosure is a large collection of deities, raised upon a platform, called by the natives 'The Court of Mahadeo.'" Though the gods in the Hindu books are represented as continually quarrelling with each other, and their devotees take up their quarrels, not only at the temple of Bisheshwar, but throughout the city which is regarded as Shiva's own, they are seen side by side, as in perfect amity, and there is not a single god who does not secure the special devotion of some worshippers. It is, however, required of all who dwell in Kasee, or frequent it, to acknowledge that Mahadeo is entitled to supreme homage, and that to him in the first instance obeisance must be made. The symbol of Shiva, or Mahadeo, which is found wherever he is worshipped, is the *Linga*, a conical stone, which does not in itself suggest any impure notion, but which is intended to be a vile representation. In this famous temple this conical stone receives special honour. There, too, are figures of Shiva himself in all his hideousness, with his three eyes, covered with ashes, and his eyes inflamed with intoxicating herbs. Outside the temple there is a figure cut in stone of a bull seven feet high, sacred to the god, as this is his favourite animal for riding. Within the quadrangle there is a well called *Gyan Bapee*, the well of knowledge, to which it is said the god betook himself when he was expelled from his former temple by the bigot Emperor Aurungzeb. On this account the well is deemed specially sacred. It is surmounted by a handsome low-roofed colonnade with forty pillars. It is covered with an iron grating, in which there is an aperture for small vessels to be let down into it, which when full are drawn up, and the water thus drawn is highly prized. As from day to day a large quantity of flowers are thrown into it, it may be supposed how horrible its water and how offensive its smell; it is a wonder the people are not poisoned by it.

We must not proceed further with this description of Bisheshwar's temple. Those who wish for more information can find it in the ample details given by Mr. Sherring.

To this temple thousands resort every day. It is open, and priests are present, we are told, twenty hours in the twenty-four. It is only shut from midnight till four in the morning. The temple itself holds a very small number, and the entire quadrangle would be crowded by one of our large congregations. The people press into it in one continuous stream, toll a bell to draw the attention of the god, make their obeisance, pour on the object of their worship a little of the Ganges water from the small brazen vessel they have in their hand, throw on it some flowers, give a present to the attendant priests, go round the building with their right hand towards it, and pass away to give place to others.

How does the visitor regard this scene? Apart from the consideration of the dishonour done to the ever-blessed God by worship rendered to images representing gods that are no gods—by which, if a Christian, he must be painfully affected—there is much in the scene before him to impress him with the sottish folly into which man can sink in his religious views and practices; and there is nothing to draw forth his regard and sympathy, except it be the fervour, the deep though mistaken fervour, of some of the worshippers, especially of the women, who may sometimes be seen with children in their arms teaching them to make obeisance to the idol. In Roman Catholic worship there is much which, as Protestants ruled by the Bible, we rightly condemn; but in the gorgeous vestments of its priests, in the magnificence of many of the places in which they minister, in the grand strains of their music and in their processions, there is much to impress the senses and awe the mind; but in the worship carried on in the temple of Bisheshwar it is difficult to find a redeeming quality. The whole scene is repulsive. The place is sloppy with the water poured out by the worshippers, and is littered by the flowers they present. The ear is assailed with harsh sounds. The ministering priests—Pundas as they are called—are, as a rule, coarse-looking men, with shaven head, save with a long pendent tuft from the crown, with the mark of their god on their forehead, and are very scantily attired. They clamour for a present when a European appears, and if given it is declared to be an offering to the god of the place. Among the crowd you see men with matted hair and body bedaubed with ashes, who have broken away from all domestic and social duties, and devote themselves to what is called a religious life. Some of these ascetics are no doubt impelled to follow the life they lead by a superstitious feeling, but many are idle vagabonds ready for the practice of every villainy, who find it more pleasant to roam about the land and live on others than support themselves by honest labour. The people dread their curse, but many give them neither respect nor love. At a place like Bisheshwar's temple there is always a host of ordinary beggars, who clamour for alms, and receive from some two or three shells, called *cowries*, sixty of which go to make up a halfpenny, from others a little grain, and from the more liberal or more wealthy a small coin.

From this stirring scene you have only a few steps to go to find yourself in the large mosque built by the Emperor Aurungzeb on the site of the old temple of Bisheshwar, which was thrown down to give place to it. The contrast is very striking. You have left the bustling, noisy crowd, and see only a few individuals in the attitude of devotion—now standing with folded hands, then on their knees, then with forehead touching the floor, engaged in supplicating the Invisible One. Instead of grotesque and repulsive images meeting your view, you see very little ornament of any kind, and are impressed with the severe simplicity of the lofty building. The more one knows of Muhammadanism, the more grievous are its defects and errors seen to be; but in the simplicity of its mosques, which has nothing in common with the sordid barn-like bareness too characteristic at one time of many places of worship in our own land, there is much from which Christians might learn a useful lesson.

Within a stone's throw of Bisheshwar's temple there is a host of temples, none of them very large, some of them small, but most covered with carving, to some extent for mere ornamentation, but chiefly for the purpose of illustrating the objects of Hindu worship. If you visit them you will see everything is accordant with the great shrine you have left. You will see Shiva, sometimes seated on a bull, sometimes on a dog; his hideous partner Durga, with her eight arms and her ferocious look, indicating her delight in blood; Hanuman, the monkey-god, with his huge tail; Krishna engaged in his gambols; Ganesh, the god of wisdom, with his elephant head and protuberant belly; and many others beside. Everything you see is wild, grotesque, unnatural, forbidding, utterly wanting in verisimilitude and refinement, with nothing to purify and raise the people, with everything fitted to pervert their taste and lower their character; and yet, I must add, with everything to give a faithful representation of the mythology prepared by their religious leaders. The pundits who wrote the sacred books of the Hindus were men of great talent, of abundant leisure; and it is a marvel to me, of which I can give no explanation, how they spent their days in spinning the wildest legends, and in setting forth their gods as performing the most fantastic, capricious, foolish, and wicked deeds, when they had a clear canvas before them, and might have filled it with something worthy of our nature, and worthy of objects to be worshipped.

Aurungzeb's mosque has two lofty minarets, rising about a hundred and fifty feet above its floor, and thus having from the river an elevation of two hundred and fifty feet. From a boat on the river the visitor has the nearest and most impressive view of the city, with its peculiarities as the high place of Hindu worship. If he proceed to the top of one of the minarets, which is reached by a steep, dark spiral stair, he will have a most commanding and extensive view of the city, the river, and the country for many miles around. He will see that while the streets in the centre of the city are long and narrow, and have very lofty houses, beyond these the roads widen, and many of the houses are poor and mean. As his eye falls on the part beyond the most crowded portion, he will observe here and there fine mansions with gardens around them, evidently belonging to the wealthy portion of the community, but surrounded by poor streets.

After seeing what I have endeavoured to describe, the traveller is well pleased to get back to his boat, and to drop down the river to Raj Ghat, the northern end of the city, where, after his fatigue, he is happy to find a conveyance to convey him to the European station more than three miles distant.

During my residence in Benares I often made this trip from Assi-Sungam to Raj Ghat, generally in company with strangers. The last time I made it I was accompanied by the late Dr. Norman McLeod of Glasgow, and the late Dr. Watson of Dundee. They were greatly interested in what they saw, and repeatedly said the reality exceeded their expectation. Dr. McLeod was specially eager to see everything that could be seen, and in his own strong genial way expressed the feelings excited by the strange scenes before him.

I must press into the concluding part of this chapter, as concisely as I can, some additional facts which call for special notice.

The city as it now stands is quite modern. Though foundations dug up, and pieces of masonry seen in existing buildings, testify to its antiquity, we are told by those who are best qualified to judge that there is not a single house or temple the erection of which can be relegated to a more remote period than the reign of Akbar, who was a contemporary of our Queen Elizabeth.

Various estimates have been given of the number of

temples. According to the census of 1872 the number is 1,454. This does not include smaller shrines in niches in the walls, which may be reckoned by thousands. The temples are constantly increasing in number; at no previous period were there so many as at present. Traders and bankers have prospered greatly under our rule, and, if devout Hindus, they deem themselves bound to devote a part of their wealth to the erection of a temple. A regard to their honour as well as to their gods prompts them to this spending of their money.

So far as I have been able to ascertain, the temples of Benares have very little of either funded or landed property. The vast sum required for the support of the priesthood comes mainly from the offerings of the people.

The "Imperial Gazetteer" of India gives no account in its last census of the castes of Benares, but we are sure that many thousands of the inhabitants are Brahmans. They are greatly subdivided, and are so different in rank and occupation that they keep as separate from each other as if they had no caste in common. The Pundas officiate in the temples; the Gangaputrs, the sons of the Ganges, minister at the waterside; the Purohits are the family priests; and the Pundits, the most esteemed of all, are the learned men who study the Shastres, and expound them to the people as occasion requires. Hindus generally have their Gurus, religious guides, who perform to them very much the work done for Roman Catholics by father confessors. These may be family priests, learned men; or, in the case of the lower castes, the lower orders of Brahmans. A vast number of the sacred caste have nothing to do with religious services. They are engaged in various businesses. A considerable number are cooks in the houses of the wealthy, as from their hand all can eat, while they in many cases would consider it an intolerable insult to be asked to eat with their masters. Not a few are beggars.

There are places in Benares to which people resort almost as much as to the temple of Bisheshwar. Among these I may mention the tank of Pishachmochan, a word meaning deliverance from demons, as bathing in it is considered very efficacious in securing this end, and the temple and tank of Durga at a place called Durgakund. At this latter place there are many hundreds of monkeys—some say thousands, though this is doubtless an exaggeration—which scamper about in all directions, and fare well at the hands of Durga's worshippers. These animals are deemed gods and goddesses, and woe to the person who does them any harm.

The monkeys are not the only animals deemed sacred at Benares. All who have heard anything about the city have heard about the well-fed lazy bulls prowling about the streets, and insisting on making free with the goods of the vegetable and grain sellers. These are no longer to be seen going about in their former fashion. I shall have something to say afterwards about them.

Mr. Sherring gives an account of forty melas, or religious festivals, in the course of the year in Benares. The principal of these are the Holee, the Saturnalia of the Hindus, the Ram Leela (the dramatic representation of the life of Ram as given in the epic poem, "The Ramayan"), and the Pilgrimage of the Panch Kosee, when the people make the circuit of the city, and halt for the night at certain assigned stations. On the occasion of eclipses vast numbers resort to Benares from all parts of India.

Benares has long been considered the Oxford of India. Its learned men have from ancient times been famed for their learning, and the aspirants for Hindu lore — all members of the same caste with themselves—have from generation to generation sat at their feet. They have had no grand academic halls in which to give their prelections; they have taken no fees from their pupils; they have met in very humble rooms, or in the open air in a garden under trees; but both teachers and students have been characterized by an assiduity and a perseverance which the most laborious of German scholars rarely attain. The very modest requirements of these learned men have as a rule been met unasked by the princes and wealthy of the land.

In 1791, a very short time after Benares was brought directly under British rule, a Sanscrit college was founded by the payment of certain pundits, who were left to carry on their work unchecked by any authority, or even suggestion, from without. It is said that pundits of the highest repute refused to have anything to do with the foreigner. In 1853 a very fine Gothic structure, said to be the most imposing building erected by the British in India, was opened under the name of the Queen's College, for the accommodation of students in both Western and Eastern learning. Here both English and Sanscrit are studied, and under the first Principal, the late Dr. Ballantyne, vigorous, and I hope to some degree successful, effort was put forth to infuse Western literature, philosophy, and science into the pundit mind.

I have mentioned the number of Muhammadans residing at Benares. It is officially stated they have 272 mosques, of which that of Aurungzeb, with its lofty minarets, is the largest. Hindus must have looked with horror on the sacrilegious deed by which this mosque was erected on the site of the demolished temple of Bisheshwar; but the power of the bigot emperor was so great that they could do nothing more than invocate curses on his head. The close neighbourhood of this mosque to the most frequented temple, and the remembrance of the building which formerly occupied its site, have produced a bitter feeling towards the followers of Muhammad. Early in this century there was a furious contest between the two classes of religionists, which lasted for some days, and was at last quelled by the military. During the fight every conceivable insult was offered to each other's feelings, and lives were lost. The Muhammadans suffered most, and since that time they seem to have been cowed, so that there has been much less fighting between them and their Hindu neighbours than in some other cities in the North-West.

The city has two great squares, occupied as market-places, in which goods of every description are exhibited and sold in the Eastern fashion. They present a stirring scene of an afternoon, which is the principal time of business.

In the census of 1872 the occupations of all males above fifteen years of age are noted. I give some of the items—

Alms-takers	184
Beggars	3,490
Barbers	979
Pundits	96
Priests (temple or ghat)	2,809
Purohits (family priests)	1,273
Servants	14,309

I suppose the distinction between alms-takers and

beggars is that the former class deem it beneath them to ask, but have no objection to take alms, while the latter class both ask and take. Among the latter, beside the blind and helpless, many able-bodied men make beggary their profession. On one occasion, in the neighbourhood of Benares, I met a man in the prime of life who said he had just returned from a long journey. On referring to his business he frankly said that he had never had any other occupation than that of a beggar. This was his hereditary profession. We have no Poor Law in India. The people, from varied motives, are ever ready to give aid to those who cannot support themselves, and in addition exercise an indiscriminate charity, which has a demoralizing effect.

The census informs us there are in Benares 16,023 masonry houses, and 21,551 mud houses—that is, houses many of which are of mud moistened and dried as the walls rise—and others of sun-dried bricks. I do not wonder at the disappointment felt by some who have been much impressed with the front view of the city, and have then traversed its streets.

Till recently, from the commencement of our rule, our Government has never been at peace with all the native rulers of India. In various ways we have come into collision with them, and the final result in every case has been their overthrow. The deposed rajahs have as a rule been sent to Benares, as if our Government wished to compensate them for the loss of their dominion by conferring on them special religious advantages.

On the opposite side of the Ganges, a little above the southern end of the city, is the town of Ramnuggur, with a population of 10,000. It is the residence of the Rajah of Benares, who is simply a large landowner, and has no authority beyond that which wealth confers. His palace, or rather fort, is close to the river. Behind the town, close to the Rajah's garden, there is a large tank, and a temple facing it which is remarkable for the exquisite carving on its walls illustrative of Hindu mythology.

I end this account of Benares by an extract from Macaulay's Essay on Warren Hastings, in which, in his own high rhetorical fashion, which so readily yields itself to exaggeration, he describes the city. If I remember rightly, there is no mention in his biography of his having visited the North-West, and his description is therefore not that of an eye-witness.

"The first design of Warren Hastings was on Benares, a city which in wealth, population, dignity, and sanctity was among the foremost in Asia. It was commonly believed that half a million of human beings was crowded into that labyrinth of lofty alleys, rich with shrines, and minarets, and balconies, and carved oriels, to which the sacred apes clung by hundreds. The traveller could scarcely make his way through the press of holy mendicants and not less holy bulls. The broad and stately flights of steps which descended from these swarming haunts to the bathing places along the Ganges were worn every day by the footsteps of an innumerable multitude of worshippers. The schools and temples drew crowds of pious Hindus from every province where the Brahmanical faith was known. Hundreds of devotees came thither every month to die, for it was believed that a peculiarly happy fate awaited the man who should pass from the sacred city into the sacred river. Nor was superstition the only motive which allured strangers to that great metropolis. Commerce had as many pilgrims as religion. All along the shores of the venerable stream lay great fleets of vessels laden with rich merchandise. From the looms of Benares went forth the most delicate silks that adorned the balls of St. James's and of Versailles; and in the bazars the muslins of Bengal and the sabres of Oude were mingled with the jewels of Golconda and the shawls of Cashmere."

CHAPTER VIII.

BENARES AS A MISSION SPHERE.

HINDUISM, like all other religions, has its points of contact, we may say of agreement, with Christianity; but in its main features and tendencies it is intensely antagonistic, and this antagonism may be conceived to have its keenest edge and greatest force in the city from which it has for ages maintained its sway over the millions of India. If any religion could be considered entrenched by local advantages beyond the possibility of overthrow, Hinduism might be declared secure at Benares, if not against assault, at least against defeat.

People in all ages, all the world over, cling with varying degrees of tenacity to the views and practices which have come to them from their fathers. Jeremiah said, "Pass over the isles of Chittim, and see; and send unto Kedar, and consider diligently, and see if there be such a thing. Hath a nation changed their gods, which are yet no gods?" Hinduism in its present form is comparatively modern; but the people generally know nothing of its history, and they regard it as an inheritance from the most ancient times. It comes to them as the gifts of gods and sages, which it would be sacrilege to reject. There is much in the religion itself to bind the people to it. Its numerous ceremonies, sustained by the largest promises, give the assurance of a great reward. In discharging their religious duties they have often to endure toil, undergo privation, and make sacrifices; but the more they do and suffer, the greater is the complacency with which they regard their religious position. There is one thing Hinduism does not demand of its devotees. It does not demand a radical change of character or of life. Its every requirement may be met without abandoning evil dispositions and practices. It can be easily supposed how strong a hold a religion like this has on its votaries, and how especially strong its hold must be in the city where it has been enthroned for ages.

In our day much is said about heredity. Facts illustrative of its power over the features, character, and life, not only of individuals but of communities, are patent to all. Whatever heredity can do it does in infusing the spirit of Hinduism into the very blood of the people of Benares, who have been so long dominated by it. The mastery it has obtained over them is shown by the whole tone of their minds and the whole bearing of their life. If sincerity and enthusiasm be the essential requisites in religion, the inhabitants of this city have all they need, for these qualities are possessed by them in a high degree. Then, in such a city there is felt the almost overpowering influence of thousands from day to day, and of vast multitudes on occasion of high festival, performing the same rites, worshipping the same gods, and animated by the same spirit. The peculiar thrill of pleasure given by a great assembled eager host to every individual composing it; the sense of importance it gives to each, as if on him rested the concentrated honour of the gathering, does much to bind people to a religion which receives such services from millions. If for a single year these daily services and periodical gatherings were intermitted, Hinduism would be greatly weakened.

In addition to the domestic, social, and public influences which guard and uphold the existing state of things, there is the tremendous power of personal gain and honour. The honour, the wealth, the very subsistence of large influential classes, are bound up with the maintenance of idolatry. The Pundits, the guardians and expositors of their sacred books; the Pundas who minister in the temples; the Gungaputrs who serve at the river side; the Purohits, the family priests; the Gurus, the father confessors and guides of the people; and the Jyotishees, the astrologers, with their families and relations, would be stripped of their honour and gain, of their very means of living, if Hinduism was at once abandoned. Benares is a great commercial as well as religious city. If it ceased to be Hindu, we cannot suppose its commerce would be paralyzed; but as a considerable part of its ordinary trade is dependent on the thousands of pilgrims who resort to it, on the money they expend on food, on gifts to the priests, and on the purchase of articles exposed for sale, great loss would be in the first place incurred. The many artisans now employed in making images of stone and brass, would find no purchasers for their goods. In addition to the pecuniary loss which directly and indirectly would fall on all classes, the whole community would feel the glory of Kasee, the Splendid City, had departed, when, stripped of its sacredness, crowds of pilgrims no longer filled its streets, frequented its temples, or bathed at its ghats. They would feel as the Jews did in their dark and disastrous days, when the ways to Zion were untrodden, and there was the silence of desolation within its gates.

When the peculiarities of Benares are in any degree realized, the work of making known the gospel to its inhabitants may appear formidable to the extent of hopelessness.

It is formidable, very formidable, but it can appear hopeless only when we forget the command of our Saviour to preach the Gospel to every creature, when we forget the power of the truth, the adaptation of the Gospel to the human heart, its past triumphs, and the promised aid of the Holy Spirit. The very strength of this fortress of idolatry should call forth the courage of Christ's soldiers by directing their eyes to Him as their great and glorious Leader. Such was the courage of the Apostles and their immediate successors, when instead of going to small towns and villages, and working from them towards the cities where the Gospel might be expected to meet with the most determined opposition, they assailed at once with their spiritual weapons the high places of idolatry, of power which claimed worship as well as homage, and of learning which aimed in its own strength, and aimed unsuccessfully, at the solution of the deepest questions which affect mankind. They went to Ephesus, to Rome, and to Athens, and secured in them a measure of success, which prepared the way for a mighty revolution throughout the Roman Empire.

Towards the end of the last century, when there was a great awakening of the missionary spirit, devoted Christians, animated by apostolic example, formed the purpose of going with the Gospel to Benares. Robert Haldane sold a fine estate, that with a band of chosen companions he might preach the Gospel to its inhabitants. He was obliged to abandon the enterprise by the prohibition of the East India Company; and then, in company with his brother and others similarly minded, he turned to home mission work, which for a time was prosecuted by them with ardent zeal and great success.

In 1781 the city and district of Benares, which had for some time paid tribute to our Government, were brought directly under our rule. We are sure no Christian missionary would have been previously tolerated in Benares for a day. He could not speak of Jesus Christ as the Lord of all and the Saviour of the world without implying that Mahadeo and the other gods of Benares were no God. His teaching would be speedily discerned in its antagonism to the genius of the place, and would ensure his speedy expulsion, if not his death. To the present hour no missionary is allowed to plant his foot in Mecca, or Medina, the sacred cities of the Muhammadans. Till a very recent period, when the Pope's political power came to an end, no Protestant minister was allowed to open his mouth in proclaiming the Gospel in Rome. The mild Hindu can be as fanatical as the Muhammadan and the Roman Catholic in resenting an attack on his religion, and in persecuting its opponents.

We have no historical records from which we can learn how Buddhism was overthrown in India; but, as we have already observed, we have reason to conclude it was not overthrown by argument and persuasion, but by fire and sword. The intense hatred shown to the Gospel by those who are imbued by the spirit of Hinduism will not allow us to doubt that, if they had the power, they would forbid all Christian effort, and especially such effort in their sacred city. They were long under the rule of the Muhammadans, and were subjected by them to grievous indignities, which they were helpless to avert or resent; but their attachment to Hinduism, instead of being diminished, was inflamed by the treatment they received, and during the semi-independent position they held previous to coming under our sway they had both the power and the will effectually to prevent the entrance of a new antagonistic religion. The superior strength and daring of the English were so signally shown in the overthrow of Rajah Cheit-Singh by Warren Hastings, that opposition to the new *régime* was seen to be hopeless, and the people quietly submitted to their new rulers. So far as they knew the temper and policy of the English, they might conclude their religion would at their hands not only be safe from violence, but protected from every attempt at proselytism. The policy which would have left Hinduism undisturbed was successfully opposed by the Christian feeling of England, and the way was opened for the Christian missionary into the very fortress of Hindu idolatry. For this entrance we are not in any way indebted to the mildness of Hindu religionists, but to the resolute, persevering, courageous effort of men of God, who contended successfully against the worldly selfishness which would have doomed the millions of India to perpetual night.

We have observed that mission operations were tentatively begun in Benares in the second decade of this century. The work was carried on in a very quiet unostentatious manner. Some time elapsed before any open aggressive effort was put forth. If Bishop Heber's counsel had been followed there would have been no departure from the first timid mode of action. He says in his journal, "The custom of street preaching, of which the Baptist and other Dissenting missionaries in Bengal are very fond, has never been resorted to by those employed by the Church Missionary Society, and never shall be so long as I have any influence or authority over them. I plainly see it is not necessary, and I see no less plainly that though it may be safe among the timid Bengalees, it would be very likely to produce mischief here. All which the missionaries do is to teach schools, read prayers, and preach in their churches, and to visit the houses of such persons as wish for information on religious subjects." If the good man had lived a few years longer he would have seen ministers of his own Church forward in modes of action which he disapproved, and would doubtless have wished them God-speed, as his successors in the diocese of Calcutta have done. The Bishop of Lahore, Dr. French, took a prominent part for years in outdoor preaching.

The missionary has of course met with opposition in many forms; the opposition has often been keen and bitter, but it has not taken the form of violence to person or injury to property. The Gospel has been for many years proclaimed in the most public places in Benares, crowds have heard it, and no hand has been raised against the preacher. In the memoirs of the Rev. William Smith, of the Church Mission, who was indefatigable in evangelistic labour, than whom none was better known in Benares, it is mentioned that on a few occasions mud was thrown at him, but it did him no harm. On one occasion, after a very keen discussion, when my Hindu opponents had been extremely angry, on coming out from the place a native Christian by my side was struck on the head by a stone, which was evidently intended for me. Happily the young man speedily recovered from the blow. The night was dark, and the act was not brought home to any one. The people present expressed indignation at the deed. On another occasion a man drew his sword half-way out of the scabbard (it was the fashion of the time to go about armed), and said he would gladly cut off my head, because I was trying to turn away his people from their religion; but he knew if he did he would be hanged, and as he wished to live a little longer he restrained himself. He gave me a scowl, which showed how ready he was for the crime if he could commit it with impunity. On another occasion most vigorous drumming was carried on above our heads, which made speaking and hearing impossible. As after many years spent in Benares I cannot recollect any more violent acts than those I have mentioned, the reader may infer how little reason we have to complain of danger to life or limb.

Nothing approaching the treatment of Dr. Kalley by the Popish priests of Madeira has been ever experienced by any missionary in Benares at the hand of Hindu priests. The perfect security, with which in ordinary times we went about our work, is in marked contrast to the experience of many a labourer in the home mission-field, not only in the early days of Methodism, but down to our own time, to say nothing of the violence to which the Salvation Army has been exposed. The fact that we belong to the ruling race, and that it is understood by all an attack on us will be promptly and severely punished, has had, no doubt, much to do in enabling us to carry on our operations so quietly and safely. There has been an ebullition at times on the occasion of baptisms, but it has soon subsided. Gradually the people have come to understand us sufficiently to be convinced we are bent on promoting their good, and they regard us in consequence with a friendly feeling. Most pleasant proof has been given that many of the inhabitants of Benares have come to look on missionaries not only with respect but affection. I well remember gratifying acts of courtesy and kindness, which could not have been prompted by sinister motives.

I must not omit to say that while missionaries have carried on their work openly and boldly, they have felt themselves bound to treat the people courteously, and to abstain from the use of violent and abusive words. There are places where they do not deem themselves entitled to declare their message—such as sacred places where worship is being carried on. Mr. Smith, of the Church Mission, once mentioned to me that he had for a short time taken his stand close to one of the bathing places, but the priests and people were greatly excited by his presence, and he deemed it proper to retire.

While at Benares the Gospel has to encounter peculiar opposition, it has some marked advantages as a mission-field. The missionary, as he moves about, meets with people from all parts of India. While these speak different languages, many know enough of the languages spoken at Benares to admit of a measure of intelligent intercourse with them. Vast multitudes come from the widely extended region over which the Hindustanee and Hindee prevail. While many go to Benares, we may suppose the great majority, urged by the gregarious feeling so powerful all the world over, happy to find themselves among the multitude, hoping to get some religious benefit, and sure at any rate, as they acknowledge, of amusement, we cannot doubt there are among them earnest souls—how many it is impossible to say—who are ill at ease, and have a craving for rest and satisfaction. These persons are in the state of mind to which the Gospel is specially adapted, and it is very desirous for the missionary to come into contact with them. Missionaries have fallen in with persons of this class, and among them there have been pleasing instances of conversion. There are individuals now in distant parts of India living Christian lives, who were led to embrace Christ as their Saviour by what they heard at Benares. Many Christian books have been circulated among pilgrims to the sacred city. These are taken to their homes, we may hope sooner or later to be read by them to their spiritual benefit. Again and again bread cast on the waters has been found after many days.

The greed of the Pundas and Gungaputrs of Benares is notorious. Many a poor pilgrim has suffered from their exactions, and we may suppose that reverence for the sacred city has received a shock under such treatment similar to that which Luther experienced on his visit to Rome. While Hinduism is no doubt greatly strengthened by the resort of the people to Benares, much done and endured there is well fitted to alienate the more thoughtful of the visitors; and so far as they are alienated from the prevailing superstition, the more likely they are to listen patiently and candidly to the Christian preacher.

I conclude these remarks on Benares as a mission sphere by observing that marked success there would have a marvellous effect on the evangelization of India. The news would soon spread that Hinduism was drying up at its fountain, and that its power could not be much longer maintained. We know that Hinduism itself has undergone great, we may say radical, changes, since Kasee became one of its principal seats, if not its head-quarters. There Buddhism was first preached, and from it Buddhism went forth to all Eastern Asia. There it was for a time predominant, but Hinduism again obtained supremacy, and drove its rival from the field. For centuries, Hinduism under the form of devotion to Shiva Mahadeo, the Great God, as they delight to call him, has had full sway. Is his dominion to last for ever? Are the people to be for ever in the slough of idolatry and superstition? We cannot believe that they are, until we abandon all trust in Him who rightly claims all human hearts, and whose grace is sufficient to enforce these claims. We know not when, we know not how, but we do know that even in Benares, as all the world over, our blessed Saviour will take to Himself His great power and reign. Even now entrance has been gained for the truth of God, hearts have been won by it, and Christian churches have been formed. The first-fruits have been gathered, and the harvest will come. Are we allowing imagination to take the reins at the expense of judgment, when we indulge the hope, that as in former days Buddhist preachers went forth from Benares to the millions of Eastern Asia with the lessons of Gautama, the Brahmans of Benares, accepting Jesus as their Saviour, will go forth with His Gospel to diffuse it far and wide among the nations of India, and then, with their converts, make their way to the remotest East? Let us not say, "If the Lord would make windows in heaven, might this thing be?" but rather, "Who hath despised the day of small things?" The Messiah "shall build the temple, and He shall bear the glory."

CHAPTER IX.

MY SECOND YEAR IN BENARES.

IN beginning this chapter it is fitting I should mention that shortly after entering on my second year an event occurred of transcendent importance to me, which has contributed to my personal comfort and missionary usefulness as nothing else could have done—my marriage with the object of my choice, who has been, through God's great goodness, spared to me through all the intervening years.

Before the close of my first year I had a striking illustration of the vicissitudes of Indian life, and of consequent difficulty in prosecuting the missionary enterprise. On reaching Benares at the end of March, 1839, I found three missionaries of our society, Messrs. Buyers, Shurman, and Lyon. Within a month of my arrival we were joined by a German missionary and his wife, Dr. and Mrs. Sommers. Towards the end of autumn Mr. and Mrs. Lyon left, owing to the failure of Mrs. Lyon's health. They were followed three months afterwards by Dr. and Mrs. Sommers, owing to Mrs. Sommers' illness. My second year was advanced only a few months, when Mr. and Mrs. Buyers, after a residence of nearly ten years, departed for Europe. Dr. Sommers had remained too short a time to render any service.

Mr. Lyon had made excellent progress in the language, and promised to be a very efficient missionary; but, to our great regret, he was obliged to leave. Mr. Buyers was in his prime, and was well equipped for service. Thus within eighteen months the staff of the mission was reduced from five to two, and one of these too young and inexperienced to do anything more than help his senior brother. In June, 1841, we were joined by the Rev. D. G. Watt, and early in 1842 by the Rev. J. H. Budden. These much-esteemed brethren still survive, and have done excellent service in the cause of Christ; but both suffered much from the climate, and their stay at Benares was too short to admit of their doing there what their hearts were bent on doing.

I have not the means of comparing our Indian missions with missions in other parts of the world, but I believe our losses by the failure of health have greatly exceeded theirs. The climate of the South Sea Islands, of South Africa, and of the West Indian Islands, is far more favourable to European health than that of the parts of India in which most of our missions are. The longevity of many of the South African missionaries bears remarkable testimony to the salubrity of their climate.

This failure of health and consequent abandonment of the work is one of the greatest trials missions in India have had to encounter, and is a formidable obstacle to success. Instances have not been rare when, after great expense has been incurred, the missionary or his wife has suddenly broken down—the wife perhaps more frequently than the husband—and a speedy return to England has been the result. The name appears in the Report as an agent, but no work has been, or could have been, accomplished. In other cases the stay has been too brief to have admitted of efficient service. A considerable time must elapse before the missionary, however zealous and able, can acquire such an acquaintance with the language and people as will enable him to do his work in a satisfactory manner. When one has fully entered on the work, there is frequent interruption from illness and weakness induced by the severity of the climate. When I transfer myself in thought to my first two years in Benares, and from my vivid remembrance of the vicissitudes of our mission during these years look down through all the succeeding years not only of our mission, but of other missions in Northern India with which I am well acquainted, I am painfully struck with the bitter disappointments of missionary Societies in the prosecution of their work. They have responded to the urgent appeal for reinforcement, and in not a few cases no sooner has the reinforcement been gained than it has been lost. The Societies formed of late years for Zenana work have suffered from this cause more than even the older Societies. They have suffered in a degree which must have been very discouraging to their managers and supporters. Happily a considerable number of all Societies have been able to remain at their post, and some have remained so long as to give an average length of missionary service, which hides the fact of the extreme brevity of the period spent by many in the foreign field.

The question here suggests itself, Has this speedy abandonment of the work been always necessary? Has there been the endurance demanded of those who have professed themselves consecrated to a missionary life? Has the return to England been accepted only when the compulsion of circumstances left no alternative, and then accepted most reluctantly? With every desire to think of others as favourably as possible, without any breach of charity, it must be acknowledged there have been cases of departure, where I think a more resolute spirit would have kept persons at their post. This I trust holds true of only a few. I know some who soon left to whom the abandonment of the work was a bitter trial. Nothing but the thought that to remain would have been to fight against Providence took them away. To go back to the cases of failure during my early period at Benares, I may mention that the departure of Mr. and Mrs. Lyon was absolutely necessary; and those who know the subsequent career of my friends, Messrs. Watt and Budden, need not be told that if health had permitted Benares would have been for many years the sphere of their labours.

As the withdrawal of missionaries has often been caused by the failure of the health of their wives, some have thought it would be well to have celibate missionaries in a country which has so severe a climate. To this there is the obvious reply that missionaries, like others, are human beings, and a restriction on them which wars with human nature would be found very pernicious, as it has ever been. Then, the wives of missionaries, when they are what they ought to be, are very efficient and, indeed, necessary missionary workers, and in many cases their labours are as useful as those of their husbands. In well-ordered missionary families the people see what a happy Christian home is, and they are assured of a sympathy in their trials and cares which they could not expect from unmarried missionaries. Some Societies, our own among the number, have accepted as missionaries to India persons engaged to be married, but they have required them to remain for a year or two unmarried after going out to test their fitness for the climate; and, in the event of the test being successfully stood, to give them an experience which will enable the newly married wife to enter with less strain on her Indian life. This may be a wise arrangement, and yet there is often a restlessness till the marriage takes place, and time spent in going to the port of debarkation, which carries with it some disadvantages.

We dare not retreat from this great work of evangelizing India on account of the vicissitudes of which I have been speaking, or on account of other very formidable obstacles which oppose us. To do so would be to act a craven part. Agents must be found for the prosecution of the work, and we must hope with the improved advantages of an Indian career the failures will be fewer than in the past; but whatever they may be, the Christian Church must go forward. One obvious inference from the facts I have stated, is the extreme desirableness of a native agency. The natives of the land, when found fit for the work, have always been highly prized. Many of this class are now labouring in different parts of India, and there is every reason to hope that in coming years the native agency will grow largely in extent and efficiency.

During my second year in Benares I entered on every department of mission work, and had many opportunities for intercourse with the people. In my turn I preached to the native Christian congregation, went with the missionaries and catechists to the city, and engaged in teaching the boys attending our primary schools. I saw the great gatherings of the people at their religious festivals, and realized their character, and the nature of the work to which I had devoted my life, more than I had previously done. Instead of following chronological order, my object in these reminiscences will be best attained by endeavouring to present to my readers those aspects of Indian and mission life which, during my second year, made a deep impression on my mind, an impression which was deepened by subsequent experience.

CHAPTER X.

THE RELIGIOUS GATHERINGS OF THE HINDUS.

CROWDS pass through the temples of Benares every day, pay obeisance, and present offerings; but on ordinary occasions there is no combined act of worship conducted by a leader, as is common in Christian assemblies. On occasions of special urgency—the failure of rain, its unseasonable fall, the fear of famine, or the dread of a great calamity coming on the community in some other form—sacrifices are offered up by priests in the presence of great multitudes, in which all present unite. These are very special and occasional services, for, as a rule, all over India persons and families act apart.

Hindus are, however, eminently social, and in their religious services full play is given to the social feeling. This is shown by their melas, or religious gatherings, which are held all over the country, and are extremely popular. Some of these melas are local, and have only a local attendance. Those to which crowds from places far and near resort are held in so-called sacred spots. Many are periodical, and are held at fixed periods of the year in honour of their gods, and in celebration of their exploits. Others, again, are held on special occasions, and of these eclipses are the most attractive.

In the course of my second year I saw a good deal of these festivals. I have a vivid and very unpleasant recollection of the Holee of that year, the Saturnalia of the Hindus, which is held at the setting in of the hot weather. It lasts for several days, during which the people act as if freed from every moral restraint. There is a general cessation of labour; the people wander about, indulge in the wildest freaks, address to women who venture out the vilest words, leap and dance as if possessed of the spirit of licence, and throw red colouring-matter on those they meet, without respect of persons; till all seen in the streets, with their besmeared faces and soiled clothes, have a most disreputable appearance. The night is rendered hideous, and sleep well-nigh impossible, by the drumming, fifing, and shouting of the revellers, kept up till break of day. During this period many think themselves at liberty to do what at another time they would deem very culpable. Not a few partake of intoxicating drink, and if native statements be true they give themselves over to the grossest licentiousness. Europeans, as a rule, except it be necessary for them to go abroad, remain quietly in their homes while the Holee lasts, and mission work is for the time well-nigh suspended. When, however, Europeans have occasion to go out they have little reason to fear insult, as even in the Holee season they are regarded, if not with respect, at least with a dread which restrains the revellers. The hurtful influence of this season of licence can be conceived. I have always observed that for some time afterwards the boys in our schools were sleepy and listless.

On the night of the Diwalee mela, held in honour of Lakshmee, the goddess of wealth, the whole city is illuminated, tiny lamps are seen everywhere, friends give presents to each other, sweetmeats and parched grain are distributed among the poor. High and low give the night to gambling. The belief is entertained that if they fail to spend the night in this manner they will in their next birth be turned into frogs, or some vile reptile.

The most popular festival of the year at Benares and over the North-Western Provinces is the Ram Leela, the Play of Ram, when the life of Ram, a very popular incarnation of Vishnu, is dramatized. This drama is acted in the open air in different parts of the city, in the presence of admiring thousands. The people see Ram and his faithful spouse Seeta forced to leave their royal home by the intrigue of his mother-in-law; they see them in the forest, where Ram leads the life of a hunter; they see Seeta carried off by Rawan, the Demon King of Lunka (Ceylon); they hear Ram's cries of bitter distress on finding his beloved Seeta gone; they see him informed that Rawan is the ravisher; they see him setting out with the divine monkey Hanuman, and his army of monkeys for the rescue; and they rejoice with him in the taking of Lunka, the destruction of Rawan, and the rescue of Seeta. The story furnishes abundant material for a drama, and the people enter with the greatest zest into the different scenes. A huge figure of Rawan is made of wood and paper; it is set on fire, and the crowds, looking on, make the air resound with their shouts. During this mela two things are united which in Hindu estimation well agree—amusement and devotion. They regard the Ram Leela as a religious service, which they are bound to render to the conqueror of Rawan, and while rendering it they are at once performing duty and receiving pleasure. They continually call such a service *tumasha, show, fun,* and they regard its life and sprightliness a pleasing contrast to the sombre and staid services of the Christian Church.

Before the conclusion of my second year an eclipse of the moon occurred, which drew to the city the greatest assemblage of human beings I had ever seen. The Hindus place high among their deities the sun and moon, and render to them daily worship. Between the gods and the demons there is perpetual war, and victory inclines at one time to one side, at another time to another. In Hindu mythological annals many instances are recorded of the gods having been reduced to the utmost extremity. We are told that eclipses are caused by the demons endeavouring to swallow the sun and moon; and religious services on these occasions have a double benefit—the worshipper secures a high degree of merit, of which he will reap the reward one day; and the demons are driven off from their prey by the drumming, the shouts, and the merit of the assembled people, to the great relief of the endangered gods. The most extravagant promises are held out to those who bathe in the Ganges, at any time in any part of it; but bathing on the occasion of an eclipse, and especially in so sacred a place as Benares, is meritorious in a degree which is incalculable. The Pundits, the religious leaders of the people, have, it appears, access to the council of the demons, for the exact time of the coming attack is known by them so long before hand that the people far and near are prepared for its approach. In fact, if it did not come on, if the demons withdrew from their intention, there would be great disappointment. Brahman missionaries go great distances to inform the people the eclipse is to take place, and to press on them the benefit they will receive by bathing at Benares on that occasion. On their return they are accompanied by those whom they have succeeded in persuading. Leaving the mythological for the scientific platform, we had better mention that the Hindu astronomers have for ages been able to calculate eclipses; and now they need not trouble themselves to make calculations, as European almanacks are in their hands to give the requisite information.

For a few days previous to the eclipse of which I am now to speak, the unusual number of strangers in the city made it evident some great event was about to occur. From the morning of the appointed day the people poured into the city in a constant stream. As evening came on I made my way into the city on foot, but before reaching its centre I found the streets so blocked that I despaired of getting to the riverside. I retraced my steps, and by a road skirting the city made my way to Raj Ghat at the northern end. There I remained till the eclipse commenced. Many were near, but they were few compared with the crowds pressing towards the chief bathing places. When I arrived at Raj Ghat the confused sound of a great multitude fell on my ear, but no sooner did the eclipse begin than the thousands on the river's brink and crowded on the ghats, as with one voice raised a shout so loud and prolonged, that I should think it must have been heard for miles. I was on a high bank of the river, and could see distinctly the people below rushing into the stream. I could not but think of what must be occurring where the crowd was so dense that individual motion was well-nigh impossible. It was reported next morning that three or four hundred persons had been trampled to death or drowned in the rush to the river when the eclipse began. This was afterwards declared to be an exaggerated statement, but it is certain many lives were lost, though how many was not ascertained, as a number were carried away by the stream. Special care was afterwards taken by the authorities to prevent such catastrophes. After stopping some time at Raj Ghat I returned to my home, musing on what I had seen, and longing for the time when the millions of India will seek cleansing and life, where alone they can be found.

Towards the end of 1840 I went to Allahabad, seventy miles north-west of Benares, to take part in evangelistic work at a great mela held there annually, as I thought I might be able to render some help to my brethren. Allahabad, called Pryag by the Hindus, is at the confluence of the Ganges and the Jumna, and all such places are deemed sacred. It is said there is a third river, the Suruswatee, once visible but now underground, and the place is therefore called Tribeni—the threefold stream. Pryag has been for many years a famous place of pilgrimage, and every year a mela is held, which is at its height for some seven days, but is kept on for weeks. It is held in the cold weather, December or January; and, next to Hurdwar, where the Ganges issues from the mountains, draws a greater crowd than any other mela in Northern India. Bathing at Tribeni is peculiarly meritorious in some years, and in these there is a vastly increased attendance. Except on the occasion of eclipses there is no such gathering even at Benares; but very many who go to Allahabad, before returning to their home, often a distant home, pay a visit to the sacred city.

At one time the Government imposed a tax on pilgrims to this mela, but it was taken off in 1838 or 1839.

The mela is held below the fort, on the land lying between the Ganges and the Jumna at their point of meeting, on a great stretch of sand, which is covered in the rainy season. In December and January the west wind blows freshly over the place, and as there is incessant movement, soon all present are so covered with dust that they look like millers.

A gathering like this at Allahabad is always embraced for evangelistic purposes. Missionaries and native brethren are thankful for the opportunity afforded them of preaching the Gospel to many who have come from places to which no missionary has ever gone. The missionaries at Allahabad gladly welcome and hospitably entertain the brethren of other missions who join them at these annual gatherings. Large tents are put up, with the front open towards the road, and there the preachers from morning till evening, preacher succeeding preacher, address the people, while hearers succeed hearers. A few individuals stop a long time, as if rapt up in what they hear, as if they were drinking in every word; others stop a considerable time; while many, after looking on and gaping for a few minutes, hold on their way. Every now and then questions are asked, objections are started, and a discussion ensues. When the questions are in any measure serious and reasonable, much benefit results from such discussion. The interest of the people is quickened, and opportunity is afforded for explaining, defending, and enforcing the truth as it is in Jesus. Sometimes the questioner is neither serious nor reasonable, and then the danger is of the discussion turning into a wrangle, which does more harm than good. Prominent transgressors in this line are the Pundas, specially interested in the mela, who do all in their power to set the people against us. At this first great gathering which I attended—I found it was the case afterwards on similar occasions—there was less mere idle discussion than there is where the missionary carries on his work from day to day. In addition to preaching-stations, there were bookstalls where portions of the Scriptures and Christian tracts and books were disposed of. On to the time of this mela there was a large gratuitous distribution among persons who from their look and manner were deemed suitable recipients; but for many years it has been found best to charge a small price, without adopting a hard and fast line against giving away.

It is very difficult, rather impossible, to estimate the effect produced by evangelistic services on such occasions. They have not been fruitless as to conversion, but if we look simply at results of this kind it must be acknowledged they are very limited. Instances have occurred of persons having been so impressed that they have followed missionaries to places far away from Allahabad; but their courage has failed them, and they have after a short time disappeared. One advantage is secured—the Gospel is kept before the minds of the people, and some knowledge of it is carried to the remotest parts of the land. Books and tracts are taken to places which missionaries have never visited. It cannot be doubted that such services have their part in preparing the people for the new and better state of things which every Christian longs for and expects.

At Allahabad I had an opportunity of observing the peculiarities of a great Hindu mela. The morning was devoted to bathing and the performance of religious rites. As the forenoon came on, the merchants of every class set out their wares in tents erected on sites appointed for them, with their opening, so far as possible, away from the side exposed to the wind. Goods of every description, useful and ornamental, cloth, grain, cooking vessels, trinkets, and sweetmeats, were exhibited to tempt purchasers, and buying and selling went on as vigorously as if the people had come together solely for that end. Crowds were in constant motion, going from place to place to see what could be seen, and stopping where there was any special attraction, or, as happens in our own crowded streets, stopping where a few were incidentally collected. By the afternoon, singers, experts in tricks, and show-people of every description, commenced their operations, and were sure of admiring crowds. The merry-go-rounds were largely patronized. Hour after hour was thus spent.

A few cooked food early in the day, but the vast majority staved off hunger—in some cases by partaking of cakes reserved from the previous evening meal; the greater number, I believe, by partaking of sweetmeats made with flour, sugar, and melted butter, of which an enormous quantity was offered for sale. As evening came on they scattered themselves over the ground lying between the Ganges and the Jumna, and set to the preparation of their one proper meal for the twenty-four hours. The plain was alight with their fires. Nothing can be simpler than their cooking. They make what they call a *choola*, an elevation in the shape of a horseshoe of a half-foot or a little more of moistened mud, or stone if they can get it. If the traveller be of a respectable caste, he takes care to make no use of the *choolas* which former travellers have left. They may have been set up by impure hands, and so he makes one for himself. It is convenient to have two such *choolas*, that they may put on the one a small pot with rice or *dal*, a kind of pea, in it, and on the other a girdle for bannocks of unleavened dough. Cooking is, of course, largely women's work, but men are as expert at it as women, and are continually seen preparing their meal. I have never travelled with a native who seemed to think he was called to an unusual or unpleasant work, when required to cook his food. All he needs is a couple of small cooking vessels, which he carries with him, a little fuel, good water, meal, and a spot on which he may set up his humble hearth. I have seen this work done by pundits, learned men, who showed no indication of shrinking from it as if it trenched on their dignity. Indeed the pundit in a party that has few facilities for cooking has, as I remember well in one instance, this honour conferred on him on account of his caste being higher than that of those who are with him. All of every caste can eat what he has prepared, but he helps himself first, and eats apart.

To return to the mela. The evening is well advanced before the repast is over. We might suppose that after the stir of the day all would be ready for sleep, and no doubt many lie down and sleep soundly; but quite a number are too eager for the enjoyment of the fair to give themselves to rest. Singing, drumming, and boisterous mirth go on till the small hours of the morning, as I have known to my unpleasant experience—not at Allahabad, but elsewhere when I have been in their close neighbourhood.

How do the vast multitudes who attend a mela, such as that of Allahabad, dispose of themselves at night? Their arrangements are of the simplest kind. Many wrap themselves in their sheet or blanket, if they have one, and lie down on the ground without any idea they are enduring hardship. Others rig out a temporary tent with sticks and a blanket over it, creep under this, and deem themselves luxuriously accommodated. This gathering at Allahabad is in the cold weather, and if the nights be very cold, as they sometimes are at that season, no doubt many suffer severely. Every now and then heavy rain falls, and then, as may be supposed, the suffering is extreme. Sanitary precautions are of the utmost importance where such vast crowds meet and remain together for days, and these are taken by the authorities. They cannot, however, provide against suffering caused by bad weather. Occasionally cholera breaks out, and then the scenes witnessed are appalling. At the mela of 1840 the weather was good, and there was no indication of disease among the people. Some years afterwards we were travelling towards Allahabad at an early period of the mela, and met crowds fleeing from it on account of the outbreak of cholera. Here and there we saw corpses at the side of the road, occasionally without one person near, at other times with a weeping group around, who were preparing to carry off the body to some rivulet to have it burnt, or, as it often happens, to have it scorched, and then left to be devoured by jackals and vultures. Some had held on their way with weary limbs till the fell disease seized them, and then they succumbed, lay down, and died. We remember stopping where a young man was dying, with two or three sorrowful ones around him. We spoke to him, but got no reply. His glazed eye told he was beyond all human help.

One of the first things I saw at this Allahabad mela was a quantity of human hair, and was told that it had been cut off after the fulfilment of vows, reminding one of a custom to which we find frequent reference in both the Old and New Testaments. I also saw a very disgusting sight—men in stark nudity, sitting in a very composed dignified fashion, and women approaching them with folded hands, and paying them profound homage. These were deemed men of great sanctity, whose blessing brought signal benefit, while their curse entailed terrible calamities. At an early period of our residence at Benares we sometimes met these naked creatures in the streets; but for many years they have disappeared, as there is a magisterial order that they be flogged for their indecency, however loud may be their pretension of sanctity. At Allahabad there were many devotees with their tangled hair, besmeared bodies, and *very* scanty clothing—if what they had on could be called clothing. These are yet seen all over the country. The time has not yet come for stringent orders in these cases.

On the occasion of a gathering such as that of Allahabad a stranger sees no sign of the separating influence of caste. The people move about and mix with each other as freely as people do in Europe when assembled in large numbers. There is nothing in caste to prevent people conversing with each other and being on friendly terms; but the friendliness must not go the length of eating together or of intermarriage. There are indeed large classes deemed so low, so outside the pure Hindu castes, that, so far as is possible, their touch is shunned, and they are not allowed to enter temples; but even these may be spoken to and caste purity retained. We have not in Northern India a class so low that they must hide themselves when a Brahman appears, as Pariahs have to do in some parts of Southern India. In fact, at Hindu melas one receives a pleasing impression of the social character of the people, when he observes their good humour and friendly intercourse.

We do not wonder at the popularity of these gatherings. The social feeling is as strong among the Hindus as among any people on the face of the earth. The vast majority lead lives of monotonous toil in places where there is no excitement greater than that of ordinary village and hamlet life, and to them it must be a great pleasure to resort to the gatherings of their people, where religion, business, and amusement are very happily combined, and where there is so much to interest, exhilarate, and gratify them. These times are to them the red-letter days of the year, without which life would be intolerably dull. Resort to these gatherings no doubt involves them in toil, in expense, and sometimes in great suffering; but they do not shrink from the cost, as they anticipate the expected benefit.

There cannot be a doubt that Hinduism is greatly strengthened by these melas. Judaism was greatly strengthened by the people according to the Divine command going up thrice every year, at appointed times, to the place where the name of the Lord was, and by their repairing in vast numbers once a year to their sacred capital after they had become widely scattered among the nations. Muhammadans, by long journeys and perilous voyages, make their way to Mecca and Medina, their sacred cities, and make it a point to be present at the most sacred season, when many thousands are assembled. These pilgrims return to their homes more devoted than ever to Islam. It would be strange if Christianity, which above every other religion aims at producing and sustaining the feeling of universal brotherhood, did not avail itself of this social feeling, to which so much scope is given in human religions, and which is so potent in confirming the devotion of their adherents.

Our blessed Saviour, the Head of the Church, has by the institution of Churches, and the instruction given to them through His Apostles, provided for the fellowship of His people; and the occasional gathering of the members of different Churches, to which the principles of the Gospel point, and to which it gives the fullest sanction, presents precious opportunities for the manifestation and exercise of the brotherliness so characteristic of the kingdom of heaven which our Lord came to set up on the earth.

CHAPTER XI.

THE OBJECT OF MISSIONS, AND VARIOUS MODES OF OPERATION.

THERE is no difference of opinion among missionaries as to the object for which they have gone to the heathen. They are all agreed their object is to make known the Gospel, the message of salvation, to all to whom they obtain access, to explain its nature, and press its claims on their acceptance. To this nothing can be held superior; to this everything must be deemed subordinate. To place anything above it, or even beside it, would be to lose sight of the very *raison d'être* of their missionary calling.

There may be, however, and there often is, a difference of opinion as to the line of operation best fitted to secure success. Missionaries find themselves in presence of widely-separated classes, who must be approached in different ways, and it is the part of wisdom to find out the most direct path to their understanding, conscience, and heart. About these modes of operation there has often been marked diversity of opinion, some pleading for one mode, and others for another. It cannot be denied that in the discussion thus carried on there has often been one-sidedness, resulting in some cases from natural liking, in some from special fitness, in others from the peculiarities of the sphere into which missionaries find themselves introduced so that they fail to realize the peculiarities in the qualifications, likings, and spheres of their brethren, who are as eager as themselves to bring the people to the feet of the Lord Jesus. Hinduism is a strong fortress, and those who assail it by hurling at it—if I may so speak—the red-hot shot of exposure of its errors, and the fire of the truth as it is in Jesus, act very unwisely in depreciating those who are quietly preparing the ammunition required for carrying on the siege, or are undermining the foundations, and thus preparing for entering the breach. The erection of the Christian Church in India is a most arduous, and at the same time a most glorious, enterprise, and a variety of workmen is required. Those who handle the trowel and the hammer act very unwisely in depreciating those who plan the structure, clear away the rubbish, and lay the foundation, or who in other ways help on the building. These illustrations require no enlargement. They indicate the views which every succeeding period of my missionary career has led me to entertain with increasing firmness. The translation and revision of the Scriptures, the preparation of Christian tracts and books, teaching in schools and colleges, taking charge of orphanages, the going among the people in city, town, and hamlet, wherever they can be reached, to speak to them about the Saviour of mankind; attending to secular work, such as the erection of buildings, keeping accounts, and gathering money—all are legitimate departments of missionary work, and the choice of them by missionaries ought to be determined by the exigencies of missions, by personal fitness, and by providential indications of the course which should be pursued. I would go further, and say that the preparation of grammars and dictionaries, the giving of time and strength to literary work, may in certain circumstances, in the case of men of peculiar qualifications, be deemed work worthy of a missionary, as thereby he may do much to further the cause to which he has devoted his life. Readers will readily recall names of illustrious men, who were deeply imbued with the missionary spirit and did eminent service, who were also remarkable for their literary achievements. It would, however, be very undesirable that literary ability and industry should be the most prominent characteristics of a large portion of the missionary band. Devotion to literary work is, with rare exceptions, incompatible with the active life which must be led by those who would come into close contact with the people, and by personal intercourse strive to bring them to the Saviour.

Some individuals have gone to the mission-field with the firm resolve to do the work in only one way. Such a resolve has ever seemed to me most unwise, savouring more of wilfulness than of holy steady purpose to do the Master's work. The missionary ought to go out ready to part with every preconceived notion at the call of providential direction and the Spirit's guidance, prepared to do with all his might whatever he may have the opportunity of doing for the advancement of Christ's kingdom, however little may be his natural liking or supposed fitness for the work.

Like most missionaries, I went to India with my liking for certain forms of work; but like nearly all who have been long in the field, there is scarcely any department in which I have not some time or other been engaged, though for some departments I have had little aptitude and, I may say, no liking, and from which I would have escaped if I could. To have held back would have been dereliction of duty, and this conviction overcame my reluctance.

PREACHING TO THE HEATHEN.

Without any depreciation of other departments, preaching to the heathen—what is commonly called in India Bazar preaching—ought ever to hold a prominent place.

Evangelistic work is carried on wherever access to the people can be obtained. In Benares, our primary schools, of which I shall speak presently, were taught in verandahs open to the streets. These were utilized as preaching-stations. The boys were first examined and taught; a few invariably gathered around, and we turned from the boys to the bystanders, and spoke to them so long as they were willing to hear, or we were able to speak. In addition to these verandahs we had humble buildings erected on the most available spots, for the double purpose of schools and preaching-stations. To these little chapels we could retire from the noise of the streets. In them we had morning and evening service; but as the hot weather advanced the heat was well-nigh intolerable in the city in the evening, and evening work was suspended till we got cooling by the first burst of rain.

We every now and then betook ourselves to the shade of a house or a tree, where we spoke to the passers-by. On the occasion of great gatherings we took our stand at the roads by which the people were pouring into the city, or making their way out of it. Every place was deemed suitable where we could get hearers, and could hope for any degree of attention. At some spots the crowd was so large and noisy that there was no use in trying to make ourselves heard. As we went about we spoke to individuals and little groups as opportunity was presented to us.

Some missionaries who laid themselves out for this department made it a point to go every year, with their native assistants, considerable distances to the great melas, and spend days, sometimes weeks, in setting before the assembled crowd the great truths of God's Word. Others, again, made it a point to travel during the cold weather, so far as home duty allowed, to preach the Gospel through the country; some within a limited area, confining themselves to certain towns and villages, and visiting them again and again, while others made very extended tours. It was my privilege for years to take part in these intineracies, and I remember with peculiar pleasure the opportunities they afforded for intercourse with the people.

What in India is called Bazar preaching is very different from the ordinary preaching of ministers in this country, both in its mode and in the circumstances in which it is conducted. When accompanied by a few native Christians, we begin by singing a hymn and offering a short prayer. Then those present are addressed. Often one of our Lord's parables, or some striking fact or passage from the Scriptures is taken as a text. Sometimes a remark by one of our hearers, or something of general interest which has just occurred, gives the key-note to the address. The great doctrines and facts of Scripture are mainly dwelt on, and the more simply and directly they are set forth, the more are we satisfied our duty is efficiently discharged. In our preaching the first place is assigned to the life and character, the words and deeds, the death, resurrection, and reign of our blessed Saviour. Suitableness is a valuable characteristic of preaching everywhere, and among no people is it more important than in speaking to the Hindus. They are very fond of figures, of illustrative instances, and when these are happily applied they produce a marked effect. In the character of the gods and goddesses, and in Hindu notions and practices, there is much which is open to attack, and some avail themselves largely of this opening to assail the cherished belief of the people; but as a rule it is far better to assert and enforce truth than to confute error, though truth does at times require error to be directly exposed. The native brethren are much more inclined to aggressive speech than the missionaries. They know their own countrymen well; they are familiar with their modes of thinking and of acting, they are well acquainted with the doings attributed to their gods, and they are ready to attack them with unsparing severity. On one occasion a catechist, more zealous than wise, began his address with the words, "Your religion is altogether false," which so provoked his hearers that they did not hear another word, and went away in indignation. Afterwards I sharply reproved him for his indiscretion, as I had at times to do to him and others.

Occasionally a missionary is quietly heard, and if heard attentively as well as quietly he is gratified with the reception he gets, and hopes that good is being done. It is seldom, however, in a city like Benares that a preacher is allowed to go on long without interruption. If a considerable number assemble we are almost sure to find, before we conclude, some among them ready to speak, and the object of those who thus come forward becomes speedily apparent. Some are eager to interrupt the preacher. He has scarcely announced his subject, and has had no opportunity of explaining and illustrating it, when he is interrupted by the words, " You have spoken a long time " (the long time has perhaps not been five minutes); " let me speak a little while." As a rule, in this case the missionary appeals to the fairness of his audience to give him a patient hearing, that they may really know his views, and may be in a position for coming to a right judgment regarding them. Often the appeal is successful, and our eager disputant is compelled to remain silent. When the address is over discussion is welcomed; and, as I have observed about preaching at the religious gatherings of the people, if conducted with reasonableness and good humour it is fitted to do good. We are thankful when there is the appearance of candour, even though there be not earnestness, when those who speak seemingly desire to know exactly what we do hold, as thereby an opportunity is given for the clearer and fuller statement of the Gospel. I have a pleasing recollection of many instances when persons were evidently impressed with what had been told them of the Lord Jesus Christ, and of the claims He has on man's love and trust.

It must be acknowledged that this has not been the mood of most of our hearers where we are well known. Many are eager to defend their own position as Hindus, and to attack Christianity because it wages war with their religion. Heathenism in ancient times, heathenism now as we see it in India, was and is very liberal. It is ready to let Christianity alone, if Christianity will let it alone. It is the exclusiveness of Christianity which is so offensive. We are continually told that Christianity is excellent for us; we are most welcome to maintain our adherence to it; and it is surely fair to let them alone in the enjoyment of their religion. Because they are not let alone, because we contend that their religion is dishonouring to the living God and hurtful to themselves, because we affirm that Christ is the one Saviour and the rightful Lord, they are eager to find something in our books and views which they can assail, and by which they can show our position to be untenable.

There is nothing we hear more frequently than that all religions lead to the same goal, as all the roads of a country lead to its capital. To this we reply that those who wish to go to Calcutta in the east are not likely to reach it soon if they set out on the road to Lahore in the west. The east and west are opposite, and yet they are not opposed; but good and evil, righteousness and unrighteousness, are essentially opposed, their fruits are opposed, and those who practise them are sure to find themselves at last in places as distinct from each other as light is from darkness, as happiness is from misery.

Traditional religion is strong, except in peculiar seasons when the tide of public opinion runs in the channel of religious revolt. From the lips of Hindus we hear continually, "We must walk in the ways of our fathers. What our fathers believed we believe. What our fathers practised we practise. No good son leaves his father and mother. No good wife leaves her husband for another." To this objection we have various replies. We tell them they do not walk in the ways of their ancient fathers, for they did many things, such as eating the flesh of cows, which they abhor, knew nothing of the gods they worship, and were not fettered by caste as they are. What we say about these Hindu ancestors gets little credit, as the people generally know nothing about them. We remind them that among themselves there have been tribes that have from generation to generation lived by thuggery and dacoity (murder and robbery). Ought the children of these murderers and robbers to walk in the ways of *their* fathers?

I have often referred to the Khonds in the hills of Orissa, who, till the horrid practice was stopped by British interference, enticed children from the plains, fed them well, treated them kindly, and then on a fixed day murdered them, tore limb from limb, and scattered the bleeding fragments over the fields as an offering to the Land Goddess to secure an abundant harvest. I have asked, "Ought these people to walk in the ways of their fathers?" To this question I have never received an affirmative reply.

We have reminded the people their fathers were as prone to err as we are; that we ought to weigh in the scales of truth and justice what they did, in order to the imitation of them when right and the forsaking of them when wrong. If they were with us, provided they were really wise, they would wish us to embrace the good of which they knew nothing, but which was now presented for their acceptance. With all their regard for their fathers, there were things unknown to them—as, for instance, the potato for food, and the railway carriage for travelling. If the potato was good for the body, as many of them showed they thought by partaking of it, might not our religion be good for the soul? If they resorted in crowds to the railway carriages even when going on pilgrimage to their sacred places, if in their earthly travels they found these carriages so serviceable, might they not find the religion of Christ, if candidly considered, the best vehicle for carrying them to heaven? We have much sympathy with the feeling of reverence for ancestors, but they are not entitled to tyrannize over their descendants.

We tell them we do not wish them to leave their father's house, but to return to it; not to leave the husband, but to return to the true husband.

At first sight the worship carried on at Benares seems so absurd that one wonders how a reasonable being can say anything in its defence. Many years ago I had a visit from an English gentleman who was travelling through India, and he expressed his surprise we had such limited success in turning the people from worshipping such ugly misshapen stones. He evidently thought that by quoting some of the passages of Scripture in which the wickedness and folly of idol-worship are exposed, he could silence idol-worshippers, and secure their speedy conversion to the living God. If he had come into contact with the people he would not have found their conversion such an easy matter. I have never met a Hindu who would allow he worshipped the material objects before which he bowed down. However illiterate he may be, he is ready to maintain that he worships the god represented by the image, and who is actually dwelling in it in a mysterious manner, after some sacred words have been uttered over it.

We are often told in defence of Hinduism that it is a symbolical representative religion, and that as God is vastly beyond our comprehension, we cannot, except by symbols, attain any conception of Him. We have often to say in reply, that as we cannot see our own spirit, and yet know how real, how dominant it is, so far less do we know the Supreme Being, and yet we have abundant evience of His existence, character, and government. Of Him no fitting image can be made, and every such attempt is unworthy of Him, and degrading and demoralizing to us. The representations of God in Scripture under sensible forms are of high value to us in our weakness; but when reproduced in material substances, such as wood and stone, they have been ever found to foster low, materialistic views of the Most High. If we must betake ourselves to such symbols, let us have those which inspire lofty thoughts. What is there in these grotesque idols to help us in rising to the living God? Hindus who know English have quoted Cowper's address to his mother on getting her picture, "Oh that those lips had language," and we have been asked, "Was not Cowper helped in realizing his mother when looking at her picture?" To which there is the obvious reply, "Cowper's mother was truly represented. Is God truly and fittingly represented by the idols you worship?"

The gods are continually represented as mediators through whom we approach the Supreme. "When we seek the favour of a king we approach him through his ministers; when we wish to propitiate a judge we try to secure a friend who will plead for us: and thus by the gods we get access to the Most High." To this we reply that as creatures we may each one go directly to God, for He is always near us, and we can never be far from Him; but as sinners we need a mediator. As the necessity for a mediator is acknowledged, we have an excellent opportunity of showing how worthy Christ is of being trusted as the Mediator, related as He is by His essential nature to the Most High, and to man by the nature He has assumed. A favourite figure with the Hindus is that the gods are a ladder by which they ascend to the Supreme; and we could not have a figure more adapted to our purpose, as it leads us to show that Christ is the very ladder we need—He by His Divine nature reaching heaven, and by His human nature being set upon the earth. His infinite excellence and His propitiatory sacrifice assure us that this ladder is so strong that it can bear the weight of the whole of the human family in their ascent to God.

Few things have been a greater stumbling-block to the Hindus than the crucifixion of Christ, and we have to dwell continually on the fact that it was not by the failure of His power, but by the ardour of His love, He endured this death. Some of the gods, Shiva and Kalee in particular, are propitiated by animal sacrifices, as blood is specially pleasing to them. The need of sacrifice to deliver from the consequences of sin is dimly discerned by the people, but they have such distorted views on the subject that it is difficult to convey to them the Christian idea of propitiation.

The learned men of India have been singularly wanting in what may be called the historic instinct, and we need not wonder at finding the people generally destitute of it. The evidence for Christianity drawn from its history makes no impression on them. Historical facts and the wildest legends are received by them with equal readiness. When speaking of the miracles of our Lord, and enlarging on their peculiar features of power and goodness, I have been pleased to witness an attention which led me to hope that a favourable impression was being made; but more than once my hope has been dashed to the ground by one of my most attentive hearers saying, "You have been telling us of your God. He did excellent things, and you do well to worship Him; but listen to me, and I will tell you what my gods have done." And then my hearer has become the speaker, and has dilated on the wonderful feats of his gods, such as Krishna lifting up a mountain and holding it on his hand above his worshippers to shelter them from the angry bolts of Indra; and has triumphantly asked, "Is there anything similar to that in your Bible?" To which we have readily replied, "There is not, but there is what is more worthy of God." The most illiterate of the people are very familiar with mythological stories, and if listened to will go on to relate them with the greatest gusto, and at the greatest length.

Our doctrine of salvation by grace alone, and not in any degree by man's merit, is often declared to be fatal to morality. This is often said in our own country, and we need not say what we advance in its confutation.

The doctrine of previous births has taken full possession of the Hindu mind, as accounting for the character and events of the present birth. This belief in transmigration has a very hurtful effect on the people, as it leads them, when suffering for their conduct, to attribute their sufferings to births of which they do not profess to have any remembrance, instead of blaming themselves for the course they had pursued. We have to show the baselessness, the unreasonableness, and the injurious tendency of this notion. The doctrine of a blind fate determining everything is widely held. The greatest criminals coolly assert it has been their fate to have done what they have done, and, of course, to suffer as they suffer. The moral nature of the people, though benumbed, is happily not destroyed, and to it we appeal against a notion which levels all moral distinctions.

Pantheism, it is well known, lies at the foundation of Hindu Polytheism. It may be indeed doubted if there has ever been a Polytheistic system apart from a Pantheistic element. The Hindus generally cannot work out the Pantheistic theory, as the Pundits do, but the most illiterate are familiar with its commonplaces, and are ready with their avowal. We often hear, "Is not God everywhere? Does He not pervade all? Is He not all? Is not all evolved from Him, as the spider's web is evolved from its body? Does not all emanate from Him, as the stream flows from the fountain and rays from the sun? Are we not all portions of Him? We may worship anything and everything if only we see God in it. There are differences in the sparks from the central fire, some far brighter than others. The gods are the brightest sparks, and therefore they are specially worthy of worship." In reply we have to insist on the difference between the Creator and the creature, between the Ruler and His subject. We are often told it is God that makes us speak and act, and we are puppets dancing as He draws the strings. In protest against this doctrine we appeal to the acknowledgment they themselves make of the essential distinction between right and wrong, the one to be done, the other to be shunned, and show that if their Pantheistic notion be accepted the distinction is obliterated, and the floodgate is open to the commission of all wickedness.

The most advanced thought of Hindu philosophy is that all is Maya, illusion, the play, the amusement of the Supreme, who leads us to believe that we are, that we have a separate existence, which we have not; but at last the illusion will come to an end, all will be absorbed in Brahm, as the water in the clouds falls into the sea; there will be no conscious existence in the universe. Brahm himself will glide into a profound slumber from which he will awake after a vast season of repose. A rope lying on the road is taken for a serpent, but it is only a rope. There are hundreds of suns glancing on the waters, but there is only one sun. In reply we contend that illusion implies reality; that if there was no reality illusion would be impossible. If there was no serpent a rope would not be taken for it. If there was no sun there would be no suns glancing in the waters.

The question has been often discussed, Have the Hindus any idea of a living, personal God? It is unquestionable they often speak as if they had. They often say, "Does not God see? Does He not know? Will He not punish us if we do what is wrong?" It is difficult to say to what degree this notion has been formed and cherished from intercourse for ages with Muhammadans, and how far it comes from the demand of the human spirit for the living God. Some eminent Sanscrit scholars tell us that the Vedas teach Pantheism, while others assert that in their most ancient teaching they assert the doctrine of a living, personal God. From this divided opinion it is plain that the teaching of the Vedas on this vital subject is ambiguous. At any rate there cannot be a doubt that the modern Hindus have some notion of God as a living, conscious One apart from His creatures, although it is held with Pantheistic and Polytheistic notions, which are antagonistic to it, and greatly weaken its influence. Its being held at all is very serviceable to a missionary in the prosecution of his work.

In a city like Benares many have acquired a considerable acquaintance with the Bible, and these endeavour to find flaws in it to show that our religion is as assailable as theirs.

I must not go further into these details of evangelistic work. As I am giving them my past life comes vividly to my remembrance. I remember its pleasures, and also its difficulties and trials. I feel as if I was engaged in preaching to the Hindus among whom I have spent a great part of my life, and discussing with them the great questions which affect God and man. I am consequently in danger of saying more than can be interesting to my readers.

In Benares it is rare to have only Hindus for our hearers. We very often have Muhammadans also, and they are our most eager and bitter opponents. All I can now say about them is that they are bent on entrapping us with questions about the Sonship of Christ, the Trinity in the Godhead, the authenticity of the Scriptures as we now have them, the alleged incompleteness of Christ's prophetic office, as proved, they think, by the promise of the Paraclete as well as by the predictions in both the Old and New Testaments. Among Muhammadans we have met individuals who seemed sincere inquirers after truth, who seemed bent on ascertaining what is true and discovering what is false. We have been gratified with their apparent candour, humility, and reasonableness. We must acknowledge these have been a small minority compared with the many whose pride and bigotry have shut up their mind against everything we had to advance, and whose sole aim has been to assail Christianity and Christians.

In the prosecution of the evangelistic work, which I have endeavoured to describe, missionaries come into contact with all classes. The seed of the word thus sown far and wide may remain for a time hidden, but we have every reason to hope it will some time spring up and bring forth abundant fruit.

CHAPTER XII.

SCHOOLS.

FROM the commencement of Missions, schools have received much attention, and have absorbed a large part of mission agency. These schools have been of different orders, many primary, a number secondary, and a few educating the pupils up to the University mark for degrees. I have had a great deal of experience in teaching and superintending primary and secondary schools, and I have seen something of the institutions of the highest class. I now speak of schools for boys and young men. Girls' schools will receive attention in a subsequent chapter.

I do not know any mission in Northern India where elementary education has been entirely neglected. Some have done much more in this department than others, but all have devoted to it a measure of attention and effort. We had at one time ten schools of this class in different parts of Benares. In these humble schools many have learned to read, write, and keep accounts, and have thus been fitted for discharging efficiently their secular work. Their minds have been furnished and their character improved by useful information communicated to them. Above all, Christian instruction has been imparted. The schools have been frequently visited by the missionary and his native assistants for the special object of reading with the pupils portions of the Scriptures, and inculcating the lessons they contain. Thus readers for our Scriptures and Christian books have been prepared, who we may hope come to their perusal with weakened prejudice from the kindly feeling with which we are regarded. A favourable impression has thus been made on the minds of parents as well as of pupils.

I have already mentioned that these schools have been utilized for preaching-stations, and have been well adapted for this purpose. They have been carried on at small expense. The great drawback has been that with few exceptions the teachers have been Hindus. They have been of the Kaisth, the writer caste, who are as a caste less imbued perhaps with Hinduism than any other. When Christians have been available their services have of course been thankfully secured. For some years the Hindu element has been gradually withdrawn from the teaching staff. Two of the early teachers in our time became Christians, one having been baptized in our Mission, and the other in the Church Mission at Benares.

The whole state of primary education in the North-West, I may say in India, is on a very different footing from what it was in 1840. Great progress in every department of education has been made since that time. Considering the vast importance of primary education, the advancement has not been so great as might have been expected, but there is every prospect of its being largely extended in the immediate future. It is hoped that one outcome of the Education Commission which is now sitting will be the gathering into schools of many thousands of the young who have been hitherto neglected.

In most Missions of any standing, even where the chief attention has been given to direct evangelistic work, some provision has been made for secondary education. A school with this object was established in our Mission in 1845. It was taught in a well-sized native house, and was afterwards transferred to a larger building. It had successive superintendents, the late Mr. Sherring, Mr. Blake, and myself. It was a longer time under Mr. Sherring than under any other, and in it he laboured very diligently and efficiently. It received the name of the Central School, as our idea was to transfer to it the best boys from what we called the Bazar schools. It was intended to allow none to enter who had not made some progress in reading their own language, but we found this exclusion impracticable, and we were obliged to form an elementary department. English was taught, and the higher classes were introduced to geometry, algebra, history, especially Indian history, and other similar branches of a liberal education. Almost all when they entered were ignorant of English. Those who remained a considerable time made fair progress, a few made remarkable progress; and we were happy to find that many on leaving us obtained responsible situations, which they continued to hold to the satisfaction of their superiors.

For years under successive superintendents the Head Master was a Christian, Babu Ram Chunder Basu, who is now most usefully employed as a lecturer to educated natives. His great attainments, his diligence and teaching power, did much to promote the prosperity of the school.

In our Central school a very prominent place was given to Christian instruction. Every day Scripture lessons were given by Christian teachers; on Saturday, for years, a lecture was delivered to the assembled school; and on Sunday morning a service was held, at which there was a good voluntary attendance. The effect of the prominence thus given to Christian teaching was shown early in 1857, when on a plan arranged by the zealous public-spirited Commissioner of the Benares Province, Mr. Henry Carre Tucker, there was a gathering in the city of the pupils from all the schools in the province who choose to attend to submit to an examination in Scripture knowledge. Prizes in money and books were given to those who proved themselves most proficient. A great number of lads and boys made their appearance, and the high place taken by the pupils of our Central school showed how well they had been taught.

Some missions provide for taking their pupils on to the University standard. Among these the missions in the Presidency cities have held, and from their peculiar sphere must continue to hold, the first rank. I have already observed nothing interested me more, nothing delighted me more on reaching Calcutta early in 1839, than the sight of many young men and boys taught in the institutions of the Church of Scotland and of our own Mission. It was most exhilarating to see so many bright youths studying our language, introduced to Western knowledge, and, above all, led to the fountain of truth in the Word of God. Dr. Duff was not the first in establishing in Calcutta an institution for the teaching of English; he was not the first in establishing a Christian school; many were before him in this good work: but he was the first in setting up an institution on a large scale on a thoroughly Christian basis, in which English was to have the first place, and in which provision was made for carrying the students on to the University standard of Europe. In 1843 the missionaries, on account of their adherence to the Free Church, were obliged to give up their buildings in Cornwallis Square, and to seek accommodation in another part of Calcutta, where they have continued their scholastic work with great zeal and efficiency. The institution in Cornwallis Square has been conducted for many years with remarkable success by the missionaries of the Established Church of Scotland. All the missions in Calcutta have taken part in this work, and have sent forth bands of well-educated young men, who have acquired a large acquaintance with the Word of God.

Similar institutions have been formed throughout the country. As may be supposed, these vary greatly in resources and efficiency. Years ago our Central school was transferred from a rented house in the city to a large purchased house in the suburbs, where, under the name of the High School, it has continued to flourish. Many of its students have successfully passed the Entrance examination of the Calcutta University, and a considerable number have passed the First Arts examination. It has always stood high in native estimation, has had a large attendance of pupils, and is reckoned one of the best institutions of the kind in the North-West. The change from the Central school, with its secondary education, to the High school, with its arrangement to carry on the pupils further, was made by the late Mr. Sherring, and to his assiduous care and efficient management its success is largely due. It maintains its character under the superintendence of our friend Mr. Hewlett, who has arranged for the opening of a B.A. class.

I have mentioned the University standard. For many

years after our going to India there was no University in the land. The establishment of Universities in Calcutta, Madras, and Bombay, and the introduction of the grant-in-aid system, have effected in the educational department a change so great that it may be called a revolution. The studies in mission schools are to a large extent what they were, but they have come under new conditions, which greatly alter the proportionate attention given to them, and the degree of zeal with which they are prosecuted. Under the grant-in-aid system missionaries are allowed full liberty in giving Christian instruction to their pupils. The only thing required by the Government Inspector is that the secular education be such as will entitle the school to a grant. If formerly a mission school egregiously failed in fitting the pupils for the positions in life to which they were looking forward, it rightly lost favour, and was soon deserted. Now there is a new urgent necessity for efficiency, and the healthy stimulus thus given is in itself a marked benefit; but if care be not taken the opportunity for imparting Christian instruction is impaired, which formed the main inducement for missionaries taking part in the work.

The effect of the change is most marked in our higher schools. There is a widely spread and intense ambition for University honours. Not only in the Presidency cities, but in the great cities of the country, a crowd of boys and young men are eager for admission to the University circle. This eagerness springs from the desire for honourable distinction, which is as strong in the minds of Indian youth as in any youth on the face of the earth. It springs, perhaps, still more from the fact that the University stamp, attesting educational proficiency, is a high recommendation in favour of applicants for well-paid situations. It would be hard to say how far a love of knowledge contributes to this eagerness for study. It would be uncharitable to affirm it is altogether absent, but it would be shutting one's eyes to potent facts to suppose it furnishes the greater part of the motive power. Owing to various causes, such as the want of opportunity, of capacity, and diligence, the great majority of students do not aspire higher than the Entrance examination; but even to pass this successfully is considered a great feat, and many are proud of achieving it. The Calcutta University has a high standard for degrees, and those who acquire them are entitled to be considered well-educated men.

The effect of this eagerness, we may say this rage for University distinction, on mission schools can be easily conceived. The great question with the student is, "How can I get to the University goal? What are the studies which promise the quickest and largest success?" The studies which do not lead to this goal have little attraction; while those that lead to it, and just in proportion as they lead to it, are eagerly pursued. Our Scriptures have no place in the University curriculum. The consequence is that the student, whose supreme aim is to acquit himself well when he goes up for degrees, and estimates studies by their bearing on his success, gives to the Bible only the attention required by the rule of the institution he attends, and he often gives that attention reluctantly; so that even the knowledge he cannot fail to acquire can scarcely be expected to tell on his heart and conscience. Every hour given to the Bible he is apt to regard as taken away from the studies which he most highly values, and in which, with all his application, he finds it difficult to attain proficiency.

It is undeniable that mission schools have been, and are, popular with the people of India. From the Report just published of our Benares Mission it appears that at present there are 1,265 pupils in its schools, boys and girls. Various things have conduced to this popularity. Missionaries as a class have acquired a firmly established character for attention to their pupils and kindly treatment of them. They are credited with good motives by many who have no drawing to Christianity. Then, for a considerable time no charge for tuition was made, the pupils being simply required to pay for their school books. Since fees have been taken they are, I believe, generally lower than in Government institutions; though, on the other hand, these have scholarships and prizes which are far beyond any pecuniary advantage mission schools can offer. There is, of course, in our schools the possibility of the pupils' ancestral religion being weakened, or even abandoned, but the hope is entertained both by them and their parents that the danger will be escaped. While the main motive for resorting to our schools is secular advancement—undoubtedly a right motive, if kept within due limits—the missionaries, while earnestly desiring the temporal welfare of their pupils, are actuated by a still higher motive, which they constantly avow. Till the establishment of the University, boys and young men, while prosecuting the special object for which they had put themselves under tuition, with few exceptions showed no disinclination to Christian instruction. A portion of the school-time was allotted for it, and to the work of that time many cheerfully applied themselves. Some became deeply interested, and a few were led in consequence to avow their faith in Jesus. With the new University system a new order of things has come in, which has placed Christian instruction under great disadvantages.

In consequence of this change some have advocated the entire withdrawal of mission agency from the schools where the higher education is imparted. It has been said, "Why should missionaries from day to day be doing the work of mere secular teachers, in hope that during the short time allotted for Christian instruction to young men, indisposed to receive it, they can secure their spiritual good?" If they withdraw, what then? The alternative is the loss of influence over a class that may be expected to take the lead in all movements of their people, and their transfer to teachers who are, in many cases, the avowed and bitter foes of Christianity, and whose object will be to imbue them with their own sentiments. There is abundant testimony to the fact that the pupils of mission schools regard missionaries with a friendly feeling, and diffuse that feeling in their respective circles, and also show respect for the Gospel even when they argue against it to justify their adherence to their ancestral religion. May it not be hoped, too, that in many minds a conviction is left that Christianity is the religion of heaven, although there are formidable obstacles to that conviction obtaining sway over the heart and life? There have been instances where the conviction has broken through every obstacle, and has been avowed by open profession of faith in Christ. Our Missionary Societies may well shrink from the abandonment of a sphere which furnishes the opportunity for favourable influence over so many minds—and minds, too, which are sure to be very influential in the community.

The preferable plan has been adopted. It appears from the latest statistics that the number of students in mission schools is greater, and the course of study more advanced, than at any previous period. I am not aware that any of the missionaries in the higher institutions have proposed to abandon them on account of the new state of things. While giving themselves cheerfully to the imparting of the education which their pupils are eager to acquire, they put forth resolute steady effort to counteract the secularizing tendency of their studies. The assembled school is opened with prayer, Scripture lessons are given, and, taught as they are by Christians, the pupils are under Christian influence during all their school hours. It is common in the North-West, and I suppose in other parts of India, to have services in the schools on Sabbath morning, at which the attendance is voluntary; and at Benares, at least, the attendance has been very encouraging. Of late Sabbath schools, apart from day schools, have been established in many missions, with every prospect of success. The attendance is large, and in some places a number of parents are present. These schools are carried on largely on the English and American model. The international lessons are used, pictures and books are given as prizes to attentive scholars; and they have a yearly treat, in conducting which care is taken against the violation of caste. The American Episcopal missionaries have taken the lead in this new departure.

It has been often remarked that our higher schools can show very few converts. The conversions have not been many, and yet they have not been so inconsiderable in number as they have been represented. When we look at our mission agents we find that a large proportion of our most efficient men, the men that have done the best service, have come from these schools. At the great

Missionary Conference at Allahabad in 1874, at which I was present, they acquitted themselves in a manner which attested their mental power and Christian earnestness, and gave one a high opinion of their fitness for evangelistic work among their countrymen. At the late Decennial Missionary Conference in Calcutta they took a prominent and effective part. It is, indeed, a matter for deep regret that of late our accessions from this quarter have been few; but when hope has been at the lowest ebb one has appeared here and there to strengthen it by avowing himself a follower of Christ.[1]

In reference to our schools, in reference to our work generally, it is important to keep before our minds the great power of public opinion. Many are the things which go to form it; it is very subtle in its working; the most acute and observant mind cannot estimate its force: but when once widely formed its effects are remarkable. In India public opinion is formed much more slowly than in a land like ours; the constitution of society presents a stronger front to its action. But there too it works, and when it works on till it has obtained overmastering power we may expect to see a marvellous change. We cannot doubt that missions have a high place in forming this opinion; and among mission agencies I believe there is no one which has told and is telling more beneficially on the people than our mission schools.

[1] At the Calcutta Conference there was much discussion about schools, especially of the higher order. Experienced educationalists gave expression to their views, some stating in strong terms the aversion to Bible lessons shown by many of the pupils; while others, among whom Mr. Miller of Madras was prominent, represented the pupils as generally willing to receive Christian instruction.

CHAPTER XIII.

ORPHANAGES.

ALL over India missions have had orphans under their charge, but from personal knowledge I can only speak of the North-West.

The need for these institutions was most pressing in 1838 and 1839. I remember hearing, on my arrival at Benares, the most harrowing account of the fearful sufferings of the people over a great extent of country. The famine had been sore in the land. People fled from their towns and villages, hoping to reach a more favoured region; but travelling through districts as destitute of food as those they left, they received no help, and perished miserably. The weak and the very young were the first to succumb. Many struggled on, eating grass or anything that could allay the pangs of hunger, in the hope of reaching the cities where they could expect relief from their own people, and still more from their English rulers. At that time Agra was the seat of government for the North-West, and as the famine was specially severe in that district, so great a multitude poured into it that, notwithstanding the strenuous effort put forth by Europeans, official and non-official, helped by wealthy and benevolent natives, only partial relief could be afforded. The means of communication between one part of India and another were, even at that time, far better than they had been in the days of native rule; much had been done to improve the roads, but owing to the distance of places where food was comparatively abundant, and the length of time and the expense incurred in conveying it to the afflicted districts, timely help was not obtained. Many children were abandoned, and the authorities sent out orders to their subordinates to rescue these waifs and feed them till arrangements could be made for their support.

Missionaries felt themselves called on to offer their services in this dreadful emergency, and the offer was readily accepted. The large expenditure for which they thus became responsible was met by a small allowance made by Government for each child, by a grant from a Famine Fund which had been raised, and by contributions received by missionaries from friends to help them in this new undertaking.

The institutions then established have become permanent. The places left vacant by the death of many of the first inmates, and the entrance into active life of those who survived, were soon filled by others who had equal claims on Christian compassion. On the occasion of great melas children are often lost, and in not a few cases their parents are never found. In the great cities, by the death of parents, and by the abandonment of children—sometimes through extreme destitution, at other times by unnatural indifference—helpless little ones are cast on the pity of the public. From country places forsaken children are sent to the head-quarters of districts. In seasons of scarcity, which frequently occur, and especially in famine years such as 1861, large additions are made to the number of orphans. With these causes operating to produce the class from which orphanages are recruited, there is no likelihood of the time coming when they will not be needed. The people, as a rule, are undoubtedly kind to children; but when we consider the great poverty of many, the extreme difficulty with which they obtain the necessaries of life, there is no reason to wonder at the cases of destitution which are continually presenting themselves. In our own country, with all its advantages, we have numerous orphanages, where many are sheltered and trained for useful life, who would otherwise be thrown as waifs on the surface of society.

When orphanages were first formed in Northern India, great hope was entertained they would not merely relieve present and pressing distress, and do good to a large number of destitute young persons, but would tell powerfully on native society, and lead to the formation of a large, strong Christian community. The sufferings of the people afflicted by famine were deplored, they were regarded with deep pity; everything was done which could be done to relieve them, but it was hoped that out of this calamitous state of affairs would be evolved, through the overruling of Providence, a signal moral and spiritual benefit to the people generally. Here was a large band of boys and girls taken out of native society, cut off from idolatrous training and associations, and made over in the most plastic season of their lives to be moulded by those whose supreme aim would be to strengthen and elevate their character, and prepare them for a happy, useful, and honourable career. It was hoped that when these children thus trained grew to manhood and womanhood, they would go out among their countrymen striking examples of moral and spiritual excellence, and would by their manifest superiority make a greater impression on the minds of the people than could be made by the preaching and efforts of missionaries. A worthy chaplain sent out a pamphlet advocating the gathering by Government of all the orphan children in the country, and, if I remember rightly, of all the children with whom parents were willing to part, and the placing of them in institutions where they should be brought up as Christians, and as members of the Church of England. He maintained that if this was done, in the course of a few years a great number would go out to native society to leaven it with Christian sentiment, and with loyalty to the British Government. He drew a glowing picture of the good that would be accomplished if this policy were adopted and vigorously carried out. Few were so hopeful as my friend, but many did anticipate great results.

It cannot be doubted that orphan institutions have done much good; but I think none will maintain that the sanguine hopes with which they were begun have been realized. There have been obstacles in the way of success which might have been partly foreseen, but which could not have been fully anticipated. Many of the children brought to the missionaries were so sickly and emaciated, that they soon died in spite of all the attention bestowed on them. The mortality has been at times most depressing. There was no vitality to resist disease. The effort to preserve life was in many cases frustrated by the vitiated taste of the children, which led them to eat lime, earth, garbage of any kind on which they could lay their hands, in preference to good food. They were closely watched, but it was impossible to watch them so closely as to prevent them from doing that which hurried them to the grave.

The orphans were of different ages, from very early youth to fourteen or fifteen. The elder ones were steeped in the spirit of the class from which they came—as a rule the lowest class of the community; and the younger ones had in their very blood hereditary qualities which put obstacles in the way of successful training. We do not believe there is in blood the overpowering efficacy which some have attributed to it; if it had, responsibility would cease, and the effort to raise certain tribes and classes would be hopeless; but we believe it has a strong influence, and we think we have seen clear evidence of its hurtful effect on Indian orphans. There were these difficulties to begin with. And then it was impossible to bring these children under the happy influence of an orderly living family. In our own country it has been found highly conducive to the right bringing-up of orphans, to the repressing of evil tendencies, and the drawing forth of the finer elements of character, to secure for them domestic training to the utmost extent circumstances will permit. The keeping of many together, not merely taught together, which is very desirable, but eating together, sleeping together, constantly acting and reacting on each other, is found very unfavourable to the formation of the right character, however careful, wise, and kindly the superintendence may be. In India, where hundreds of orphans were brought at once to mission premises, this gregarious life was unavoidable. Besides, it is impossible to separate orphans from the community around so completely as to leave them unaffected by its moral atmosphere.

There was of course a difference in the qualifications of those who undertook this great charge, some being more fitted for it than others; but this we say with the utmost confidence, after an intimate acquaintance with the working of some of the larger orphanages, and a general knowledge of others, that they have been managed with a laboriousness, a patience, a wisdom, and a kindness, deserving of the highest praise. Those in charge acted as parents, so far as that was possible, but in the nature of things there could not be the close attention and the fond personal affection to each of ordinary domestic life. We remember cases where children were committed to well-ordered Christian families with happy results, but for many years after orphanages were founded there were no such families to receive them.

With the exception of orphans sent to Baptist Missions, they were as a rule baptized at once, and were thus brought within the pale of the Christian Church to be trained for the love and service of Christ. The first place was given to Christian instruction and training. All were taught reading, writing, and arithmetic. Those who proved themselves capable of receiving a higher education were continued at school, in the hope of their becoming qualified for offices such as those of teacher and preacher, for which mental and moral fitness was indispensable. The great majority were early taught a trade. In the larger orphanages a variety of trades was introduced—tailoring, carpentry, baking, dyeing, carpet-making, printing, bookbinding, and farming. Some of these trades, after much labour had been bestowed upon them, were given up, as it was found the orphans could not compete with native workmen. They had not the energy and aptitude possessed by those who followed their ancestral occupations, and who had been from their earliest years familiar with the conditions of native trade. Hopes were entertained many would betake themselves to farming. These hopes have been only partially realized. On land secured by the Church Mission of Benares, at a short distance from the city, orphans when they grew up were settled; but few took kindly to the work, and most soon abandoned it. There are now a few Christian families on the ground, but the larger part of the land is let to ordinary native agriculturists. In some places, such as Goruckpore and Shahjehanpore, the experiment has been successful. A greater number have continued at printing and bookbinding than at other trades. Co-operative associations of native Christians have been formed at Allahabad for printing, and at Futtygurh for tent-making, which I believe continue to prosper. These associations are under unfettered native management. A considerable number who have come out of orphan institutions have followed the trades they were taught, and have succeeded in getting employment in different places. Many were trained as servants, and in that capacity they are scattered over all Northern India. These have been joined by not a few who were taught trades, but did not continue in them, as they deemed service easier and more profitable. This is much to be regretted as native Christians in service are exposed to many disadvantages and temptations from their fellow-servants, and too often from their European masters and mistresses. The position of a capable artisan is far superior.

It must be acknowledged by those who have the kindest feeling towards the orphans, and who wish to entertain the most favourable opinion of them, which truth will permit, that they have often been wanting in energy and self-reliance. There has been a tendency to lean unduly on those to whom they have been indebted for the preservation of their lives, and for everything which makes life desirable. They have been accustomed to call them, in the language of the country, *ma, bap*—*mother, father*—and to expect everything to be done for them as if they were still helpless children. This can not be said of all, but it must be acknowledged this unduly dependent spirit has been often shown. A greater wrong could not be done to orphans, when grown to maturity, than to treat them as children, unable to make their own way in the world. This would be to destroy all strength of character, and turn them into abject, and at the same time discontented, paupers. Few have been so destitute of common sense as to have supposed that in this way they were to be supported, but there has been a tendency to expect the missionaries to set them out on a career of self-support, and remove all obstacles in their way without any special effort on their part, and when difficulties have arisen to fall back on their missionary friends to set them out afresh. When these expectations have not been realized, they have been disposed to view their guardians as having failed in parental duty and affection. We have known cases where the rough experience of life has taught self-dependence, and thankfulness also for the treatment, which at the time was regarded as unkind, but had led to lasting benefit. So far as we have been able to ascertain, the ordinary feeling among those who had been inmates of orphan institutions, and of their descendants, has been one of affection and gratitude to those who have watched over them and provided for them in their days of helplessness, and who have toiled and in many cases suffered to promote their temporal and spiritual good. When travelling we have met many of this class, and have been much gratified by the spirit they have shown.

Some have come out of orphanages well equipped for the highest work by character and attainments. As teachers, catechists, and native preachers, these occupy honourable and useful positions, and have been a great blessing to the Church and the world. In the course of our residence in India we have seen many of the missions in the North-West, but our acquaintance with them is too slight to enable us to mention the number given by orphanages to the higher class of native agents. We have known several who are worthy of all respect, confidence, and affection.

To the question, "What is the general character of the large community of native Christians formed of orphans and their descendants?" it is difficult to give a satisfactory reply, though easy enough to give one's impression. A characterization of communities is one of the most common and at the same time most unsatisfactory of operations, as the data for its being done well are so wide, recondite, and difficult to grasp. As I proceed I shall have occasion to give my views of native Christians generally. All I can now say about orphans and their descendants is, that considering what human beings are, as shown from age to age, considering the circumstances and surroundings of those of whom we are speaking, the moral and spiritual results are what might have been expected, though not all that had been wished for and hoped for. Sanguine spirits had hoped that they would have had a striking superiority to their fellow-countrymen, which would have drawn forth their wonder and led them to inquire whence the superiority had come; but no one will maintain this has been the case. A few, I believe very few, have turned out utterly reprobate. The character of some who have not lapsed into gross wickedness has been very unsatisfactory. Many are respectable members of society, and make the profession of religion implied in attending public worship and calling themselves Christians. A considerable number show in different ways spiritual character. What more can be said of congregations composed of those whose advantages have been immeasurably greater? It would have been a most pleasing, but at the same time a most remarkable and unparalleled result, if orphans brought up under the charge of missionaries had gone forth a united band, with no defaulters, to maintain the cause of God among their countrymen, by a life so adorned with excellence that its testimony to Christ could not be resisted. The result actually attained, though chequered, is sufficient to show that orphan institutions have by the Divine blessing done much good, and that the faithful labour bestowed on them has borne gratifying fruit.

CHAPTER XIV.

MISSION TOURS.

IN our own country, under the pressure of life, many hail the release from toil and the refreshment of spirit promised by the annual summer trip. So in India missionaries avail themselves of the cold season to sally out for the prosecution of their work. Their main object is to make known the gospel to the many whom they are sure to meet wherever their tent may be pitched, who have never heard the name of Jesus, except perhaps amidst the bustle and noise of a mela, and who but for itineracies would remain in total ignorance of the Saviour of mankind. The missionary who does not keep this before his mind as his chief aim is unworthy of the name. While this object is pursued, another is sought which missionaries deem very legitimate. Health is indispensable for the efficient discharge of their duties, and travelling is found very beneficial to the health of their families as well as to their own. Touring in the cold weather, by the new strength it gives to the body and the refreshment it gives to the spirit, has been found to prepare them for a new campaign at home as nothing else could have done.

Some missionaries have kept themselves within a limited sphere not far from their homes, visiting the same places again and again, obtaining a personal acquaintance with many of the people, and endeavouring to deepen any impressions which may have been made. Others have travelled for weeks, sometimes for months, over hundreds of miles, visiting the towns and villages on their route, and speaking about the things of God to all whom they have met.

During my long residence in India it was my privilege to undertake tours of both descriptions. I never stopped at home during the cold weather—we are not in India in the habit of saying "summer and winter," but "hot weather and cold weather"—except when justice to my colleagues, or the necessities of the mission, compelled me to stay. There were seasons when my colleague was, either from inexperience or ill-health, unable to do the home work; or, as happened more than once, I had no colleague at all, and in these circumstances it was obvious duty to remain at my post. Even then I commonly managed to get out a little into the surrounding country. On some of our tours we were put to no small inconvenience, and we were not strangers to hardship; but we look back to them with much pleasure, and think how much we would like to set out on them again if circumstances permitted.

At an early stage of our residence at Benares voyaging on the Ganges was a favourite mode of enjoying the cold season. There were budgerows, vessels with two tolerably sized rooms, available for hire at a moderate charge. It was indispensable to have with the budgerow a small boat for the accommodation of servants and for the cooking of food. On a few occasions I took a trip on a vessel of this description with my family, moving up and down the river, and halting towards evening near a town or village, which I could visit for the purpose of speaking to the people about the Saviour. The country is so populous that there was no difficulty in mooring our little craft in the evening near some place where hearers could be collected. It was seldom on any tour in the North-West we were allowed to forget that we were in the region of the sacred river, which receives from the people divine honours, and which in their belief confers inestimable benefit on all who bathe in its waters. When on the bank of the river, its alleged virtues formed a frequent subject of remark and discussion. There, as elsewhere, we had to tell them that Ganges water, however good for refreshing and cleansing the body, cannot wash away one spot from the soul. We had to tell them frequently, that as the washerman who puts clothes into a box and carefully washes it with the expectation of their coming out clean and white will be acting a very foolish part, so they were acting an equally futile part if they supposed that the water of the Ganges, so useful for the body, had any effect on the spirit. In answer to the remark that Ganges water could not do what other water could not, as it had nothing peculiar in its composition, I have been gravely told that two things exactly the same to the senses may be essentially different; and the proof given was that the river Kurumnasa, which means the destroyer of merit, takes away all merit from those who bathe in it, while bathing in the Ganges secures an untold degree of merit, extending not only to one's own past and future, but to an untold number of ancestors and descendants!

When on the Ganges or its banks one continually sees proof of the implicit trust placed in it. We remember being awakened very early one morning long before dawn by a person bathing close to our boat, in a quivering voice which showed he was chilled by the water, long and earnestly imploring the favour of *Gunga Ma*—Mother Ganges.

There is no part of India, mountain or plain, where serpents may not be encountered. One evening, when returning to our boat from a village on the banks of the river, I was walking warily on a narrow path half-covered with grass from both sides, when I saw before me what I first supposed to be a rope. I halted, and immediately a serpent glided away. That evening, before reaching the boat, I saw at least a dozen of serpents at their evening gambols over the ruins of a house. I walked quietly on, deeming it the best part of valour to leave them undisturbed. If they observed me they showed no inclination to approach me.

For many years voyaging on the Ganges has gone out of fashion. Native boats laden with produce and wood continue to ply, but the budgerows and pinnaces, which Europeans could hire, have almost entirely disappeared. There are various reasons for this change. The current of the river is very rapid in some places, which makes the work of dragging against it very slow and tiresome; there is sometimes the danger of collision with other boats. The high banks of the river here and there prevent the country from being seen, and at other places there is a dreary stretch of sand. Though the weather of the cold season is very steady, a storm might come on, and if it did neither boat nor boatmen could be trusted; for the boat, never of the best material, was often sadly out of repair, and the boatmen were ready, when danger appeared, to throw themselves into the water and make for the shore, leaving the passengers to shift for themselves. There was, indeed, the pleasantness of sailing on a broad river; the air was very fresh; there was no leaving of the temporary abode from day to day; the trouble of a shifting camp was escaped, though occasionally there was inconvenience from the indispensable cook-boat not keeping sufficiently near. Opposed to these advantages were the disadvantages I have mentioned, which were always felt to be serious drawbacks; and when the roads had been improved, and journeying facilities increased, travelling by land obtained so decided a preference, that the river has been well-nigh abandoned by Europeans.

Some seasons our touring was confined to a narrow range, not extending beyond thirty or forty miles. We every now and then spent a few days within a few miles of the city. Our first journey of any considerable length was, at the end of 1840, to the mela at Allahabad, some seventy miles north-west of Benares, which I have already mentioned. At the end of 1842 I made a tour along with my wife and child to Agra, more than four hundred miles from Benares, which occupied us about three months. On this tour we passed through Allahabad, Cawnpore, Futtygurh, Mynpoorie, and other well-known places. Early in 1847, accompanied by a brother missionary, we went to Almora, nearly six hundred miles distant, travelling with our tents to the foot of the hills, and spending six or seven weeks on our way. We left Almora for Benares in October, and reached it early in December, having taken Meerut, Delhi, and Allygurh, as well as Cawnpore and Allahabad, in our return route. Our long journeys many years afterwards were performed with few exceptions under new conditions, and with much greater expedition.

If my readers are in thought to accompany us on those journeys, it may be well to state the circumstances in which we travelled, the weather we had and could generally expect, our travelling arrangements, the state of the roads, and the aspects of the country through which we passed.

As to the weather, it was generally delightful. We had from day to day an unclouded sky, with the sun rather strong as the day advanced, but with a refreshing breeze, which made it thoroughly cool in the shade, even cold sometimes, so that one was inclined to go out into the sunshine to get warmth. In the daytime warm clothing was pleasant, and at night, especially in tents, our blankets and wraps came into full requisition. There was a steadiness in the weather exceeding anything known in our climate. We have known weeks without any shading of the sky. There were, however, occasional breaks. Now and then clouds gathered from day to day, and at length came down in heavy rain, which was most welcome to the farmers, especially when it came as it often did, about Christmas. Thunder storms might be sometimes looked for, accompanied by sudden and severe gusts of wind. These days of atmospheric disturbance were sufficient to make us, as travellers, appreciate more highly the weather with which we were ordinarily favoured.

The greater part of the country through which we travelled is very level. Beyond Chunar, indeed, which is sixteen miles from Benares, and Mirzapore, which is thirty miles distant, there is a great extent of low hill-country. These districts we visited several times. The most of our journeys were in the wide open plains of the North-West. The country, though level, is by no means uninteresting. You receive as you travel a very favourable impression of the productiveness of the land

and the industry of the people. In the cold weather you see, as far as the eye can reach, a sweep of growing corn, wheat and other grains, which give the hope of an early and abundant harvest. Towns and villages meet your view on every side. If you get to a slightly elevated spot you are struck with the number of wells you see in the fields, dug for the purpose of irrigation. In the great region lying between the Ganges and the Jumna, called the Doab—the country of the two rivers, the Mesopotamia of Northern India, over a great part of which we travelled for the first time at the end of 1842 and the beginning of 1843, and which we have often traversed since—there is no extensive forest near the Trunk Road. In all directions, however, you see clumps of lofty and shady trees, and occasionally groves of considerable extent. Trees have been largely planted along the road, and within every few miles there are groves, where travellers get their tents pitched, and where they are thoroughly protected from the glare and heat of the sun. Even in the coldest part of the cold weather tents pitched in the open become quickly too heated for comfort. In the groves the deep shade cast by the widely-spread branches and the thick foliage sometimes darkens the tent too much for reading and writing; but outside, on a chair before a small table, if that be required, one can spend hours very pleasantly reading or writing, as it may be, and listening if inclined to the cawing of the crows, the cooing of the doves, and the notes of other birds, while the gentle breeze rustles through the trees, and the children, if any, play with their toys under them.

Natives, when they travel, as I have already mentioned, manage things in a fashion which we are not able to imitate, but which I have often been inclined to envy.

Let them have flour, water, a little wood for fuel, if not in its stead dried cow-dung, and they partake with relish of the meal their own hands have cooked, conscious of no want and complaining of no hardship. The relish is increased if they can get some of the ordinary vegetables of the country. With the meal over, after chatting a while over the Hookah, the "hubble-bubble" as English people call it, the pipe which sends tobacco smoke through water, they wrap themselves in the blanket which they carry with them, and sleep soundly under a tree, when, as is often the case, no Sura, a native resting-place, is at hand. If rain comes on they creep into a place where the rain cannot reach them, if such a place be available. A few Europeans have at different times tried to follow the habit of native travellers, and in very exceptional cases it has been successful. The ordinary result has been the speedy ruin of health.

Our habits compel us to travel in a different way. When a missionary is alone, though he cannot travel as a native does, he can put up, and does put up, with inconveniences to which a family cannot be exposed. The family, however, requires a change as well as himself; and when wife and children are with him, as they often are, the house is shut up at home, home servants are taken, and travelling requires only a slight addition to the domestic staff. An additional horse is needed for the conveyance (in India a conveyance is not a luxury but a necessity); two tents are required, one to be sent on over-night, while the other is kept behind for occupation; along with the tents, slight portable beds, bedding, small folding-table, cane chairs, and cooking-vessels. These goods of the moving household are laden and forwarded on carts called Hackeries, drawn by oxen. Highly paid officials manage as they travel to have with them many of the luxuries and even some of the elegancies of life, but missionaries are satisfied if they get necessaries. As we travel we manage, though not always, to get milk, fowls, and eggs, and occasionally a kid. Whatever beside we need must be taken with us.

When the weather is fine, the roads good, the horses and bullocks strong and manageable, and the attendants efficient, touring in the North-West in the cold weather is very pleasant. If travelling be prosecuted from day to day, the custom is to rise very early in the morning at the earliest dawn, or before dawn, when the morning-star appears, and to rouse the camp. This was my part when travelling with my household. The watchman wakened me, and I wakened all around. We got quickly ready, and set out on our journey of twelve or fourteen miles. The mornings were not only cool, but often sharply cold. On arriving at the end of our stage, it might be as early as eight or half-past eight o'clock, we should find, and often did find, the tent pitched, which had been sent on over-night, the table spread commonly under a shady tree, the water boiling, food prepared; and then with a keen appetite we sat down to breakfast. When the afternoon was a little advanced, the cart arrived with the tent and other things left behind, and was soon pitched for our night occupancy. Towards evening the day-tent was taken down, and was sent on over-night with everything requisite for the next day. When all the circumstances were favourable, everything went on with an ease and regularity which made us feel at home while away from home, and gave us at the same time the constant variety of new scenes.

The circumstances were not, however, always favourable. They were sometimes the reverse. The new horse was unmanageable, the bullocks were weak and could not draw the carts, the servants were remiss or incapable, the roads were in some places shockingly bad, we were left for hours without tent and food, and, as I have said, the weather now and then was wet and stormy. We had sometimes an amount of trouble which made us half regret we had left home. Ladies are generally very patient in such circumstances, but children are sorely tried. The difficulties we encountered in some of our early journeys were such that we now wonder how we got out of them, and succeeded in getting on at all. The touring in favourable circumstances, which I have described, is not however a mere ideal. Happily it was often with us a reality. On setting out things required to be adjusted. Time was required for getting things into their places, and for each person learning to do the work assigned him. When once we got into travelling trim, and our people were what they ought to be, things went on with the regularity of clockwork.

I have mentioned our long tours in 1842 and 1847. On these journeys we had a good deal of pleasant smooth travelling, and we also encountered some of the difficulties of which I have spoken. The Trunk Road from Allahabad to the North-West was in excellent condition in 1842–43; but from Benares to Allahabad it had been allowed to get out of repair, and the roads diverging from the Trunk Road on one side to Futtygurh and on the other side to Agra we found very bad. The story of our difficulties is well remembered by us, but it must be given very concisely. At one place a wheel of our conveyance broke in the middle of a stage, and after some delay we succeeded in getting an Ekka, a small native conveyance drawn by a pony, on the narrow platform of which the members of our party who could not walk were squatted as they best could; while the rest of us walked. We sent on word of our trouble to our missionary friends at Futtygurh, who kindly arranged to get us on to their hospitable abode, and to get our conveyance repaired. Three days after leaving Futtygurh our best horse died, from sheer fatigue in drawing our conveyance through the sand. This threw us on having it drawn by bullocks at the rate of a mile and a half, or at the utmost two miles, an hour, over a very bad road, which jolted us frightfully.

As we travelled we saw many things which drew our attention and excited our interest. Most of the villages along our route were surrounded by high mud walls, and had only one entrance by a great strong gate, which was shut at night, reminding us of the insecurity from which this part of India had emerged when it came under British rule within the memory of men then living. Villages thus fortified, if sufficient watch was kept, were quite secure against the sudden raids of Mahratta horsemen, or the attacks of robbers, to whose unwelcome visits they were always exposed. The former state of insecurity was also suggested by the number we met armed to the teeth, by shield on the breast, sword at the side, and matchlock on the shoulder. The insecurity had to a great extent come to an end, but the habit of going armed continued.

Along the road at convenient distances there were Suras for the convenience of travellers, which people in England, when speaking of Eastern lands, call Caravanserais. These are generally open spaces, surrounded by mud walls, with sheds at their sides for people who are willing to pay a very trifling sum for the luxury of sleeping under cover, and, if they like, for having their horses near them. Carts and oxen are always in the open. Sellers of grain and wood are always there with everything native travellers require. If a bedstead—a low four-footed article with rope for its bottom and mattress—be preferred to the bare ground, it can commonly be procured for three-halfpence for the night. When in the evening we were near these places we went to them, and saw the poor weary travellers setting to the preparation of their simple meal—with most the only cooked meal of the day—with apparently as great contentedness as we have when after a fatiguing day we reach an hotel, and, having given our orders, know that speedily we shall sit down to an ample repast. Many of these Suras have been built at the expense of well-to-do natives impelled by different motives, for love of name—*nam ke liye*, as the natives say, a motive for which their countrymen continually give them credit—for the acquisition of religious merit, and from benevolent feeling. These places are called Dhurmsalas, places erected by righteous, good men.

On this our first long journey in the country, we were impressed by the amount of traffic we saw on the road; and this impression was deepened on future occasions. We seldom travelled a few miles without seeing carts drawn by bullocks and laden with goods. We saw rows of camels, walking in single file, each attached to the one before and the one behind by a string. These belonged chiefly, though not exclusively, to Afghans, and were laden to a large extent with the products of their country. Every now and then we came across elephants, sometimes with a stack of tender branches on their back, which form a large part of their food, and at other times with persons seated sometimes on a howdah, sometimes on a pad. There were many foot-passengers, not a few with heavy loads on their heads. When these came in sight of a well, how quickly did they step up to it, throw off their burden, drop into it their brass vessel attached to a string, draw it up, and take a long, deep draught of the precious water! As I have observed them I have thought of the words, "With joy shall ye draw water out of the wells of salvation." To these poor toiling people the wells did appear wells of salvation. On some days we met bands of persons—chiefly men, with a woman here and there among them—with bamboo rods across their shoulders with a basket at each end, their travelling gear in and on one basket, and a vessel with Ganges water in the other. Thousands of these pilgrims travel every year over Northern India, going from one shrine to another, and pouring on certain images the water of the sacred river.

In our journeyings we had a singular immunity from thieves, a greater immunity than we had in our house at Benares, which was several times visited by these unwelcome intruders, though we always kept a watchman. All over the North-West, I suppose all over India, thieves abound. Whole tribes have for generations followed theft as a profession, and have betaken themselves to honest work only when compelled by finding their occupation perilous. They have had as their associates the idle and dissolute of other castes. Tents, as I have observed, are commonly pitched in shady groves, and in consequence admit of being approached unobserved, and a sharp knife in a skilful hand can easily secure an entrance on any side. Travellers have piquant stories to tell of the cleverness and impudence with which their property has been taken away. A missionary friend of ours awoke one morning to find that during the night everything in his tent had disappeared on which thieves could lay their hand. We had a large experience of tent life, but we have happily no story to tell about any similar loss. I do not remember our having had even a night alarm, though I well remember the difficulty we often had in preventing our guardians from sending forth unearthly cries, which made sleep impossible. My habit was, wherever we halted, to make my way to the headman of the adjoining village or town, and to place our encampment under his care. We were generally told there were thieves in the neighbourhood; we were sometimes told they were numerous and daring. We always stated our readiness to pay for watchmen, and we told the headman that if he did not send trustworthy men we should hold him responsible. We thus paid a sort of black-mail, but we thought the small sum paid well expended as insurance for the safety of our property. Some travellers take watchmen with them. This we never did, as we thought ourselves safer in the hands of men on the spot. Many a time as we lay down in our tent did we think how strange it was that, far away from our European brethren, in a strange land among a strange people, we could compose ourselves to sleep with as little fear, and with as strong a feeling of security, as if within locks and bars in our own country. We thought, with thankfulness, that we were under the ægis of our own government, even when we were in places where Englishmen were seldom seen, but where, notwithstanding, our prestige was fully recognized.

At all the places through which we passed on our first

long tour, Allahabad, Cawnpore, Futtygurh, Mynpoorie, and Agra, we were treated with the utmost kindness by the American and English missionaries, and by other Christian brethren, some of whom have been life-long friends ever since.

We were interested in all the places we saw on this tour; but Agra—Akbarabad, as natives always call it, the capital of Akbar, the most remarkable emperor who ever ruled over India—had for us, as for all who have visited it, peculiar attractions. When at some distance from the city we saw glistening in the sun the lofty dome and the still loftier four minarets or towers of the Taj Muhal, that wondrous mausoleum of the purest marble, built by the Emperor Shah Jehan for a favourite queen. On our arrival we lost no time in going to it. On subsequent visits to Agra we renewed our acquaintance with it, and on every new occasion its exquisite beauty and lofty grandeur enhanced our admiration. We also saw the Motee Musjid, the Pearl Mosque as it is called, built of marble, and called the Pearl Mosque, as I suppose, on account of its beauty and symmetry; the grand tomb of Akbar at Secundra, six miles from Agra; and other objects of interest. I am not to attempt a description of these world-famed buildings of Agra. They have been often described, and by none perhaps better than by Bishop Heber in his journal, which is now little read, but which gives a more graphic and accurate account of the parts of India he visited in 1825 than any I have seen elsewhere. Of the Taj and other grand structures of the Muhammadan emperors, he says they look as if "built by a giant and furnished by a jeweller."

While deeply interested in much we saw in this tour of 1842–43, on it, as well as on all subsequent tours, our great evangelistic object was kept steadily in view. On this occasion I was accompanied by a catechist. In the early afternoon, when we might hope to meet people released from the work of the day, we repaired to the neighbouring village. Often we found a large tree at the entrance to the village, with a stone seat close to its trunk, and on it we sat down. If there was no such seat a small native bedstead was often brought—such a thing as a chair was unknown—and we were asked to sit, while the people politely stood, till at our request they sat, which they can well do on their haunches. We entered into conversation with those who gathered around us. We asked if there was any pundit, any learned man in the village; and if there was we were happy to see him come, as we knew the people would look on us with less suspicion if he was present. In many places they were so unaccustomed to the sight of Europeans that they looked on us with a mingled feeling of curiosity and fear. We tried to put them at ease by speaking about something in which we knew they were deeply interested, such as their fields and crops, and as soon as we well could we made our way to the subject of religion. We read those passages from our Scriptures which we thought most fitted to arrest their attention. We aimed at setting forth the great facts and truths of revelation with all the simplicity, conciseness, and earnestness we could command. We repeated what was not understood, or was misunderstood, and endeavoured to make it plain by familiar illustrations.

We met with varied reception. In some places the people were so stolid, that even the catechist, one of their own people, seemed to make no impression. On many occasions we were heard most patiently, and were treated most courteously. Now and then, especially in the larger places, and where markets were being held—these are held weekly in central places, sometimes twice a week, and are well attended—there was much noise and great interruption. At times we encountered strong, bitter, and captious opposition. On the whole we met with far less opposition, and with a much more patient and respectful hearing, than at our stated work in a city like Benares. Often we were thanked for our visit, and were told our teaching well deserved consideration. Not infrequently the remark was made, "What you say is very good, but we never heard it before; we understand it very imperfectly, you will be leaving to-morrow, and we shall forget it all." We parted with such persons with a heavy heart. We always halted on the Lord's Day, and often on other days, when we met with encouragement and circumstances permitted.

Kunauj, now a poor, decayed town, composed chiefly of low mud-built houses, with not one fine building in it so far as I remember, was, as I have already mentioned, for ages the most famous city in Northern India, the capital of sovereigns ruling over extensive regions. The Brahmans of Kunauj continue to hold the highest rank in the Brahmanical hierarchy, but I believe only a few reside in Kunauj and its neighbourhood. As we learned it was only a few miles off the Trunk Road, we determined to halt a day for the purpose of visiting it. We accordingly went to it one morning, and remained in it some time, looking at the mounds which cover the ruins of its palaces, and which is all that remains to tell of its former greatness. A number gathered around us, with whom we conversed. They seemed so much interested in what we said about the Saviour, that we promised to visit them on our return. We accordingly arranged to remain a Sabbath at the part of the Trunk Road nearest to Kunauj. Reaching it on a Saturday we sent on a small tent, and early next day, accompanied by the catechist, I made my way to the town. There we remained the entire day, and I have seldom had such a day of pleasant toil. The people came in crowds, and talk on the highest subjects was kept up from hour to hour. The catechist, after a time, left me to visit some persons he knew in the neighbourhood, and I was left alone to unfold the doctrines of Christianity, and to answer the questions put to me. I more than once said, "I must have rest." All went out, and I lay down on a piece of carpet on the floor of the tent. Some one soon peeped in; "Have you not had rest now, sir?" and so I had to get up and resume my work, not over well-pleased the catechist had left it all to me. Since that time Kunauj has had visits from missionaries, and they have had many hearers, but I have not heard of any fruit gathered from these visits in the form of converts.

I was greatly impressed with one visit I received on this tour. We had got over our morning journey. I was, I suppose, more tired than usual, for in the forenoon I lay down on our travelling bedstead to rest. I heard a voice at the tent door, "Ṡahib, sahib!"—"Sir, sir!"—and I said, "Come in." In came a native well dressed, and looking as if tired with a long walk. I told him to sit down on the carpet, which he did, and he then proceeded to tell me the object of his visit. He said in substance: "Last night you were in a village twelve miles from this place, and you there spoke much of an incarnation, an '*autar*,' which had for its object the deliverance of man from the power and punishment of sin. One who heard you last night told me something of what you had said. I have long been a worshipper of the gods of my fathers, but I have got no rest, no satisfaction. I have heard much of incarnations, but I know of no sinless one. Not one of them has done me any good. Have you certain information of one that can deliver me and satisfy me?" I need not say what I said in reply to this great inquiry. We talked long and earnestly. I found he could read, and I gave him a Gospel and some tracts. He professed to be much interested. I begged him to give me his address that I might communicate with him. He did not pointedly refuse, but no address was given to me, apparently from the fear, so common among the people, of the reproach and suffering which will come upon them if they be suspected of an intention to abandon their ancestral religion. I parted with the man praying, that he might be led to the Saviour. Often, often have I thought of him; often have I hoped that what was said that forenoon had sunk into his heart; but I have never seen him, never heard of him, since that time.

I have mentioned that early in 1847 we went to Almora, in the Hill Province of Kumaon, and towards the end of the year returned to Benares. Before our departure we had the pleasure of seeing the completion of a work which had made a great demand on our time and attention, and had caused us no small anxiety—the erection of a new place of worship in the Grecian style, in the place of the small mud building in which we had hitherto met. This was our first essay in building, and our inexperience led us into many mistakes, which we tried to avoid in future work of the kind. The building cost above £1,200, fully twice the sum we had calculated.

Through the liberality of friends its entire cost was met within six months of its opening, and it has proved of great service to the Mission. The opening services were conducted in Hindustanee and English. The late Rev. J. A. Shurman preached with great power in Hindustanee to a crowded congregation composed of Christians, Hindus, and Muhammadans, and I preached in English to a large European congregation. We were greatly encouraged by the liberal collections made at these services.

I must defer to a later period of this work what I have to say about Kumaon, to which we paid several visits, and where we spent the last years of our Indian life. Our journeying to and from Kumaon in 1847 was partly over the ground traversed on our trip to Agra in 1842–43, and partly over new ground, as one may see by looking at the map of Northern India. The conditions of the journey were to a large extent those I have already described; but we suffered from bad roads, from our camp equipage falling behind, and I may add from inefficient service, much more than we had formerly done. On reaching Almora we mentioned to a friend the route we had taken, and he said, "Surely you have not come in a wheeled conveyance, for I am told that road is impassable." I told him the road was passable, for we had passed it, but if we had previously known what it was we should not have attempted it. Amidst the tracks we saw, we often had difficulty in deciding which was the road. Between unbridged streams with high banks, ditches, and deep ruts which caught our wheels and would not let them go, our progress was much impeded; but we toiled on. At one place we were happily helped by a company of Sepoys, whose medical officer was a dear Christian friend. In other places we were extricated by the help of villagers.

As we journeyed in these circumstances we were not in a mood to be amused, but I was amused one day by the contrast between a romantic lady and an unromantic "sais" (*anglicè*, groom). The Hills had come grandly into view, but unhappily we were fast in a ditch. The lady looking to the "sais" said, "Sais, do you not see the hills?" To which he most dolefully replied, not lifting his eyes as he spoke, "Madam, what can I see? We are stuck in the mud."

One day we took full ten hours to go twelve miles. When we came to the end of our stage we found we had to encamp for the night in the low scrub of the forest, with stagnant water all around us. There was a hut at the place with two native policemen to help travellers, and we were told by them that there had been for some days in the neighbourhood what is called "a rogue elephant"—an elephant which, for some reason known only in elephant councils has been driven out of the herd, and is so enraged by his expulsion that he is ready to run amuck at every person and animal he sees. This was not pleasant intelligence. We found native carts at the place, ready to proceed in the morning to a market to be held at the foot of the hills; and after a very uncomfortable night, much disturbed by the cries of the beasts of the wilderness, we set out, the people shouting to scare the elephant, which, though ready for mischief, is frightened by noise. We saw no trace of him. When the day was well advanced we reached a rest-house close to the hills, with a brawling stream behind it, with which our children as well as ourselves were delighted, one of them clapping his hands and saying, "Water clear and bright!"

We had our first and rather perilous hill journey the next day, but my account of it and subsequent journeys in the mountains must be reserved for another time.

We went to Kumaon by the most direct route through Futtygurh and Bareilly. We returned by a longer route *viâ* Meerut and Delhi. Our difficulties on our way back were somewhat different, but they were quite as great as on our upward journey. Some of the streams we had to cross were not fordable, and we had great difficulty in getting ourselves ferried over. A few nights were spent in exceeding discomfort, our carts not having come up with our tents, and we were shelterless and supperless—rather, if I may coin such a word, dinnerless. One night cover was got for my wife and children, but a missionary brother and myself remained out all night, with no possibility of obtaining rest, as a pack of jackals were gorging themselves on the carcase of a bullock, and making the most hideous noises. As the night was cold, and we had no bedding, it was perhaps well the jackals were there, as otherwise we might have been tempted to lie down on the bare ground, which we could not have done with safety to our health. When once we got to the Trunk Road, which we had from Delhi to Benares, our travelling difficulties were at an end, and we got on most comfortably.

At Delhi our tents were pitched in an open space near the house of Mr. Thompson, for many years the Baptist missionary in that city, whose widow and daughters were afterwards so barbarously murdered by the mutineers in 1857. With him and his family, and with some other Christian friends there, we had much pleasant intercourse during the few days we remained. We of course saw the sights of the grand old imperial city—the Juma Musjid said to be the largest mosque in Asia, a most commanding building on a small rocky elevation, to which you ascend by a lofty flight of steps, and which has a most magnificent court paved with granite inlaid with marble; the palace, so far as it was open to visitors; the Chandnee Chauk, the great open street and market-place with a fine stream of water flowing through it; and, at the distance of a few miles from the city, the remarkable tower, the Kootub Minar, 240 feet high, erected by the Muhammadan conquerors who first made Delhi their capital. For miles around there are ruins of mosques, mausoleums, palaces, and splendid mansions. For a description of Delhi, as for the description of Agra, I must refer my readers to Bishop Heber's Journal.

During this journey to and from Kumaon we carried on, so far as circumstances permitted, the missionary work I have already mentioned. Our experience while prosecuting this tour so closely resembled that of which I have already given an account, that it is unnecessary to enter into details.

As on our visit to Agra in 1842–43, so on these journeys of 1847 we met with the greatest kindness from our missionary brethren, some of whom we had afterwards the privilege of entertaining at Benares. It mattered not whether they were Episcopalian, Presbyterian, or Baptist, English, Continental, or American (at that time there were no Methodist missions in Northern India), we received a cordial welcome, and though formerly unknown to each other we at once felt at home. We sometimes felt in much need of help, and it was most readily afforded. To some other Christian friends we met our grateful acknowledgments are due.

CHAPTER XV.

RETURN TO BENARES.

VOYAGE TO ENGLAND AND RETURN TO INDIA, A.D. 1847—1857.

WHEN two more years had passed, during which we were enabled to carry on our work with few interruptions, we found that, beneficial though our visit to the hills had been, we stood in need of a still greater change, and of a more thorough bracing of both body and mind. Health again began to fail, and we felt unequal to the work devolving on us. We accordingly left Benares for Calcutta towards the end of 1849. As our children were young, and travelling by land was both fatiguing and expensive, we hired a budgerow and sailed down the Ganges. Our voyage lasted over four weeks. It gave us the opportunity of touching at a number of places, Ghazeepore, Buxar, Monghyr, Dinapore, Patna, and Berhampore, in most of which we had the pleasure of meeting missionary brethren. Towards the end of January we embarked on the ship *Monarch*, and after a prosperous, though not a rapid, voyage we arrived in England in May, 1850. The only place at which we touched was St. Helena. We lay off it the greater part of a day, but none were allowed to land as we had measles on board.

I will dismiss our stay in England in a few sentences, as it is no part of my plan to give English reminiscences. Like other missionaries on leave, I visited many places in England and Scotland on behalf of the Society of which I was an agent. At the expiration of our leave in the autumn of 1852 medical opinion forbade our departure. By the autumn of 1853 health was so improved that the way was open for our return to India.

After a season of severe domestic trial, which delayed our departure, my partner, myself, and two children embarked on board the *Indiana*, one of a new magnificent line of steamers plying to India round the Cape of Good Hope, in November. The voyage extended to eleven weeks. The weather throughout was remarkably favourable. We touched at the Islands of St. Vincent, Ascension, the Cape of Good Hope, the Mauritius, Point de Galle, and Madras. We landed at most of these places, and this took away in a great measure the weariness of a long voyage, which I must say we felt increasingly on every successive occasion. We were detained at the Cape for three or four days, which gave us an opportunity of getting to the top of Table Mountain, and of visiting the vineyards a few miles out of Cape Town. We were hospitably entertained by Mr. Thompson, and attended his services on the Lord's Day. Mr. Ellis, who was at the time at the Mauritius, kindly came on board as soon as the *Indiana* came to anchor, and took us on shore to the house of our missionary, Mr. Le Brun. We attended his service—it was the Lord's Day—and were delighted to see so many present, several of whom we were told were refugees from Madagascar. The congregation was well-nigh entirely composed of people of colour, varying from the brown of the mixed race to the jet black of the negro. The white dresses formed a striking contrast to the dusky faces, many of which, dark though they were, were lit up with an expression indicative of intelligence and contentment. The service was conducted in French, which continues to be the language of the island, although many years have elapsed since it became a British possession. After the service we were taken to the house of the Secretary to Government, who hospitably entertained us. We embarked the next day. As we were proceeding to the shore we were struck with the familiar sounds of the Hindustanee language from the lips of Indian coolies. We were sorry we could exchange with them only a few passing words. During the few hours we were off Madras we had the pleasure of landing and seeing some of the missionaries there.

After a short stay in Calcutta, we set out for Benares. The journey was performed in a new fashion. We purchased a conveyance, and arranged to have it drawn by relays of coolies all the way. Arrangements were made by an agent in Calcutta to have word sent on in advance, so that at every sixth or eighth mile coolies might be in readiness for us. Before 1839 the great Trunk Road from Calcutta to Delhi had been made, but the streams and ravines were for the most part unbridged, and consequently travelling by a wheeled conveyance was very slow and difficult. By 1854 the road had been greatly improved, many bridges had been made, and thus the facilities for travelling were much increased. At every twelve or fourteen miles there were rest-houses for European travellers, called "staging bungalows," all built on the same plan at the expense of two wealthy natives, each with two rooms and a bath-room attached, a bedstead in each room, a table, and two or three chairs, with a man in charge to take a small sum from each traveller for accommodation, and ready to furnish him with a good Indian meal at a very moderate rate. At some of these we stopped for rest and food. Our party consisted of our family, and a lady friend who wished to travel with us. Desirous to get on quickly, we were sometimes in our conveyance twenty hours out of the twenty-four, and dosed as we proceeded the best way we could. We met with no adventure worth relating, and were glad after ten days' journeying to find ourselves once more in our old dear abode. We had a most hearty and gratifying welcome from our brethren, both European and native. We reached it on a Saturday. I told the brethren that after my long absence, and entire disuse of the native language during that period, I must be a hearer the next day. They said that could not be, as the people were expecting me to officiate. Thus urged I ventured to conduct the service, and I was agreeably surprised to find that old scenes seemed to revive my knowledge of the language, and to bear me through with unexpected ease.

We resumed work at Benares recruited in health, and refreshed in spirit, and prepared by the experience of previous years to prosecute it with new effectiveness. We had a sense of the difficulties of the work, its trials and discouragements, and of the absolute necessity of Divine help in order to its being rightly prosecuted, which we could not have had at an earlier period; and we had at the same time a deeper realization of its greatness, blessedness, and final certain triumph. The missionary has little of the spirit of his office, and little fitnesss for it, who at every successive stage of his course is not increasingly bent on honouring his Master and promoting the good of the people among whom he labours, and who is not at the same time increasingly thankful for having been called to so high an office, while deeply humbled at his own unworthiness and his many shortcomings.

During the three years under review, our native Christian congregation was larger than it had been at any previous period, and, I am sorry to say, larger than it has been in later years. There were at that time about twenty Christian households in the mission compound, and several Christian families came from a little distance. There was a printing-press in our neighbourhood, which gave employment to a number of our people, and others succeeded in getting situations which gave them comfortable support. It was a gladdening sight, when the gong was struck for worship, to see them making their way to the chapel, and to find them, when assembled there, well-nigh filling the place, all cleanly clad, and devoutly engaged in the service of God. Many a time was my heart full of joy and hope when ministering to them. We had, indeed, our difficulties and trials. These are never long or far from us wherever we may be. There were inconsistencies and lapses among the native Christians which grieved us; but their general conduct was good, they were at peace with each other, and in some there were marked indications of growing piety.

Our tours during the cold weather of these years were mainly confined to the country within thirty or forty miles of Benares. Our only tour of any length was in January and February of 1857, when we went on the Calcutta road as far as Susseram, more than a hundred miles distant; and, leaving the Trunk Road, made our way to the rock of Rohtas, overlooking the Soane, where there are extensive remains of an imperial fort. We lodged one night in one of the deserted halls, of which there were several in a fair state of preservation, and we were told that to these the tigers of the surrounding forest occasionally resorted. During the Mutiny this fort was for some time the headquarters of a rebel chief. With the exception of this tour to the east of Benares, to which I shall afterwards refer, our experience in these itineracies closely accorded with that of former years. During this period the school and preaching work of the mission was steadily prosecuted by the catechists and missionaries.

Towards the close of 1856, and at the beginning of 1857, there were two interesting gatherings at Benares. The one was the meeting of boys and lads from all parts of the province for a Biblical Examination—of which I have already given some account. The other was a Missionary Conference, which was largely attended and efficiently conducted. The facilities for travelling were not so great as they are now, but they were such as admitted the presence of a number of missionaries from distant places. We parted deeply thankful for the pleasant and profitable intercourse we had had with each other. Little did we think of the terrible storm which was so soon to break over us, in which several of our number were to lose their lives.

CHAPTER XVI.

THE MUTINY OF 1857–58.

NO one who was within the range of the hurricane of 1857, no one who was even on its edge, can ever forget it. When we now look back, we marvel that a single European in that part of India was spared to tell of its fierce struggle, its sad sights, and its fearful perils. The annals of the Mutiny are furnished in volumes filled with ample details. Its causes and consequences have been largely discussed. My narrower and humbler aim is to describe that terrible outbreak so far, and only so far, as it came within my own experience and observation. My narrative will, however, be better understood by stating briefly the causes, which, in my opinion, led to this great rising against us, and by giving an outline of its progress before reaching Benares, where we then resided.

CAUSES OF THE MUTINY.

Our position in India is very peculiar. The history of the world presents no parallel. A great continent, containing a number of nations, possessed of an ancient civilization, some of them composed of races given to war and noted for their prowess, with a population amounting at present to 253 millions, has been brought under the dominion of a country of limited extent and limited population like ours, separated from it by many intervening countries, and accessible only by thousands of miles of ocean. That continent has not been subjected to tribute, and then left to its native rulers. Over by far the greater part of India these rulers have been displaced, and British rule has been established. Where native rulers remain, they are bound to administer their affairs in accordance with the views of the Sovereign Power. Over a part of the Indian continent the rule commenced more than a hundred years ago, and from decade to decade it has extended till it now embraces its present vast proportions. It extends beyond India. In the North-West we have entered into what properly belongs to Afghanistan, and from Burma a large extent of territory has been taken; so that the east as well as the west coast of the Bay of Bengal has come under our rule. To all appearance the rule is as firmly established as if it had come down from ancient times.

It would be a great mistake to suppose that India had been conquered for England by its own people. If they had been left to themselves, no part of it would now belong to us. The small European force has always been the backbone of our armies; but in every battle native soldiers have formed the great majority. The French gave us the example of employing native soldiers to place their country under European rule. In the dissolution of the Mogul Empire, thousands of warriors were ready to fight the battles of any one, European or native, who would pay them well. The example of the French was followed by the English, till India, from Cape Comorin to the mountains of the north and the north-west, came under their sway, to an extent and with a completeness and firmness of grasp never reached by the Muhammadan power in its palmiest days. Each Presidency—Bengal, Madras, and Bombay—has had its own native army, in 1857 amounting altogether to 240,000 men. In the Bengal army, by far the largest of the three, there has never been a single native of Bengal Proper. It has been entirely composed of north countrymen, to a large extent of Brahmans, and Chhatrees the old fighting caste of India, who have entered our service on account of its good pay and good treatment, though alien from us in everything by which one people can be alien from another. Many of the native soldiers have been Muhammadans, who are intensely averse to us on both religious and political grounds. Under the influence of friendly intercourse and good offices performed to each other, a kindly feeling often sprung up between officers and men; but as a body they were mercenary troops fighting for strangers, and the history of the world furnishes abundant instances of such an army being as formidable to their employers as to those against whom they have been employed. In the course of time our native soldiers were more and more trusted; important places were garrisoned by them, military stores were entrusted to them; and nothing was more natural than that in the more ambitious of their number the thought should spring up that the time had arrived for expelling the stranger, and seizing the power within their grasp. In thus acting they could make themselves sure of the sympathy of their countrymen.

The Sepoys have been treated in the matter of pay, clothing, and food, as they never were under native rulers; but they have been subjected to strict discipline, and they have been cut off from the much-prized privilege of foraging, or rather plundering. They have at different times complained loudly of unjust treatment. Alleged breach of promises of pay, and their being sent to fight our battles in foreign countries such as Burmah, China, Persia, and Afghanistan, and to parts of India foreign to them, have been prominent among their causes of complaint. They have not confined themselves to complaint and remonstrance ; they have again and again broken out into mutiny, which has led to some regiments being disbanded, and the mutineer leaders being severely punished. Years before 1857 it was asserted by persons eminently qualified to judge, like Sir Henry Lawrence, that grievous mistakes had been committed in the administration of the native army, and that our safety demanded great changes in its treatment and distribution. When one reads the statements they made, and the warnings they gave, the wonder is the mutiny did not sooner occur. Lord Ellenborough, before leaving India, declared the Sepoys were our one peril in India, and characteristically proposed we should keep them in humour by keeping them always fighting.

All other causes of revolt were light compared with the charge often advanced and believed that we were bent on the destruction of their religion. From the outbreak at Vellore in 1806, on to the great mutiny of 1857, this charge was persistently made. The Sepoys were allowed all the religious liberty compatible with military obedience ; they had every facility for following their religious customs ; they were fenced off from Christian influences as no other part of the community was ; they were solemnly assured again and again their religion would be scrupulously respected ; they had full evidence before their eyes that with few exceptions their officers had no Christian zeal. Whence, then, this charge of tampering with their religion? The explanation is to be found in the character of Hinduism. It is intensely outward. It is a matter of rite and ceremony, of meat and drink, of clothing and posture. It may be filched from a man without any act of his own by the act of another, and he may not be aware till informed that the fatal loss has been incurred. Something may be introduced into his food which will deprive him of his religion, and make him an outcast all his days. What more easy than to introduce a defiling element, such as the blood or fat of the cow or bullock, of which the Brahman or Rajpoot might unaware partake? To this intensely outward religion people of these castes are passionately attached from custom, from superstition, and still more, I think, from the consideration among themselves and others which caste purity secures. Their honour, *izzat*, as they call it, is their most valuable possession. An attack on it is bitterly resented. This honour is quite consistent with licentiousness, robbery, plunder, and even murder; but to violate caste by drinking from the vessel of a low-caste man, or eating with him, would bring with it indelible disgrace. To partake of the cow, the sacred animal, is the greatest crime which can be committed, and, if done unconsciously, the greatest calamity.

Notwithstanding the fact that the English as a people had little zeal for their religion, the Sepoys thought they saw reasons for our wishing to effect their conversion. If Christians, they would be fitter instruments for carrying out the designs of their English conquerors. They would in that case be no longer hampered by class distinctions, commissariat arrangements could be more easily made, they would have no objection to serving in foreign lands, and they would become identified with us. What was more easy than to effect the change by the manipulation of their food? Their imagination led them to interpret facts as justifying suspicion, and the supposition was enough to drive them to revolt.

The Muhammadans in India have become Hinduized to a large extent; they continually speak of themselves as a caste, and Muhammadan soldiers have shared with their Hindu comrades in the fear that the English were bent on destroying their religion. They took the most prominent part in the mutiny at Vellore in 1806. They were injudiciously required there to put on the English military hat, to shave their beards, and put on leather belts, which they maintained were made of pigs' skins; and all this was done, they said, to turn them into *Topeewalas*, Hatmen—in other words, into Englishmen and Christians.

Outside the army there have been causes, co-operating with those within, in prompting the soldiers to rise against us. Our government is a very foreign one. There is a national gulf between the rulers and the ruled, and consequent absence of the sympathy which would draw them to each other, if they were of the same people. Our government is at once expensive and strong, requiring a large amount of taxation considering the resources of the country, and able to enforce its payment. India has been greatly favoured by high-minded and able rulers; but often, with the best intentions, from want of thorough acquaintance with the native character and customs, injustice has at times been done by the decisions of our courts. Though giving security for person and property, such as India had never previously enjoyed, our government has borne hardly on some classes, such as the officials of the native states we have annexed, the numerous dependents of the abolished native courts, and the able and enterprising members of the community, for whom no suitable sphere has been open, as the main prizes in both the military and civil services are reserved for the English stranger. Then deposed princes have now and then intrigued with the army to draw it away from its allegiance.

In the spring of 1856 Lord Dalhousie laid down his office, after his long and memorable Proconsulship. So little did he anticipate the events of the coming year, that in the elaborate Minute he wrote on his retirement he satisfied himself with saying, regarding the native army, that the condition of the Sepoy could not be improved. Till the closing months of the year there was no fear of the coming storm. Profound peace reigned throughout India. War had been declared against Persia, but hopes were entertained that victory would soon crown our arms, and these hopes were fulfilled.

THREATENINGS OF THE STORM.

Towards the end of 1856 and early in 1857 there were mutterings of the storm. A number of men were selected from each regiment to be taught the use of the Enfield rifle, and for this purpose a new cartridge was required, which required to be bitten with the teeth. The report spread like wild-fire, and was firmly believed, that the cartridge was smeared with bullock's fat to destroy the caste of the Hindus, and with pig's fat to destroy the caste of the Muhammadans. The Adjutant-General of the army declared there was not the slightest ground for the statement; but the more strongly our innocence of design on their religion was asserted, the more firmly did the Sepoys believe our guilt. Paper was offered to them, and they were told to prepare cartridges for themselves; but they said the paper was dangerously glazed, and they would not accept it. Among other things causing disquietude was an order that in future all enlisting must engage to go wherever they might be sent in India or beyond. Hitherto some regiments had been enlisted only for service in India, and could not be sent out of it except by their own consent. On every side there were signs of a new era setting in, which forbode no good to the ancient customs and institutions of the land. The more aspiring spirits among the Sepoys had evidently formed the project of uniting the whole army in the attempt to drive the English into the sea, and secure power and emolument for themselves.

Various things favoured the project. It was well known that many throughout India hated the English, and were ready to join in their expulsion. Forts and arsenals were left in their keeping, unchecked by the presence of European soldiers. The mass of the European force was in the far North-West, in the Punjab, and towards the border of Afghanistan, as if there the danger lay. The Sepoys saw that if they could combine and act in concert they could with ease strike us to the ground. Then the prophecy was widely spread that our rule was speedily to come to an end. It had commenced with our victory at Plassey on June 23, 1757; and when the sun of June 23, 1857, should set, not one English face would be seen in India. Mysterious cakes, resembling our bannocks, were sent on from village to village, like the fiery cross in Scotland in former days, to prepare the people for great and startling events. Early in 1857 the ferment among the soldiers was spreading among large classes of the people.

During the cold weather of 1856–57 I spent some weeks in travelling with my family in the country to the east of Benares, on the Calcutta road. We left the high-road and made our way, as I have already mentioned, to Rohtas Gurh, a famous abandoned fortress on the top of a hill. In some of the villages to which I went to preach the Gospel the bitterest feeling was shown, especially by young men, towards our rule and religion. In one place the feeling manifested was so bitter that I thought they were prepared to lay violent hands on me. I remember remarking more than once, as I returned to the tent weary and worn out in body and mind, that a strange feeling was coming over the people, which I had never previously observed, and that I feared dark days were approaching.

THE OUTBREAK AND PROGRESS OF THE MUTINY.

At Berhampore, more than a hundred miles above Calcutta, and Barrackpore, a few miles from it, the Sepoys broke into open mutiny, which led to the leaders being executed and their regiments disbanded. The outbreak at these places made a painful impression on the entire English community, and created deep anxiety. That anxiety was increased by the reports received from day to day of the mutinous spirit shown by the Sepoys all over the country. We were told of midnight meetings, insolent conduct, and incendiary fires. The most sanguine could not but fear that we were entering a calamitous period. The most hopeful were those officers who had been long with native regiments, and were sure that whatever others might do, their men would remain staunch.

At length, on May 10th, the storm burst out at Meerut

in all its fury. I cannot enter on a detailed account of the events of that sad, memorable day. I can only in a few words mention what took place. On the previous day 87 men of a native cavalry regiment had, before the whole garrison of the place, been put in irons for repeated persistent disobedience. Though there was a large European force a native guard was put over the prisoners, who were confined in a place close to their comrades. No precaution was taken against their rescue. On the evening of the next day, Sunday, as the Europeans were gathering for Church, the Sepoys rose, murdered their officers, hastened to the parade ground, liberated their imprisoned comrades, opened the jails, raised all the villainy of the native town, massacred the Christians whom they met, men, women, and children, set houses on fire, and then set out for Delhi, the great old imperial city. There they were welcomed by the titular king and his family, and there, as at Meerut, they murdered all the Christians on whom they could lay hold. By the mismanagement of the large European force at Meerut, a small portion of which was well able to cope with the Sepoys, they did not arrive on the scene of revolt till the Sepoys had done all the mischief on which they were bent, and had set out for Delhi.

That 10th of May we remember vividly. We had had our usual afternoon service with the native Christians. In the evening we walked out in the garden. The moon was shining in an unclouded sky. Hot though the weather was we enjoyed our quiet walk, talked of the services of the day, and the threatening appearance of affairs. Little did we think of the terrible scenes which were then being enacted at Meerut.

The outbreak at Meerut awoke as with a peal of the

loudest thunder the entire English community in India, and especially in Northern India, to a sense of imminent peril. We had hitherto lived in the enjoyment of profound security. There had been uneasiness on different occasions, when our power seemed imperilled by the disasters which overtook us in Afghanistan in 1841–42, and by the life and death struggle we had afterwards with the Sikhs. Our enemies were then watching for our fall, and the reasons for uneasiness at those times were stronger than the community generally were aware of. There had been also at different times uneasiness in reference to the Sepoys, but they came to be regarded as wilful children, who might be troublesome, but who would do us no harm. In our own country, among our own people, we could not have felt safer than we ordinarily did. At the travelling season we went about, pitched our tents in solitary spots, for weeks together perhaps did not see a white face, and were treated not only with courtesy, but generally with profound deference, as if we belonged to a superior race. The people in their obsequious fashion, and with their idolatrous views, would almost have given us divine honours. All at once we realized ourselves as living in the midst of a dense alien population. Our own trusted soldiers, serving under our banners, receiving our pay, and sworn to defend us, had risen against us; and with them as declared enemies, in whom could we confide? Our obsequious servants of yesterday might become our murderers to-day. We felt ourselves at bay, surrounded by a host who might any moment fall on us and destroy us.

CHAPTER XVII.

THE OUTBREAK AT BENARES.

AT no place was the shock felt more severely than at Benares, where I was residing with my family. In no place was the danger greater. We were living in the suburbs of the most superstitious and fanatical city in the land. Again and again during the eighty years of our rule there had been riots in the city, professedly to avenge religious wrongs—riots so formidable, that they were quelled by military force. A very few years previous to 1857 the city was thrown into violent commotion, in consequence of new messing regulations in the jail, by which it was alleged, though without reason, the caste of the prisoners would be affected. The rowdy element, composed of those emphatically called *budmash* "evil-doers," persons ready for every mischief, was very strong. The Sepoys put in the forefront of their quarrel the plea that they were fighting for their religion, and where could they expect so much sympathy and help as in Kasee? Sir Henry Lawrence, writing some time previously about the mistakes committed in the management of the native army, named Benares as a place where fearful scenes would be witnessed in the event of a Sepoy rising. Intensely Hindu, though Benares be, it has, as we have already observed, a large

Muhammadan population, and in attacking us the Hindus could fully depend on their help.

Our danger was greatly increased by the vast disproportion between the native and European force—a disproportion so great, that apart from the danger of our neighbourhood to a great city, from which we might expect a host to pour out to attack us, it looked as if we were doomed to destruction. We had in Benares a Native Infantry regiment, which was believed to be tainted; a Sikh regiment, the temper of which was little known; and, a few miles off, an Irregular Cavalry regiment, composed, it was said, of a superior class of men, all, I believe, Muhammadans, but whom few could trust in the event of a rising. Our European force consisted of thirty artillery-men in charge of a battery of three guns. At the fort of Chunar, sixteen miles distant, there was a number of European soldier pensioners, of whom perhaps sixty or seventy might be effective. So unbounded had been the confidence in the Sepoys, that the artillery-men in Benares and the pensioners in Chunar were the only European force in the entire province of Benares under the Benares Commissioner, with a population of over ten millions; while in seven stations in the province there were native soldiers, chiefly infantry, but partly cavalry and artillery. Besides the English officers of the native regiments, and some half-dozen English civil officials, the only English people were missionaries of the Church, Baptist, and London Societies, and a few traders, while a few indigo planters were scattered in the country.

On the news of the Meerut mutiny reaching Benares, the civil and military authorities lost no time in consulting what should be done. The proposal that we should leave in a body for the Fort of Chunar was most wisely rejected. It was impossible to disarm the distrusted Native Infantry regiment in the absence of a European force. There was a large building in cantonments, which had been erected for a mint for the North-Western Provinces, and had been used for this purpose till the provincial mints were removed to Calcutta. It always afterwards bore the name of "The Mint." This building is in a wide enclosure, surrounded by a high wall, and it was hinted all round that in the event of a rising we should, if possible, make our way to this place. The Irregular Cavalry regiment was called in to patrol the roads leading to the station and city, and report the presence of suspicious persons. The resolution was formed to maintain a bold front, and pursue our usual course, as if we knew that succour was at hand. On every side the hope was expressed that none would give way to panic. The men at the head of affairs had the general confidence of the community.

Most happily for us and for many others there was a lull in the storm after the mutiny at Meerut and the possession of Delhi by the mutineers. There was alarm everywhere, here and there there was commotion, but there were no extensive and concerted risings. If there had been we could not have been saved. Our soldiers were returning from Persia, regiments proceeding to China were stopped on the way and brought to India, and an available force was thus placed at the disposal of the authorities. English soldiers were hastened up from Calcutta. From day to day we with joy saw them pass our gate in carriages on their way to cantonments. Great though our danger was they were not detained. A small number was kept for our defence, and the rest were sent on to relieve our sorely-pressed people farther north. Some began to hope the dark cloud over us was about to be dispersed, while others looked on our position with dismay approaching despair. As our house was in a very exposed position, a friend had at an early period invited us to take up our abode with him; but we resolved to remain for the present in our own home.

THE FOURTH OF JUNE, 1857, AT BENARES.

At length the storm burst over us. By attempts at incendiary fires and in other ways the Native Infantry regiment had shown a mutinous spirit. The necessity for disarming it was obvious to all except its own officers, but the difficulty of the measure was great. On June 4th Colonel Neil, one of those men whose high qualities were elicited by the terrible struggle on which we had entered, arrived at Benares. On the previous day a native regiment had mutinied at Azimghur, sixty miles distant. A council was held, and as there were one hundred and twenty English soldiers it was resolved to disarm the Native Infantry regiment next morning. The question was asked, "Why not now? We may be all killed before morning." Immediate disarmament was determined on. Well was it for us this was the decision, as it was afterwards found that very night had been fixed for the rising of the regiment, and the massacre of us all. The whole military force of the place was called out, the English soldiers being placed near the guns, and the Sepoys were ordered to pile their arms. The order instead of being obeyed was met by our officers and men being fired on, and the fight commenced.

We had just finished dinner when our night watchman

rushed into the room with the startling words, *Pultun bigar guya,* and *lin men ag luga!*—"The regiment has mutinied, and the cantonments are on fire." Scarcely had he uttered the words, when we heard the sharp rattle of the musketry and the crash of the guns. Our little conveyance was made quickly ready, and, with all others in that part of the suburbs, we drove as quickly as we could to the only place of temporary safety available for us, on the banks of the Ganges at the northern end of the city. The English were in different parts of the suburbs, and betook themselves to the places nearest to them which promised immediate shelter. Sir John Kaye, the historian of the Sepoy War, says that the missionaries left the city for Chunar, with the exception of one he names, Mr. Leupolt. In fact, only the Church missionaries went in that direction, and they could go in no other.

As we were hastening to the Ganges we knew from the noise of the musketry and cannon that the battle was going on, and from the cloud of smoke rising from cantonments we feared that all the houses were on fire. We went with others to the house of an English merchant whom we knew well, and then as the natives were gathering around we betook ourselves to boats on the river, and got out into the stream. In a short time a messenger from cantonments reached us with the good news that our men were victorious, and that the mutineers were in flight. We returned to the house of our merchant friend with the intention of remaining there for the night. With our party were a number of children, some of them infants, and they, poor things, were put to rest in any corner which could be found. Between eight and nine the Brigade-Major, who had been slightly wounded, and had been saved from certain death by the faithfulness of a trooper, rode into the compound accompanied by men of the Irregular Cavalry regiment. We all ran out, and were told by him that a number of English soldiers, who had just arrived from Calcutta, were on the other side of the Ganges ready to be ferried over, and that they would form our escort to the Mint, which was between three and four miles distant. In the meantime we learned all that had occurred—how the Native Infantry regiment had mutinied, how they had been joined by the Sikhs, some said by panic, by others I believe more truly, from sympathy with their Hindustanee brethren, as was shown by their after conduct; and how all had been put to flight by our band of soldiers, aided by the guns. On our side four were killed and nineteen wounded, of whom the greater number afterwards died. How many of the Sepoys were killed was not ascertained, as, with the exception of a few, the dead and wounded were carried off by their comrades.

When all was ready we set out, a long cavalcade, with English soldiers in front and behind, and native troopers on each side, our guardians then, but before the morning dawned in flight to join the mutineers. It was a calm, beautiful moonlight night, forming a strange contrast to the turmoil of the preceding hours. The road took us by our house, and as we passed the gate a servant, who had been watching for us, came out with artificially cooled water, which was very welcome. We reached the Mint about midnight, and there the whole European community was assembled. On every side there was eager talk about our position and prospects, but there was no appearance of panic or fright. The mothers soon succeeded in finding spots in the spacious rooms of the Mint—which had not been swept, and were covered with half an inch of mud—for their precious charge, and there they remained to watch over them; while the men sauntered about, or tried to sit where anything like sitting was practicable. Stray shots were heard, and from the city went up rockets, which were regarded as signals to the Sepoys outside. Most were awake as if it were full day. Between three and four in the morning, as I was sitting with two or three others on a native bedstead, a person came and said, "Where is the magistrate? The city is up." It was a false alarm; the city remained strangely quiet. As the morning broke we were all in safety, and no enemy was to be seen. Many of the English soldiers were so overcome by fatigue that they lay on the gravel fast asleep, with their muskets by their side.

In the Mint we all remained for more than a week in the greatest possible discomfort, unable to change our clothes except by going to some house outside, which some of us ventured to do. We once ventured to our house for some very necessary articles, and daily visits were paid to a barrack a short way off, where the sick and wounded were. During the day, with the blazing sun above us, and the wind blowing through the Mint with the heat of a furnace, we were obliged to confine ourselves to its large crowded rooms. The exposure was trying, but was patiently borne, and did no seeming injury to our health. At night we slept outside, most of us on the flat roof of the Mint, on bedding which our servants brought us. Our food was cooked at our homes, and brought to us by our servants, and very thankful were we to get it, though we had neither tables to sit at nor chairs to sit on. Had not our servants been faithful we should have starved, as the authorities, to prevent panic and to show a bold front, had laid in no provisions. This seems very unwise, and yet there is no doubt the bold front did much under God to effect our deliverance.

In the morning of the Sunday after the mutiny the Rev. C. B. Leupolt, of the Church Mission, preached on the parade ground. In the afternoon I was requested to preach. The soldiers, with their rifles in their hands, and the European inhabitants were my audience. I took for my text words which at once suggested themselves to my mind, "If God be for us, who can be against us?" These words of the Apostle Paul, I was afterwards told, came fraught with strength to the hearts of some present.

On Sunday evening it began to be whispered that mutiny had broken out at Allahabad. On Monday we knew all. The 6th N. I. Regiment, after professing in the afternoon their readiness to march to Delhi and fight the rebels, in the evening rose, murdered sixteen officers, six of them young lads who had just arrived, and all Europeans who came their way. Happily families were in the Fort, to which they had betaken themselves in opposition to the affectionate remonstrances of the native officers, who said it was a slur on their fidelity! The Sepoys plundered the Treasury; and it is said many of them were afterwards murdered by the villagers on account of the money with which they were laden.

As the Sepoys entirely disappeared, and the city of Benares was quiet, though the country around was much disturbed, most of us after a time returned to our homes. In our own case we found that not one of our servants had decamped, and not a pin's worth had been stolen. The very night of the mutiny a servant picked up the few silver spoons we had left on the table, and at considerable risk made his way to us to place them in his mistress's hands. Indeed, all about us acted with a faithfulness which elicited our warm gratitude.

While we were at the Mint a little incident occurred, which suggested how, in the excited state of affairs, a spark might have caused a great conflagration. Seeing a crowd of natives, almost all servants, at the gate, I went to it, and there the sentry, a little peppery Irishman, was threatening to stab with his bayonet a native servant with a note in his hand. I asked what was the matter. The sentry said, "That black fellow is mocking me, and I'll send this through him." The servant appealed to me. He said he had a note for a gentleman in the Mint, and entreated that "gora," "white man," to let him in, but instead of doing so he threatened to kill him. The mocking was, it turned out, the native folding his hands in the attitude of supplication. I explained the matter, and the man got in. The native servants were so roughly treated by some of our people, especially by the newly-arrived soldiers, simply because they were natives, that I was afraid they might leave us in a body; and if they had done so we should have been in a sad plight. One of my own servants, a native Christian, complained bitterly to me of the treatment he had received.

The quiet of Benares during this period was remarkable—I might almost say preternatural. When the fight of the 4th of June commenced, numbers were seen with drawn swords rushing towards cantonments, but when they saw Sepoys falling, and others running away, they shrank back into the city. A great dread fell on the entire population. I was told by natives the report had gone out that the English soldiers had been commanded to enter the city, and slay every man, woman, and child they met; and that in consequence, to adopt their exaggerated words, they sat trembling all night, no one daring to sleep.

In the meantime the terrible work of retribution commenced. Martial law was proclaimed, and many poor miserable creatures, charged with plundering, were hanged. Some of the Sepoys caught were blown from guns. I will not harrow my readers with details. I shunned as much as I could these bloody scenes, but on several occasions I came suddenly on them. To the present day I shudder as I think of what I saw.

THE PANIC OF JULY 6TH.

I must now come to our day of panic, July 6th. July 5th was a Sunday. We had our usual services with the native Christians. Some two hours after the evening service, a nephew of ours, then at Benares, drove into the compound, and told us we must go at once to the Mint, as a large force of Sepoys and country people were four miles off, prepared to attack the jail. This was startling news, as our house lay in the direct line between the jail and the city, and, in the event of the attack being successful, we should be the first victims. Still, we were very unwilling to stir, but our nephew was so urgent that we at last complied with his entreaty. A refugee family was in our house, and with us all crowded into a small conveyance we made our way to the rendezvous. What a scene was there! Most had arrived before us. Rain was falling, and we could not remain out. The rooms were so crowded that we could not get into them, and we had to lie for the night as we could in a dirty passage, with our back to the wall. The night passed off without an alarm, and in the morning we returned to our home, somewhat annoyed at having been taken from it, as we supposed, without sufficient reason.

On the morning of the 6th I had a strange duty to discharge for such a time—the marriage of a couple. One of our native Christians had arranged for his marriage taking place at that date. I told him that this was no time for marrying; that we who were married must abide with our families, but that those who were intending marriage should defer it to a more propitious season. He said all was arranged, and he begged me to officiate, which I did, I must say, with a bad grace. No sooner was the marriage over than I went home. After breakfast and family worship, we each betook ourselves, thoroughly worn out, to our rooms to obtain some rest. Scarcely had I lain down on my couch, when our faithful watchman came to my door and exclaimed, "If you do not go at once to the Mint you will all be killed." I asked him what was the matter. He could not tell me. He could only say, "Fly, fly." The refugee lady who, with her family, was with us, hearing the watchman's words, exclaimed, "Oh, Mr. Kennedy, do not leave us!" to which I replied, "Depend on it, I will not. Rather than that, I myself will remain behind." Our conveyance was speedily made ready, and off we started, with such a crowded coach as has been seldom seen, I, as driver, urging the poor overladen horse to his utmost speed. Natives as well as Europeans were seized with panic. There was a stream, then in full flood, close to our house, and I saw several natives throw themselves into it to swim across, at the imminent risk of their lives. As we crossed one of the great roads leading to the city, the natives were running as if pursued by demons. Right before us we saw an English lady running towards the Mint, with her bare head in the sun, which had now come out in its strength. A gentleman in a buggy drove past us, pulled in reins, the lady leaped into it, and they dashed on to the place of refuge. On reaching the Mint we found most of the Europeans there before us. I accosted a friend and said, "What does this mean?" He told us how the impression had gone out that the enemy were on us, and how the panic might have been prevented if information of the state of affairs had been given. There was danger. The host coming against us had, with characteristic procrastination, put off the attack till the morning. To prevent their approach to the city, every man and gun that could be spared were sent out to meet them.

When we reached the Mint we heard the rumour that Cawnpore had fallen. The report was not generally believed, but it was true. We were only two hundred miles from Cawnpore, and yet nine days had passed before our hearing of its fall, and we then heard of it only as a rumour.

The feeling of panic soon subsided, and as some in their haste had taken something with them, it soon looked as if we were a large improvised picnic party. For a few hours all was quiet; but in the afternoon the rattle of the musketry and the boom of the cannon told us the battle had commenced. Soon the news reached us that the rebels were in flight, and that we were again safe. Till the news reached there was anxiety, but there was little manifestation of it, except by the wives of some of the soldiers, who were wringing their hands and weeping bitterly. The night was spent by us in the greatest discomfort, huddled together, lying in our day clothes on the floor, in an atmosphere so close that I wonder we were not stifled. That 6th of July, 1857, at Benares can never be obliterated from the memory of any one who was there. It makes us understand, as nothing else could do, how much more dreadful a panic is than the most furious combat.

I must recall my readers for a little to the couple whom I had married on the morning of that memorable day. We had not been above a few minutes in the Mint, when whom did I see rushing in at the gate, out of breath, but my friends whom I had united in wedlock a few hours previously, the bridegroom a few steps in advance of the bride, who was doing her best, with little success, to save her bridal dress from being soiled by the muddy road. Grave though our position was, I could not but smile when I saw them. I went to meet them, and looking sternly at the bridegroom I said, "Chhotkan, did I not tell you this was no time to marry?" He looked at me sheepishly, and said, "Well, sir, it is now over, and I cannot help it." I had better add that the marriage has been a happy one. The husband has maintained a Christian character, and has had a prosperous career, and they both survive to the present time.

THE DAYS SUCCEEDING THE DAY OF PANIC.

On the day after the panic we all returned to our respective homes. The immediate danger was past, but the country around was in a very disturbed state. The officer commanding the station sent round a circular strongly recommending the immediate departure for Calcutta of European families, and, indeed, of all Europeans who were not able and willing to bear arms. Like many of my countrymen, I was thrown by this circular into great perplexity. Our house was out of cantonments, in a very exposed situation. We had four children with us at the time, the eldest six years of age, and the youngest a little more than three months. Their departure was indispensable. Was I to go with them, or send them away and remain behind? Some advised me to go, but we soon saw this was not the course which ought to be pursued. Officers were sending away their families, and they themselves were remaining behind. For me to desert my post at such a time, was seen by us both, would be to undo the work of my life, and it was evident my duty was to remain. Armed steamers were going up and down the Ganges, and I hoped to secure a passage to Calcutta in one of them for my family. Hearing a steamer was expected from Allahabad, we went down to Raj Ghat; and as soon as the steamer came to anchor I went on board. It was full to overflowing of refugees from the North-West. The captain told me he could not give my family even a deck passage, so crowded was the vessel. There was nothing for us but to go back to a friend's house, where we had been living for a few days. Through the kindness of a friend at Allahabad, to whom I had written, I succeeded in securing a small cabin for my family in the next steamer, and in it they made their way to Calcutta, after a detention of some days at Dinapore in great discomfort and danger, owing to the mutiny having broken out there. At Calcutta they embarked, in September, in a cargo ship for England, which they reached after a long and stormy passage. During the whole of July and August the communication between Bengal and the Upper Provinces was so interrupted, that sometimes for weeks together no certain information was received of what was transpiring. At Benares the only mails reaching were from places near us. At Calcutta the rumour went out that Benares had fallen, and that all the English people in it had been massacred, causing the deepest distress to the many there who had left loved ones behind.

BENARES FROM JULY TO DECEMBER.

From July till October the position of the English at Benares was one of great danger. We had no fighting, but we were continually threatened. We had twice or thrice an alarm, the most serious being from an *emeute* in the jail, which was soon suppressed and the leaders executed. Delhi was not taken till September, and till that was done, all who desired our overthrow were sure it was about to be accomplished. Our great peril was from Lucknow. Our small force there was besieged, it was reckoned, by 50,000 men. They were not relieved till towards the end of September. While the siege was being carried on, information reached the authorities of Benares that a plan had been formed to detach from the besieging army five or six thousand men to attack us. The plan was most feasible. The distance by the direct route was under two hundred miles. The river Goomtee, which flows by Lucknow, enters the Ganges a few miles from Benares. It was at that time in full flood, and a flotilla might be easily gathered by which, in a few days, a large body of armed men with the munitions of war could have reached us. Some of the Barons of Oude sent offers of aid, but these offers were by many considered lures to draw us into their net, that they might the more easily destroy us. Jung Buhadur, the famous ruler of Nepal, proposed to come with his brave Ghoorkas to defend us, but their presence was more feared than desired. Then in the great city near us we knew there were many plotting our destruction, and ready to rise at the first signal of an approaching foe.

So great was the danger considered, that thouands were set to the erection of a great earth fort close to the Ganges, on the site of an old Muhammadan fortress. Owing to the disturbed state of the country the commerce of the place was paralyzed; the stock of grain in the market was very low, and food was selling at famine prices. The erection of the fort gave most welcome employment to the poorer portion of the community. So great was the danger, that, acting under the advice of those best acquainted with the state of affairs, I sent to this fort books, documents, and other things which I deemed it most important to preserve. We were instructed how we were to act in the event of a sudden outbreak, the rendezvous to which we should instantly resort, and from which we might make our way together to the fort, which was being erected. It often occurred to me that our position at that time was like that of persons sitting on a barrel of gunpowder in a house on fire. So alarming were the accounts received in the daytime, that I often lay down at night uncertain what might occur before morning. Often I got up, looked towards the cantonments, and listened. Thankful that all was quiet, I returned to my bed.

During these anxious months I had abundant reason to be thankful for the decision at which we had arrived, that I should remain behind when my family left for England. In the discharge of the work devolving on me from day to day, I felt I should have been recreant to duty, and missed many opportunities of usefulness, had I gone away. Early in September, to the great grief of us all, a much-loved member of the Mission, my sister-in-law, the wife of my senior colleague, Mr. Buyers, was removed by death. She had remained behind when other ladies, who had children, left. Mr. Buyers was prostrated by the blow, and for a considerable time was unable to resume work. The charge of the Mission thus came largely into my hands. Before the end of July we re-opened our principal school in the heart of the city, of which I was superintendent, and which I visited constantly. At Benares a Depôt Hospital was opened, to which the sick and wounded Europeans were brought from the surrounding country, and there a part of every day was spent. My principal work, however, was among the native Christians, with whom I met constantly to speak about the state of affairs, to consult what should be done, to commit ourselves to God, and ask from Him guidance and protection. The firmness and courage of these Christians were worthy of the highest praise. As natives, they could elude observation far more easily than Europeans; but even where they were unknown, so entwined is idolatry with the whole life of the people, they could not be any time among their countrymen without being discovered if faithful to their Lord; and, as recreants from their ancestral religion, they were sure to be cruelly treated. They had only to declare themselves Muhammadans, and safety would be at once secured. Not one of our native Christian community thought of seeking safety by such means. They seemed resolved to brave every hazard rather than deny their Lord. At length, by the capture of Delhi in the first half of September, and the relief of the Lucknow garrison some twelve days afterwards, the dark, threatening clouds over us began to break.

From October onward the tension was loosened; but the danger was not over. Though the garrison at Lucknow had been relieved, we were forced to evacuate it, and for months afterwards the whole country of Oude remained in the hands of those who had risen against us. Over a large portion of the North-West, and in Central India, our government remained prostrate. We had been so long in danger we had become blunted to the sense of it, and remained unmoved in circumstances which at an early period would have greatly excited us.

During the recent outbreak in Egypt, the position of Europeans in that country in many respects resembled that of Europeans in Northern India in 1857. Very similar was their danger, very similar their sufferings, and very similar was the deliverance of the greater number. But for providential interposition, not one would have in either case escaped. When I look back and consider what our position was, I marvel that any of us survived to tell what we endured; and our hearts are hard and cold indeed if we are not fervently thankful for our preservation. While my narrative shows that the residents at Benares in 1857 had to pass through a season of severe trial and great danger, all acquainted with the history of that period are aware that our countrymen in other places had vastly more to suffer. In many places the rising was temporarily successful. With us, the authorities all through kept the upper hand. The result was that we were kept from the extremity of suffering to which many were subjected. The entire loss of property was the least of the trials they had to bear. Many, among whom were delicate women and helpless children, were cruelly murdered. Others saw the objects of their warmest love killed before their eyes, had to endure the most fearful privations, and had to pass through untold horrors before reaching a place of safety. Not a few sank into the grave, the victims of toil, suffering, and sorrow. At no place was the danger greater than at Benares, and at no place did the general community suffer so little.

VISIT TO ALLAHABAD.

Learning that there was no missionary at Allahabad, about seventy miles north-west of Benares, which is now the seat of Government for the North-West, I wrote in December to a native Christian there whom I knew, proposing to visit him and his brethren, and in due course I got his reply, expressing the pleasure my visit would give them. I accordingly went, taking Mirzapore on my way, where I spent two or three days very happily with the mission family. I found a tent erected for my accommodation by the native Christian brethren close to the ruins of the mission premises. What a scene of desolation the whole place presented! The houses of the European residents had been set on fire, and there they were as the mutineers had left them. There were no European families. One large house had been put in order by the magistrate, and in the wide surrounding enclosure what may be called a canvas town had arisen. Civil and military officers were continually passing up and down, and for their accommodation tents had been pitched. All took their meals together in the restored mansion, and they kindly asked me to join them during my stay. My tent was pitched close to the abode of the native Christians. I had thus the opportunity, during the week I remained, of holding constant intercourse with my own countrymen and with native brethren. From the natives I heard much of what they had seen and suffered. I was shown the scenes of the terrible events which had occurred, and as retributive measures were still carried on, I saw, in spite of myself, scenes which made me shudder. On the other side of the Ganges there were frequent skirmishes between parties sent out and bands there who were resisting our authority; the firing was distinctly heard. On Sunday I preached twice to the native Christians. In the forenoon the service was conducted in a small chapel, which had not been burnt down, because it was so close to native houses that, if burnt, the flames would have certainly spread to them. In the evening I re-opened for worship the principal mission chapel. An attempt had been made to set it on fire, but as it had not been at once successful, owing to its being very strongly built, the insurgents satisfied themselves with breaking the doors, windows, seats, pulpit, and everything which could be easily destroyed. The wreck had been cleared away, and there I preached to a goodly company, one of them a man whose arm had been cut off because he was a Christian, and who had been left as dead. His recovery was marvellous. That was a memorable Sunday to me and to those to whom I ministered. My morning subject was, "In the day of adversity consider" (Eccles. vii. 14); and in the evening, Christ stilling the storm (Matt. viii. 23–28).

CHAPTER XVIII.

VISIT TO CEYLON AND RETURN TO BENARES.

1858—1859.

DURING the hot season and rains of 1858 I suffered greatly from boils and feverishness. After applying in vain the usual means of cure prescribed, I was advised to try a sea voyage. I accordingly arranged to go down the Bay of Bengal to Point de Galle in Ceylon, and to await there the arrival of my wife from England, so as to return with her to India.

The rebellion still flickered in Bahar. A part of the road to Calcutta was in the hand of Kower Singh, a rebel chief; and travellers like myself to the capital from the North-West were on that account happy to avail themselves of the river steamers. We had the clear sky and the gentle breeze of that delightful season in Northern India. From morning to night we sat under a thick awning, reading or talking, as we were inclined, refreshed by the breeze, and interested in the various objects presented to our view on the river and its banks. The fortnight of the voyage passed most pleasantly, and I arrived in Calcutta half cured of my ailments. I was happy to find myself in time for the outgoing steamer of the P. and O. Company, on which I took passage to Point de Galle. On landing I saw the last newspaper received from England with the list of passengers for successive steamers, and from it I learned that my wife was to come a month later than I had anticipated. This left me with five or six weeks in Ceylon to dispose of myself as I best could. I made up my mind to travel through the island. I accordingly left Galle by coach the next day for Colombo, the capital. After staying there a few days I set out for Kandy, the old capital; held on to Newera Ellia, the sanatorium of the island, lying under Pedro Talla Galla, its highest mountain; ascended the mountain, made my way back by another route to Kandy, and then proceeded to Galle, where I was happy to meet my wife and child, with whom I went on to Calcutta.

When I landed at Galle I was not aware that I knew a single individual in the island, but I was not an hour at the hotel to which I went before I found myself in company with a medical gentleman, a native of Perthshire, who knew my friends; and on my arrival at Colombo I was recognized on the street, by my resemblance to my father, by a person who had never seen me previously, but who knew him. It struck me it would be dangerous for me to attempt an incognito, which, happily, I had no temptation to do. During my travels in Ceylon I met several from the North of Scotland whom I had known intimately, and among them one who had been for years my schoolfellow. My countrymen were there, as elsewhere, prominent members of the community.

I was much interested in all I saw during my travels in Ceylon. I was prepared to see fine scenery and rich foliage, but the reality greatly exceeded my expectation. On the coast between Galle and Colombo there is a considerable extent of level land, covered by the cocoanut palm, which forms much of the wealth of the people. Every part of the tree is turned to account. The wood is used for rafters, and the leaves for thatching. The kernel is an article of food, but its principal value comes from the oil made from it after it has been dried. The nut contains a liquid, which is deemed by the natives very refreshing. The fibrous husk round the cocoanut, called coir, is manufactured into ropes, matting, brushes, and other useful articles. It is largely and profitably exported. The trees are tapped for a juice, which, boiled when fresh, gives what is called palm-sugar; but when kept, becomes intoxicating. The name of the tree in the native language is "Tar"; this intoxicating juice is called "Taree," and by a well-known custom of linguistic transposition it is called by English people "Toddy." We have at Benares palm-trees which furnish this toddy, and I am sorry to say it is by far too largely used. This cocoanut palm abounds on the coast, and is always bent towards the sea, as if to welcome its breezes, or to strengthen itself against them. Away from the coast it well-nigh disappears, and trees of a very different order are seen on every side, many of them rising to a great height and covered with beautiful foliage.

The scenery in the interior is very striking. When travelling on the top of the coach from Colombo to Kandy, I might have thought myself in my own Highlands, as mountain after mountain came into view, and our road in its descents and ascents skirted precipices, where safety demanded the most careful driving. Long, winding valleys, through which rivers flowed, with falls and cascades here and there, reminded me of our finest straths. I saw no large bodies of water like our lochs.

There were two points of marked dissimilarity. The month was December ; I required no great-coat, and the rays of the sun were stronger than was pleasant. Instead of the leafless trees, and the white covering of the snow of the Scottish winter, there were trees in their richest dress, and all around a verdure of the freshest green, telling me I was in a tropical land, and in a land where heat and moisture by their abundance gave extraordinary force to vegetation. As I travelled from Kandy to Newera Ellia, and back again to Kandy by a different route, my impression of the picturesqueness and productiveness of the country was confirmed. There was one thing I did not see—the blooming heather of my own Highlands.

There is, I suppose, no country where all that is desirable can be obtained. It must be acknowledged Ceylon has its disadvantages. Its climate is that of perpetual summer, warmer indeed at some times than at others, but never approaching our heat in Northern India in May and June. It is only six degrees from the equator, and it owes its moderate temperature to its sea breezes and abundant rain. I missed the bracing coolness of Northern India in December and January. Perpetual summer is good for neither soul nor body. For bodily health and enjoyment the alternation of cold and heat is far better, as in the moral world prosperity and adversity are required for the maturing of character.

There is one evil—I do not know whether I should call it a minor or a major evil—to which both man and beast are exposed in Ceylon. We have all heard of snakes in the grass. In the fine grass of Ceylon leeches abound, and are ever ready to take their unwelcome contribution from all that come their way. They leap up on passers by, and try to exact from them their favourite food. I was often reminded by unpleasant nips that they had got hold of me. For months after leaving Ceylon I had on my limbs marks of their doings.

When travelling between Kandy and Newera Ellia, I was the guest of coffee-planters, all of them, so far as I remember, my own countrymen; and saw coffee in all its stages, from the berry on the coffee-bush on to the manufactured article ready for the market. The plant is indigenous in the island, but it was turned to little account till taken up by Europeans. The pioneers in its culture, as so often happens in such cases, are said to have lost heavily; but at the time of my visit plantations were paying well, and a large tract of land was under cultivation. I believe it afterwards ceased to be profitable, and now tea cultivation is taking its place.

At one time cinnamon was the most valuable export of the island, but by 1858 it had so decreased in value by its being produced abundantly in lands still farther east, that comparatively little attention was given to it. I was taken to the public garden in Colombo, and saw the work-people with their sharp knives peeling off the fragrant bark from the cinnamon-tree, and preparing it for the market.

Colombo, the capital, is a large, stirring, rising town. Galle is a much smaller place, and owes its importance to its being a place of call for steamers on account of its sheltered bay. It is noted for its pedlars, men who, with combs in their long hair, and clad in jacket and petticoat, might be taken for women. Their wares of jewellery and precious stones have not a high character for genuineness. Kandy, the old capital in the interior, is a small place, lying very low, and is surrounded by hills. It has a beautiful little artificial lake, and is famous for its temple, with a tooth of Buddha as its great treasure.

During the few weeks I was in Ceylon I was most hospitably entertained wherever I went by missionaries, chaplains, coffee-planters, and others. I shall always retain a grateful recollection of the kindness I experienced. From these friends I heard much about the spiritual state of Ceylon. It is well known the Dutch were the first Europeans who obtained a footing in the island. They determined to stamp out heathenism and establish Christianity, not by violent persecution, but by reserving offices of every description for those who embraced the Christian faith, by treating them in every possible way as a privileged class, and by showing official disfavour to the unbaptized. An agency composed of chaplains, catechists, and schoolmasters was appointed to bring the community within the Christian fold. The work went on with great apparent success. Tens of thousands avowed themselves Christians. It looked as if heathenism was to disappear under Dutch rule. If the Dutch had retained possession of the island, and had persevered in their policy, in all likelihood by this time Ceylon would have been a professedly Christian country, with a strong underlying element of heathen notion and practice.

No sooner was the policy of neutrality adopted with the installation of English rule, than this large Christian community melted away, and flowed into the old channel of Buddhism, which had been for ages the religion of the Cingalese. The thousands of Christians were reduced to hundreds and tens. The London Missionary Society early entered the field, but withdrew. In the parts of Ceylon where I travelled I met with Methodist, Baptist, and Church of England missionaries, and in other districts there were American missionaries. The descendants of those who once were professed Christians retain some Christian notions, and adhere to some Christian practices. Baptism is still in favour with them, but it is never administered by Protestant missionaries except to those deemed fitting recipients. If Buddhists were consistent, caste in a mild form and to a limited extent might be tolerated, but could not be approved. They are not, however, consistent, and caste is much more regarded by them than Gautam would have sanctioned, though it has not among them the rigidity it has among the Hindus. I was told regarding one boarding institution for young men, all ate together; but on returning to their homes they performed certain ceremonies which removed the defilement they had contracted. As to the general character of the native Christians, I inferred it was much the same as in India, with similar excellences and similar defects.

I went into some of the Buddhist temples. On the walls were sculptured the terrible sufferings of the wicked in the different hells into which, according to Buddhism, they are cast. The worshippers appeared to me remarkably stolid and listless, as if engaged in a work which could not be too mechanically performed. There was nothing of the animation of the Hindus when they are worshipping their gods.

I went into a large Roman Catholic church, and saw all the usual furniture of Roman Catholic worship. On the wall, the worship of demons by the faithful and their attendance at demon feasts was strongly denounced, and threatened with severe punishment; from which it would appear this was no uncommon offence.

I was struck with the massy churches built by the

Dutch in Galle and Colombo. They testify to the zeal of the first colonists, as if they were taking possession of the land for Christ, and were determined to maintain His worship, though far distant from the land of their fathers. Dutch descendants and Scotch colonists now form the most of the worshippers in these places. The Dutch language still survives, and in 1858 some of the Dutch people understood no other. For them a service is held in their own language. I preached in both of these churches at the request of the chaplains. In one of them the Lord's Supper was administered, and the communicants were addressed first in English and then in Dutch.

Towards the end of December I left Galle with my wife and child for Calcutta, taking away with me pleasing recollections of the scenes I had witnessed, the information I had received, and the kindness I had experienced during my six weeks' travels in the island.

After a brief stay in Calcutta we made our way to Benares—the first part of the journey by the recently constructed railway, and the rest, the greater part of it, by a four-wheeled conveyance, drawn by a horse, called a Dawk Garry, arrangement for a fresh horse every sixth or seventh mile being made by the Dawk Garry Company. Instead of spending three weeks on the way, as we had done in 1839 when proceeding to Benares on a steamer, and twelve days in 1853 in a conveyance drawn by coolies, we now completed our journey in five days. We were glad to rejoin our brethren, and to resume our work in Benares.

CHAPTER XIX.

VISIT TO CITIES IN THE NORTH-WEST AND TO KUMAON—VISIT TO ENGLAND AND RETURN TO INDIA.

FROM 1859 TO 1866.

FROM the time of our arrival at Benares in January, 1859, on to our departure for the hills in March, 1861, the work of the Mission was carried on in the usual way. There were interruptions from failure of health, but during the most of the period the operations of the Mission were vigorously carried on with tokens of the Divine blessing.

The principal change during this period was the greater attention given to the European population. Before 1857 the English-speaking population of Benares was very small, and as there was always an English chaplain at the place, and our Baptist brethren kept up an English service, our Mission did very little in this department. For a time we had an English service one evening in the week, but owing to the weakness of the Mission, and the pressing demands of native work, this had been given up. After the Mutiny the English-speaking population was largely increased by English soldiers, and persons connected with the Public Works. It was deemed incumbent on us to do something for our own countrymen, whose spiritual need was manifest to all. On this account English services on the Lord's Day were commenced. For a time two such services were held, one in the Mission chapel, and another in the schoolroom of the cavalry barracks. On the withdrawal of the cavalry this second service was discontinued. The service on the Lord's Day morning or forenoon in the Mission chapel has been steadily kept on till this time, has been generally well attended, and has been, I believe, productive of much good.

As the Rev. William Moody Blake, who joined the Mission in 1858, took the superintendence of the Central School, and with occasional assistance conducted the English services, the work among the native women and girls was left to be carried on by my wife, to which she had given her heart and strength from the time she became a member of the Mission in 1839, while I had the principal charge of evangelistic work among the heathen, and of ministering to the native Christians.

The most memorable episode of this period was a visit we paid to Allahabad, Cawnpore, and Lucknow, in the winter of 1859–60. We saw much on this tour which deeply and painfully interested us. I have already mentioned the desolation I saw on my visit to Allahabad at the end of 1857. During the two succeeding years the houses which had been burnt had been rebuilt, new houses had been erected, and new roads had been made. Traces of the desolation caused by the Mutiny remained, but there were on every side signs of great prosperity. Allahabad, from its position at the confluence of the Ganges and the Jumna, had always been deemed a place of great importance in both a military and civil aspect. It rose to new importance by being made the seat of government for the North-West instead of Agra, and also by becoming the central railway-station, from which it was arranged railways should ramify to Lahore and Peshawur in the north-west, to Calcutta in the east and south, to Jubbulpore and Bombay in the west, forming in Central India a connection with the railways in Southern India. This arrangement has been carried out, and now there is no city in the interior of the country which bears so close a resemblance as Allahabad to the great Presidency cities, in its churches, European shops, hotels, and roads so lined with houses that they may be called streets. As might be expected, the native population has greatly increased.

From Allahabad we went by train to Cawnpore, one hundred and thirty miles to the north-west. This place was for many years a large military station, as the kingdom of Oude lay on the other side of the Ganges. It may be well to give a very brief narrative of the terrible events which occurred there, that readers may the better understand what we saw.

On the breaking out of the Mutiny, the English soldiers and residents entrenched themselves in an open plain, which had the solitary advantage of accommodation in barracks, while they left the arsenal in the hands of the insurgents. The siege commenced on June 6th, directed by Dundhoo Punt, the Nana Sahib as he was called, the adopted son of Bajee Rao, the ex-Peshwa of the Mahrattas, whose castle was ten miles distant. On June 27th, after enduring terrible hardships and privations, our people surrendered on promise of being sent safely to Allahabad. They accordingly made their way to the promised boats; but no sooner had they been reached than they were set on fire, and the Nana in person directed a fusillade on the party. Only four succeeded in escaping, and they did this by swimming. The men were murdered, the women and children, to the number of two hundred, were taken back, were huddled together in crowded rooms, scantily fed on the coarsest food, and subjected to every indignity. The Nana's army was defeated in several engagements, and was at last utterly overthrown by the army led by General Havelock, in a battle fought at the entrance to Cawnpore. By an order of the Nana, issued by him when fleeing from the place, the women and children were murdered, and their bodies were thrown into a well. Our soldiers arrived to see to their horror the well choked with the victims of Nana's satanic cruelty. Unknown to those whom he was besieging, he had previously, on June 4th, ordered the massacre of one hundred and thirty men, women, and children, who had come from Futtyghur.

At Cawnpore we saw much to sadden us to the very core. The thrilling accounts we had read of the atrocious deeds there committed came to our remembrance with a painful reality. All along the river-side, houses, once occupied by officers, lay in ruins as the mutineers had left them. We observed flowers blooming here and there in the gardens, planted by those who had been so ruthlessly cut down. We visited all the places made memorable by the sad events of 1857. We went to the Sabadha Kothee, as it was called, the house on a slight elevation from which the Nana directed the siege of the entrenched camp. It was well remembered by us as the abode, in 1842, on our first visit to Cawnpore, of a missionary of the Propagation Society, with whom we had much pleasant intercourse. Within less than half a mile of this house lay the entrenched camp of the English—if a trench three or four feet deep, with a breastwork of earth behind it four or five feet high, deserves the name of an entrenchment. The spot was chosen on account of the barracks, in which our people could shelter themselves against what they expected to be a mere temporary assault, if an assault at all was made, as they supposed the mutinous soldiery would leave at once for Delhi, which they would have done had not the Nana stopped them by large pay and larger promises. The barracks speedily became well-nigh uninhabitable under the fire of the enemy. At last they were burnt down, and no shelter remained from the fierce rays of the sun. One could not look on the spot, and consider the weakness of the defenders compared with the strength of the enemy, supplied as they were with the guns and ammunition of our arsenal, without wondering the defence could have been maintained for a day. The defence was most heroic; extraordinary feats of valour were performed, but at last the besieged were obliged to succumb from the failure of food and ammunition.

We walked from the entrenchment, which was rapidly disappearing under the rains and heat of the climate, by the route taken by our people to the promised boats, which were set on fire as soon as they reached them. It was truly a *via dolorosa*, and we walked on it with saddened hearts, musing on the awful sufferings our countrymen had endured. On a little temple close to the ferry at which the boats lay, and on some houses near it, we saw marks of the bullets on the walls.

Since that period—the winter of 1858–59—we have been on several occasions at Cawnpore. The desolation has disappeared. Ruined houses are no longer to be seen. A stranger might pass through the place without observing anything to remind him of the events of 1857.

He would be a very preoccupied or a very stolid person who could pass through Cawnpore without making it a point to see the monuments erected to commemorate our fallen countrymen. On the site of the entrenched camp a memorial church has been raised, with stained windows and varied devices bearing the names of those who had fought and suffered there. A very handsome monument of marble, surmounted by a statue of the Angel of Peace, with a suitable inscription, has been erected over the well into which the bodies of the women and children were thrown. The ground round it is kept in beautiful order. For many a day visitors to India will look with tearful eyes and sad hearts on these spots sacred to their fallen countrymen.

Leaving Cawnpore, we crossed the Ganges and travelled forty miles to Lucknow, the capital of the country of Oude, which was ruled by a feudatory of the Mogul Empire, who had become a feudatory of the British Crown. To him our Government gave the title of King. In 1856, by an order from home, the country was taken under our direct rule on account of gross misgovernment, by flagrant and persistent violation of the engagement made with us. The Chief Commissioner in March, 1857, was Sir Henry Lawrence. After staving off the Mutiny successfully for a time, he was obliged in the end of June to concentrate his force in a half-fortified place on a slight elevation, called the Residency, as there the British representative, under the title of Resident, and his official subordinates, had their abode and offices. There the English were besieged by a vast body of Sepoys, and by the Talookdars, the Barons of Oude, and their retainers. Sir Henry Lawrence was mortally wounded on July 4th. The siege was maintained till

THE WELL AT CAWNPORE.

September 25th, when, after a fierce struggle, it was relieved by Havelock and Outram. They in their turn were besieged, but they were able to maintain their footing till November 19th, when they were finally relieved by Sir Colin Campbell. Outram remained with a force of observation at Alum Bagh, a large garden with a very high wall, outside Lucknow on the Cawnpore road; while the rest held on to Cawnpore. Sir Colin Campbell returned with his army, and took the city on March 6th, 1858. We are told that in the interval it had been fortified in a way which would have done credit to a European power. My narrative will be better understood by these facts being remembered.

As we travelled from Cawnpore to Lucknow we passed houses close to the road which still retained the loop-holes through which the enemy had fired on our troops. The earthworks hastily raised for temporary shelter still remained. We were reminded at every mile of the fierce resistance our soldiers had to encounter. At Lucknow we remained for a week, and went over all the scenes made memorable by recent events. We paid several visits to the Residency, where our people defended themselves so long and valiantly against thousands of armed men well supplied with ammunition. At every step proofs presented themselves of the desperate struggle maintained with the foe. The houses in the Residency had been so battered and torn by shells and balls that scarcely one was habitable before its evacuation, and the ruin was completed when the city was finally taken by Sir Colin Campbell. At the beginning of 1859 the whole place was a mass of ruin, with here and there a piece of tottering wall, shaken or perforated by heavy shot and ready to come down. The walls still stood, though in a very broken state, of the house in which Sir Henry Lawrence died, and the spot was pointed out to us where he had received his death-wound. A large body of labourers was employed in taking down the ruined walls and levelling the ground. We observed bones which had been dug up by them as they pursued their work.

From the entrance into Lucknow on the Cawnpore road there is a street, two miles in length, leading straight to the Residency. The enemy expected our army to advance by this street, and made provision for its destruction by digging trenches, and lining the houses on both sides with musketeers ready to pour on our soldiers a killing fire. The relieving army, guided by a person who knew Lucknow well, and had at great risk made his way to them at night from the Residency, made a sudden detour to the right, and advanced by a comparatively open route, stoutly but unsuccessfully opposed at almost every step. I had the promise of a guide to take me on foot by this route to the Residency, but on reaching Alum Bagh, the appointed place of meeting, I found no one there. I made my way, however, with very little difficulty by observing the marks of the bullets on the houses along the line traversed. I sometimes lost the trace, but soon recovered it, musing as I went along on the very different circumstances in which our countrymen a short time previously had gone over that road.

We saw other places of interest, such as the Muchee Bhawan, the fort in which our soldiers were previous to the siege; the Kaisar Bagh, an extensive garden, filled with showy, lofty houses, where the King of Oude and his numerous retinue had resided; the Chuttar Manzil, a handsome building where public entertainments were given; the gateway at which the gallant Colonel Neil

RUINS OF THE RESIDENCY, LUCKNOW.

fell—now called Neil Gate; the Secunder Bagh, a garden with a high wall, where a large body of the enemy was posted, and which was stormed by the 78th Highlanders, who shut up every exit and killed every soul, many of the Sepoys fighting desperately to the last. Two thousand bodies were taken out of the place and buried in the adjoining ground. We observed on the walls the marks of the bullets, and even the indents made by the swords and bayonets, while this carnage was going on.

A French adventurer of the 18th century, General La Martine, had risen to great power and wealth in the service of the Kings of Oude. He erected a splendid mansion in Lucknow for the support and education of boys of every creed—Christian boys to be brought up in the Christian Government's religion—and richly endowed it. Similar institutions were established in Calcutta and in Lyons, La Martine's native place. This institution has proved a signal blessing to European and Eurasian families. On the outbreak of the Mutiny the teachers and pupils betook themselves to the Residency, and under the leading of their Principal took an active part in the defence. La Martine had so little confidence in the kings whom he had served for years, that he ordered his body to be buried in a vault under the building, which he knew would prevent a Muhammadan from making it his dwelling-house. This was accordingly done.

While we were at Lucknow we were most hospitably entertained by a missionary of the Church Missionary Society, to whom a large native mansion had been made over by the authorities on account of the owner having taken an active part in the rebellion. On Sabbath I preached in Hindustanee to the native Christians, and we attended the English service held in a building which had been an Imambara, the name given to a building where Muhammadans of the Shiah sect worship.

When going from Cawnpore to Lucknow we travelled by day. We returned by night, when the moon was full. It was one of those calm, clear nights of which we have many at that season. We reached the Ganges about four in the morning. While waiting for a boat to take us across, there fell on our ears, coming from a cluster of huts close by, the voice of a singer at that early hour; and what was our delight and surprise, as we listened, to hear the words distinctly uttered of a well-known hymn in praise of the Redeemer of mankind! A short time previously the mention of that name with honour in that place would have exposed him who uttered it to a violent death. The incident was very cheering as an omen of the dawn to benighted India, when, through the tender mercy of our God, Jesus the light of the world shall shine into the hearts of its teeming population, and raise them into the sunshine of heaven.

Lucknow, as well as Cawnpore, has undergone a great change since 1859. We saw it last in 1877, when traces of the fierce conflict which had been there carried on had well-nigh disappeared; while on every side, in new roads opened up, in miserable tenements thrown down, in new houses erected, and in rubbish removed, evidence was given that the effete government of the Kings of Oude had given place to the vigorous government of their Western conquerors. Nothing is now to be seen of the ruins and desolation of the Residency. The ground has been levelled, trees planted, paths made, and the whole place is kept in beautiful order. On the

THE LA MARTINIERE, LUCKNOW.

highest spot there is a memorial cross. All out from Lucknow for miles, at the instance of friends, monuments have been raised, some of them with very touching inscriptions, in memory of the fallen, so far as the spots where they fell could be identified.

We returned to Benares with a very vivid impression of what we had seen, with a new realization of the sufferings our countrymen had endured, with deepened admiration of the heroism they had shown, and with thankfulness at once for our rescue as a people from destruction, and for the restoration of our rule.

We continued at our post at Benares till March, 1861, when the state of the Mission admitted of our obtaining a much-needed retreat to the Hills for a few months. We accordingly left Benares for Almora, and took Delhi by the way, where we remained a few days. This was our second visit to the grand old imperial city. On this occasion we visited the scene of the memorable events of the Mutiny year, as we had previously done at Cawnpore and Lucknow. We went to the heights commanding the city, where our army was encamped for months, at once the besiegers and the besieged, and from which at last they took the city, after a contest so desperate and bloody that for days the issue was doubtful. The palace, with its magnificent halls of audience and entertainment, where the Emperors of India had for ages kept their court, we found turned into barracks and an arsenal. English soldiers trod those rooms where Indian magnates had bowed before imperial majesty—giving us an impressive illustration of the transitory nature of earthly glory.

For some time after going to Almora our health improved; but as the season advanced it gave way so entirely, that our medical attendant came to the conclusion a visit to England was indispensable to its restoration. The Directors of the Society gave their kind and prompt consent to our return. We accordingly embarked from Calcutta for England, *viâ* the Cape of Good Hope, in January, 1862, and reached our destination in April.

All I have to say about the interval between 1862 and 1865 is that I visited many places in England and Scotland on behalf of the Society, did a good deal of ministerial work besides, and was kept in uncertainty about my future course by medical opposition to my going back to India. In 1864 I feared I could not return; but my health improved so much in 1865, that the medical men I consulted, to my great joy, consented to our going back. We accordingly embarked for Calcutta *viâ* the Cape, accompanied by two young missionaries appointed to Benares, in September, 1865, and reached our destination, after a prosperous voyage, towards the end of the year. We were very pleased with the thought that our traversing the Atlantic and Indian Oceans had come to an end.

The railway had some time previously been completed to the North-West, and so instead of days and weeks spent on the journey from Calcutta to Benares, it was now made in twenty-six hours.

The hot weather and rains of 1866 were spent in Benares. We felt the heat that year more than we had ever previously done, and were to a great extent incapacitated by it for the prosecution of mission work. We came to the conclusion that continued work in the plains was beyond our strength, and as we much wished to continue in the mission field, we hoped a hill sphere might be opened up. In March, 1867, we left for Almora, where, with our colleague Mr. Budden, we engaged in different departments of mission labour. Early in the cold weather we returned to Benares, and resumed our work there. As the hot weather of 1868 came on, we were again privileged to return to Almora. Towards the end of that year it was arranged that our connection with Benares should cease, and that we should begin a new mission at Ranee Khet, about twenty miles north-west from Almora.

CHAPTER XX.

KUMAON.

(1) ITS SCENERY AND PRODUCTS.

KUMAON is a sub-Himalayan region, with Nepal to the east, the snowy range, separating it from Tibet, to the north, Gurhwal and Dehra Doon to the west, and Rohilkund to the south. Including the hill country of Gurhwal, and the belt of forest and swamp lying immediately under it, of which only a small part has been reclaimed, Kumaon is about half the size of Scotland.

The province presents a remarkable contrast to the great level country beneath. Over it you travel in some directions hundreds of miles, and scarcely any elevation or depression in the land can be discerned. As you travel northward, and approach the limit of the plains, you see hills rising before you, tier after tier; and behind them, on a clear day, the higher Himalaya, with their snowy peaks, as if touching the heavens.

Kumaon is very mountainous, with as great irregularity as if the land had been fluid, had in the midst of a storm been suddenly solidified, and had then received its permanent shape. Here and there are valleys of some extent, table-lands and open fields are occasionally seen; but over a great part of the province hill is separated from hill by a space so narrow that it can only be called a ravine. The consequence is that cultivation is carried on mainly in terraces. Where the slope is gradual, and the soil fit for cultivation, these terraces, some very narrow and others of considerable width, rise one above the other to the distance of miles, with the hamlets of the cultivators scattered over the hill-side, presenting to the eye of the traveller an aspect of scenery which is not to be seen in Europe, so far as I am aware. At any rate, we saw nothing resembling it on the vine-clad hills rising from the Rhine, or in the mountains of Switzerland.

The country is well watered. It has innumerable streams, varying from tiny rills to large rivers. In travelling, we have been for days within the constant sound of running water. It has a few lakelets, but it has no large bodies of water, like the lakes which contribute so largely to the beauty and picturesqueness of Switzerland and Scotland. It looks as if the deep hollows, of which so many are to be seen, had been unable to retain the water poured into them, and had let it all flow away. A large part of the province is so steep and rocky that it cannot be turned to any agricultural purpose; and even for grazing purposes a large portion is of little use, as the grass is coarse and poor. There is a great extent of forest and brushwood. As the land slopes towards the Bhabhur, the forest is very dense and varied. The timber is of considerable value, but as there is neither road nor water carriage it must be carried on men's shoulders, and this involves an expense more than it can bear.

From what I have said about the peculiarities of Kumaon scenery, its mountains, valleys, and ravines, my readers are prepared to hear it has a great variety of climate and produce. Of hills, of which there are many from 5000 to 9000 feet above the level of the sea, the climate is delightful—warm, but not oppressively warm, a little warmer than it is in our country in summer; and cold, though not so severely cold as it is with us in winter. The rains are very heavy, but to compensate for this there is, during the greater part of the year, a steadiness of climate which forms a striking contrast to the fickle climate of England. Down in the valleys the heat is very great. Even in winter the sun is unpleasantly strong, and in summer in the deep ravines the temperature is almost as trying as in the plains. When the season has been somewhat advanced, I have been very thankful to escape from the heat of these low places to the bracing air of the hills. The English Sanatoria are of course on elevated sites.

As Kumaon has within its borders a cold, a temperate, and a tropical climate, it has a great variety of produce, and when its capabilities are more fully turned to account this variety will be greatly increased. Most of the grains found in the plains are grown in the hills. The warmer parts of the country produce superior oranges in abundance, and there is also a good supply of walnuts. Of late years apples and pears have been grown with great success, and if the farmers paid attention to this branch of horticulture they might reap a large profit. Attempts have been made on a small scale to cultivate the grape, gooseberry, and currant, but the excessive rainfall of the rainy season has been found unfavourable to them. Tea has become the most valuable product of the province. Tea-planting was commenced at the instance of Government, under its direction and at its expense, more than forty years ago; and now tea-gardens are found all over the province, owned almost entirely by our fellow-countrymen, and, with few exceptions, managed by them. At first Chinamen were employed, but they have been dispensed with, and the entire work is now done by hill people under English superintendence.

(2) THE NATIVE INHABITANTS OF KUMAON.

The hill people of Central and Southern India, the Kols, the Santhals, the Bheels, and others, as is well known, widely differ in race, language, customs, and religion, from the Hindus and Mussulmans of the plains. In Kumaon, on the other hand, the great majority are strict Hindus, worshippers of the Hindu gods, and scrupulous observers of caste rules. It would appear that when the ancestors of the Hindus, coming from Central Asia, crossed the Indus, and took possession of the country now called the Punjab, they made raids into the lower range of the Himalayas, killing their inhabitants, or turning them into slaves. The descendants of the aborigines are at present found in a class called Doms, who form the artisan portion of the population, and are also largely employed in agriculture. The Muhammadans form a very small part of the population, and are almost entirely emigrants from the plains.

The character of the hill Hindus, in its essential elements, closely accords with that of their brethren elsewhere. They worship the Hindu gods, practise Hindu rites, and are imbued with the Hindu spirit. The Brahmans and Rajpoots are proud of their position, firm in maintaining it, and shrink from everything which would invalidate it. Under native rule the high-caste spirit had full scope, for we are told that for murder a Brahman was banished, and a Rajpoot heavily mulcted; while other murderers were put to death. Such offences against the Hindu religion as killing a cow, or a Dom making use of a *huqqa* (the pipe for smoking), or a utensil belonging to a Brahman or Rajpoot, were capital offences. The power obtained by the Brahmans was shown by the fact that, when the province came under British rule, one-fifteenth of its arable land belonged to the religious establishments.

All the Hindu gods and goddesses are worshipped in the hills, but the hideous goddess Kalee is the favourite object of worship. Small temples to her honour are found all over the province, many of them in solitary places on the tops of hills, to which it is meritorious to make pilgrimages, and around which at certain seasons melas are held. We have in our wanderings fallen in with several of these temples in spots from which, for many miles around, no human habitation is seen. By far the most famous shrines are those of Badrinath and Kedarnath, in the upper part of Gurhwal, within the snowy range, where Vishnu is the object of worship, and the officiating priests are Brahmans from Southern India. Pilgrimage to these places is very meritorious, as it can only be accomplished at the cost of great toil and suffering, and at the imminent risk of life.

In addition to the gods worshipped all over India, the hill people have local gods unknown elsewhere. *Bhoots*, evil spirits, commonly supposed to be the spirits of those who have during their earthly life been noted for their wickedness, and have acquired the demon character, are believed to haunt the mountains and forests, and are the objects of special dread. Homage is paid to them to secure their goodwill and avert their vengeance. The people greatly dislike travelling at night, as that is the

TEMPLE IN THE HIMALAYAS.

season when the *Bhoots* roam about and fall on their prey. When they must move about they break off the branches of the pine-tree, and turn them into torches to frighten off both the wild beasts and the evil spirits. In the imagination which peoples hills and forests with beings outside the circle of humanity, that make their presence especially felt at night, the people of Kumaon closely resemble the mountaineers of other lands, among others those of our own Scotch Highlands, as they were till a recent period. In my early days I heard so many stories in my native Highland village of ghosts and fairies, that I was afraid to move about after sunset except when guarded by others, lest these supernatural beings should lay hold of me and carry me away.

The people have a character for industry. When one sees the difficulties under which cultivation is carried on, he is inclined to consider it deserved. They have periods of lounging, but also of very hard work. The women, in addition to household work, cut and carry wood and grass, and do much farm work—I have thought at times more than their share; but after all, the heaviest work, the carrying of great loads on head and shoulders, up hill and down hill, and the farm work requiring most strength, is done by the men. Much of the work done by them—work done by draught animals elsewhere—must tend to break down their health and shorten their days.

The Kumaonees have been described as untruthful but honest. I must say our experience has verified the unfavourable part of this description more than the favourable. So far as veracity is concerned we have not been impressed with any difference between them and other natives of India. We think their honesty has received more credit than it deserves. This is, at any rate, the opinion of the tea-planters with whom we have conversed, and who have had superior opportunities for judging. They have told us of the strict watch they have to set to guard their tea and fruit. We found that some hill servants, whom we had greatly trusted, had systematically robbed us. The character for honesty was, I believe, given to them because when they set out on their periodical migration to the plains they left their villages unguarded, and found their property safe on their return. I suppose this resulted partly from an unwritten—may I say?—honourable understanding, that as in their sparse and widely-scattered population it was well-nigh impossible to guard their goods, the rights of property should be respected; and partly from the circumstance that there was little left behind in the villages which could be carried away. So far as others, especially Europeans, are concerned, this understanding to practise honesty does not hold.

We incidentally heard of no small degree of immorality among the people, but our information is too limited to justify one in comparing them with others in this respect. There is much that is likable among them, but the general moral tone is undoubtedly low. Polyandry, which prevails in some districts in the Western Himalayan range, is I believe unknown, but polygamy is not uncommon among those who can afford it.

Cleanliness has never been considered a virtue of Highlanders. It is not—or perhaps I should say it has not been—a characteristic of the Highlanders of our own land. Among the Kumaonees it is notably wanting. The loathsome disease of leprosy has long prevailed in the province, owing to a large extent to the filthy habits of the people. To the same cause there is every reason to believe, we have to trace the outbreak now and then of the plague—*muha muree*, the great plague, as it is called—which has proved very destructive. It resembles the plague which at different times prevailed in Europe and swept away thousands. So great is the dread of this terrible malady, that on the report of its approach people flee from their villages. Cholera has been at times fatal to many, but its ravages are not to be compared to those of the plague.

(3) HISTORY OF KUMAON UNDER GHOORKHA AND BRITISH RULE.

Kumaon had been long under the rule of a native dynasty, but intestine feuds laid the country open to the attacks of ambitious neighbours. In the latter end of the eighteenth century the Ghoorkhas, a military tribe, rose to power in Nepal, the hill-country to the east, and early in this century they extended their conquests over the hill-country to the west, till they were checked by Runjeet Singh, the famous ruler of the Punjab. Their rule over Kumaon was said to be very oppressive. By raids into British territory they came into collision with the English. After a severe struggle, carried on through two campaigns, they were defeated, and forced to give up the country they had conquered to the west of Nepal, which they had held for about twelve years. Kumaon and the adjoining hill-country of Gurhwal were placed under the jurisdiction of a British Commissioner, and the arrangement made in 1816 has been maintained to the present time.

The country has made immense progress since the English took possession. The people are now under a government which aims at protecting life and property, and at treating all, high and low, with equal justice. No longer are Dom offenders against caste laws executed while Brahman and Rajpoot murderers escape. Atrocious customs have been suppressed, such as the burial of lepers alive, which was formerly largely practised. Sanitary regulations have been issued, and penalties imposed on those convicted of violating them. Fights between villages, ending in robbery and murder, are no longer permitted, though sham-fights are still allowed. I was once a witness of such a fight, when a vast number of hill people were collected, as if for a great field-day, and stones were thrown from slings in a way I thought perilous to the combatants. Roads have been made, and rivers bridged. The new roads are too narrow and steep to admit of wheeled conveyances; often they are only three or four feet in width, and are at a gradient which makes them trying for horses and for persons on foot; but they are an immense improvement on the footpaths with which the natives were satisfied till they came under British rule, and with which they are still satisfied when left to themselves. I have not had much experience of the by-paths of the country, but quite enough to have made me thankful for the new order of things. Very recently a road for carts and conveyances has been made from the plains to Nynee Tal, Ranee Khet, and Almora; but the route is so circuitous that the roads hitherto traversed will continue the chief means of communication.

No sooner was the British rule established than the effect was seen in the increase of cultivation. Mr. Traill, the first Commissioner, states that from the time of the occupation, 1816 to 1822–23, the date of his retirement, cultivation had increased fully one-third, and since that time there has been a steady advance. The population has more than doubled, for we are told that in 1823 there were 27 inhabitants to the square mile, while in 1872 there were 65. At the same time there were 797 to the square mile in the Benares district, and there was no district in the North-West Provinces where the population was under 185, while the average was 378. An immense disparity must continue between countries with such different capabilities, but the progress made in Kumaon under British rule is proportionably as great as that made in the most favoured parts of India.

Wealth has been brought into the country as well as drawn out of it. I have already referred to tea-planting as a new department of agricultural industry. Many thousands have been spent on tea-gardens—much more, I suspect, than has yet been got out of them. A tea-planter once pointed to a cluster of well-built villages, and said, "These houses have all been built within the last few years by the proceeds of wages made in the tea-garden under my charge." Then the great influx of European travellers and residents has done not a little to enrich the people in various ways, though at times the labour thus required has been very grudgingly given, as it has withdrawn them from their homes when their own work was urgent.

Of late years a new source of income has been opened up to the people by the enterprise of Sir Henry Ramsay, who has been for many years the Commissioner of the Province, and has done more for it than any of his predecessors. The hill people of some districts have been for ages in the habit of moving down *en masse* with their cattle at the beginning of the cold weather for grazing, and have returned to their mountain homes when the hot weather had set in. The country immediately under the hills is called the Bhabhur, and is quite distinct from the Turai which lies beyond. This Bhabhur is a formation of sand and shingle filled with boulders, largely covered over with soil, which produces abundant herbage in the rainy season, and is thus good grazing ground in the succeeding months. It has a large extent of forest, composed of trees of great girth and magnificent height. The innumerable streams which come down from the hills flow under the Bhabhur, and make their way into the Turai beyond, where the land becomes water-logged, and the main product is long, rank grass, growing to the height of ten or twelve feet. By a system of canals, devised and carried out by Sir Henry Ramsay, the water as it comes down from the hills is made to irrigate a large part of the Bhabhur, rendering it fit for agricultural purposes. The result is that the people now cultivate the land, beside grazing their cattle over it. They sow toward the end of the rainy season, and reap at the beginning of the hot weather, when they retreat to the hills, and are ready for the cultivation of their fields there. This addition to the arable land has been a great boon to the people. I cannot say, however, judging by those with whom I have conversed, that they are satisfied. They grumble at the new tax imposed for the construction and maintenance of the canals, and also at the tax they have to pay for their holdings in the hills, though I believe it to be very light. They would gladly have all the benefits of a firm and improving government without paying anything for its support.

Notwithstanding the extension of cultivation and the increase of population in Kumaon, we may travel for many miles over hill and forest and not see a trace of man's presence. Cover for wild beasts has been somewhat abridged, but it is still sufficient to shelter them, and to make it unlikely they can be exterminated. Both in the hills and in the country beneath, hunters of wild beasts, European and native, still find abundant employment. Not a year passes without persons, sheep, and cattle being killed by tigers, leopards, and hyenas. They live so much in the gorges of the mountains, and in the depths of the forests, ready to pounce on their prey when opportunity presents itself, that the destruction caused by them is seen, while they themselves disappear. The first thing we saw on our first approach to Almora was a horse which had been killed by a leopard the preceding night. A woman, who had been cutting grass before the door of a house we occupied for a few days, was killed an hour afterwards by a tiger in the adjoining forest. One afternoon we heard the cry of a herd, and running out we saw a goat with its throat cut, but the leopard that had killed it had disappeared in the jungle beneath. On another occasion my pony, picketed near my tent, had a narrow escape from a leopard. I have often heard huntsmen relate the encounters they have had with these terrible brutes. On one occasion I saw four dead tigers brought in by a party that had killed them a few miles from the place where my tent was pitched. Tigers are very migratory. They live in the cold weather down in the Bhabhur and the Turai, and as the hot weather advances they follow the herd up the hills on to the verge of the snow. The bears of the hills feed on fruit and vegetables, and usually make away when human beings are seen, but they are very formidable to those who attack them, or come suddenly across their path. In some places wolves abound, and children and animals require to be guarded against them; but they never hunt in packs as in Russia, and they are not feared by grown-up people. In the lower hills and the Bhabhur there are herds of wild elephants, which do much injury to the crops of the people, and cannot be safely approached. I have been again and again in their track. There are also serpents, but they are not so numerous or venomous as in the plains. The dangers to which the inhabitants are exposed is shown by the annual statistics of casualties, in which the first place is given to the ravages of wild beasts, the second to landslips, and the third to serpents.

I may end this account of Kumaon, its scenery, products, history, and people, by mentioning two stipulations in the treaty with the Ghoorkhas, when the British took possession of the land, which are strikingly illustrative at once of British policy and of Hindu feeling. One stipulation was that certain sums should be paid annually to the priests of certain temples. A second stipulation was that the slaughter of bullocks and cows should be strictly prohibited. Not a vestige of power over the country was left to the Ghoorkhas; the entire rule was transferred to the British. But our authorities, influenced at once by religious liberalism or indifference, and by deference to Hindu feeling, accepted these conditions. The first stipulation caused no trouble, but the force of circumstances has led to the violation of the second. When there were no European troops in the Province, and the only Englishmen were civil officials, officers of native regiments, and a few casual travellers, the prohibition of beef caused little inconvenience; but a large influx of English people, soldiers and others, made the observance of the stipulation impracticable. For a time it was violated, and the authorities professed to know nothing about it; but when Nynee Tal became a great summer resort, and English soldiers were located at it, beef became a well-nigh indispensable article of food, cows and bullocks were killed, and the breach in the treaty by which the country was ceded to us became manifest to all. It is said that when the high-caste officials protested against this outrage on the Hindu religion, an English official quietly said that such good Hindus were not in their proper place, that they should be transferred to their holy city, Benares. This speedily silenced the complaint, as hill people intensely dislike leaving their mountains for the plains.

The treaty with the Ghoorkhas is not the only one in which the stipulation against beef has been made when territory has been ceded. To a treaty-keeping people like the English the stipulation has been very embarrassing, so embarrassing that for a time resolute effort has been made to observe it, but it has at length broken down under what has been deemed the compulsion of circumstances. We have heard of a high-caste official consoling his brethren for the outrage by reminding them it is the nature of tigers to eat cows and bullocks, and by telling them that the English were tigers, had a similar love for such food, and as it was their nature it must be borne with. Though so shocked with the shedding of the blood of cows and bullocks, the ruling class in Nepal have shown no aversion to the shedding of human blood, as is well known by all acquainted with the history of the country. During the mutiny a friend of mine, travelling with a regiment of Ghoorkhas that had come down from Nepal to help us, saw them kill a party of mutineers who had surrendered under an oath of their lives being spared, with a savage ferocity which shocked him beyond measure.

(4) TRAVELLING IN KUMAON.

The greater part of our time in the Province was spent in the capital, Almora, and in the newly-formed Sanatarium Ranee Khet, but we frequently travelled through many of its districts. I have mentioned the improved means of communication, but vastly better though the roads be than they were in the days of native rule, travelling continues to be very expensive, fatiguing, and in some modes not a little dangerous. Travellers must either walk, ride, or be carried on men's shoulders. The first mode can be adopted only by those who have abundant strength and leisure. It was my mode during our first visit, as I was not pressed for time, and notwithstanding our residence of eight years in the plains I retained a good deal of my youthful vigour. The mountain scenery and the mountain air gave us new life. I travelled on foot some three hundred miles. On the occasion of future visits I was happy to avail myself of a hill pony. Most gentlemen and many young ladies perform their hill journeys on horseback. Happily, hill ponies are, as a rule, quiet and sure-footed; and they require to be, as the roads are narrow, in some places very narrow, and overhang precipices, down which the rider would be dashed if the pony slipped or was scared. At first, riding appears very dangerous, but after a time there is a feeling of security. I remember riding with confidence over places where at first I deemed it prudent to dismount. Scarcely a year, however, passes without riders being killed, and all who have travelled much over the country have to tell of providential escapes. The third mode, the mode adopted by most ladies, and by gentlemen who have not nerve to ride, is to be carried on men's shoulders. The palankeen and dolie of the plains are by far too heavy and cumbrous for the hills. The favourite vehicle is the *dandee*—a pole, with a piece of carpet attached, on which the traveller sits sideway, and which has belts for the back and feet. Two men, one at each end of the pole, are able to carry the *dandee* a short distance, but in journeys four are commonly employed. During the last few years a very light sedan-chair has come into favour, which is far more convenient for ladies, but the *dandee* is lighter and will continue to be largely used.

We have seen a good deal of both the eastern and western portions of the Province. In 1847 we travelled to Lahoo Ghat and Petorah Gurh in the east. On this occasion I went on to Nepal, and was told by the Nepalese sentry on the frontier bridge that without special permission from Khatmandoo, the Capital, I could not proceed farther. In 1869, in company with my much-esteemed friend the late Dr. Mather, I travelled in the same direction, and saw much of the country, as we went by one route and returned by another. During the later years of our residence we saw a good deal of the western districts, to which I shall refer when giving an account of missionary operations.

Along some of the main roads, at the distance of twelve or fourteen miles, are small rough Rest-houses, with a table, two chairs, and a bedstead, often in very bad condition. These houses are in charge of a watchman, who is often long in making his appearance, and then brings wood and water, and sometimes a little milk. For everything else you are dependent on people with you carrying supplies. Where there is much traffic there is good accommodation.

Our most memorable journey, perhaps, was one made in 1861 to the Pindaree glacier. The journey was a very fatiguing one, as the roads were so bad, and the ascents and descents so steep, that before we got half way I was obliged to leave my pony behind, and to make my way on foot, helped to ascend and descend in some places by strong hill-men, who drew me up or helped me down by a belt round my middle, while my wife and little boy were carried in *dandies*. Many of the bridges were rough wooden structures, with no parapets. As we approached the snow we suffered much at night from cold in our little tent. The hill people of the higher region we found much stronger and more unsophisticated than those we had left behind. The women seemed never to have seen an English woman or child. They were first afraid to come near us, but my wife made her way to little groups, and they seemed delighted with her, and still more with her little boy. Fatiguing and trying though the journey was, health was improved by it, and we were well rewarded for any toil and inconvenience we endured by the magnificent scenery we saw. Down the Pindaree valley came a roaring torrent, showing by its yellow tinge it came from the melted snow. We were awed as we looked up at the tremendous cliffs on either side. Pursuing our way in silence, I heard a servant from the plains, who was walking behind me, muttering to himself, "Such a wicked place I never saw in my life." We breakfasted on the glacier, and after looking at some of the crevasses we were glad to make our way back to our tent a few miles below. Next morning we retraced our steps, and it was well we did so, for as we were rapidly descending we had heavy rain, and could see snow falling where we had been. The next day the whole region behind was covered with snow, and we were thankful for our timely escape.

The details of travelling I have now given, and the previous details about the country and people may perhaps enable the reader the better to understand and realize missionary work in the Province.

CHAPTER XXI.

THE ALMORA MISSION.

STATED mission work was commenced in Kumaon in 1850. Previous to that time a few of its people had heard the Gospel from missionaries travelling through it, or residing for a few months in it. In that year the Rev. J. H. Budden, of the London Missionary Society, after labouring for a time in Benares and Mirzapore, was obliged by the failure of health to abandon all hope of continuing in the plains, and took up his abode at Almora, the capital of the Province. The society declined to enter on mission work in Kumaon; but Captain Ramsay, Senior Assistant to the Commissioner, with other friends, came forward with most liberal offers of support, and consent was given to Mr. Budden's entering into an engagement to carry on the Mission as the agent of its local supporters. For some time his entire salary and all expenses were met by these friends. Afterwards a part of the salary was paid by the Society, and for years the whole, but the friends who founded the Mission have on to the present time supported it with princely munificence. At the head of these is Sir Henry Ramsay, the Captain Ramsay of 1850, who has been for many years the Commissioner of the Province, and who continues the warm and liberal supporter of everything by which the spiritual

MISSION SCHOOL, ALMORA.

as well as the temporal good of the people may be promoted.

As the Mission at Almora was the first, so it continues to be the most important in the Province. Organized and administered by Mr. Budden, and heartily supported by friends on the spot, it has done a work which has told powerfully and happily on the entire country. From the beginning much attention has been paid to the education of the young. For a long time the school of the Mission was the only one in the Province where a superior education, at once native and European, was imparted; and still, both in the number of its pupils and in the extent of its course of study, it stands highest. From it have gone out for many years bands of young men who now fill varied positions under Government, and it is believed they are discharging their duties with greater intelligence and a higher character than those they have succeeded. In remote parts of the Province I have met persons who have spoken in strong terms of gratitude of the benefit they had received from attending the Almora Mission School. A few years ago a large, handsome structure was erected for its accommodation at great expense, towards which the natives contributed very liberally. In addition to this school-house, the Mission has valuable property in mission-houses for native Christians, an orphanage, and a book-room.

In other departments excellent work has been done. Female education has been zealously prosecuted under the direction of Mr. Budden's daughters. For many years there has been an orphanage in which destitute children have been brought up and educated. The authorities made over to the Mission a Leper Asylum they had established, and for years it has been under its exclusive charge. Much has been done for the inmates of this asylum at the cost of personal labour, great anxiety, and a heavy expenditure. Suitable buildings have been erected, the wants of the lepers have been supplied, everything has been done which could be done to mitigate their sufferings, and to secure order and cleanliness. The efforts put forth to draw them to the Great Physician to secure their spiritual cure have by the Divine blessing borne abundant fruit. When the Rev. John Hewlett was in charge in 1864–65 there was a movement towards Christianity, which resulted in the baptism of several. Since that time the work has gone on. Christian worship has been regularly maintained among them, and much labour has been bestowed on their instruction. Many have been baptized, after giving all the evidence of sincerity which could be expected, and at certain times the Lord's Supper has been dispensed. Among the lepers there have been persons of very debased character, but the conduct of most has been good, and, so far as we can judge, a number have become the true followers of the Saviour. If the Mission had done nothing more than sustain this Leper Asylum, it would have done a most Christ-like work, deserving the warm approbation and liberal support of Christ's people.

From the commencement of the Mission a service has been conducted every Sabbath in English for the benefit of our countrymen residing in Almora. Services have been held in the native language for the native Christians and natives generally.

In addition to the work of organizing and conducting the various departments of the Mission, Mr. Budden has made large and valuable contributions to native Christian literature.

LEPER ASYLUM, ALMORA.

I have seen much of the Almora Mission, and have had the privilege of taking part in conducting its operations. Among other duties which I endeavoured to discharge during two seasons was to go, along with my wife, every Sabbath morning to conduct worship with the lepers, and to instruct them. Mrs. Kennedy went besides once every week. There is no work on which I look back with deeper interest than I do on this. We first conducted a brief service of singing, prayer, and preaching. Mrs. Kennedy then took the women and I took the men to see how much of the sermon they understood, and to inculcate the great lessons of God's Word in the way of question and answer. The work was at first very trying, but gradually we became more than reconciled to it. Our heart was drawn forth in deep pity to these poor people, and we left them deeply thankful for the privilege we had of speaking to them of the Saviour, and of telling them of His compassion for the suffering and the lost.

CHAPTER XXII.

RANEE KHET MISSION.

IN accordance with instructions from the Directors of the London Missionary Society, Mrs. Kennedy and myself went at the beginning of May, 1869, to Ranee Khet, a new station twenty miles north-west of Almora, to enter on mission work there. Some time previously it had been resolved to open a new mission in the Province, and I had been appointed to commence it. After much consideration Ranee Khet was deemed the most eligible place for the extension of our work. The name means "The Field of the Queen," and was probably given to it in honour of Kalee, as it has on its higher part a small temple sacred to her, round which the hill people hold a yearly mela. The place may be described as a rough table-land, with an elevation of from 6,200 to 7,000 feet above the level of the sea. With the exception of a little land cleared on one side, the country for miles around was covered with forests of pine, oak, and rhododendron, over which the people of the valleys pastured their cattle at some seasons of the year. The attention of the Government was drawn to the place as suitable for a military Sanitarium, and engineers were sent to open up roads and investigate its capabilities. The report made by them was so favourable that a considerable outlay was sanctioned for turning it into a retreat for English soldiers from the heat of the plains.

The prospect of Ranee Khet as a European station, where soon a large population was sure to gather, was one reason for regarding it as a good sphere for a new mission. The chief reason, however, for the choice was the fact that within twelve miles around, on the sides of the hills and in the valleys beneath, there was a large accessible population, furnishing a much wider field than one missionary could well occupy.

Previous to taking up our abode at Ranee Khet I paid several visits to it, with a view to making myself acquainted with the neighbourhood and to holding intercourse with the people, many of whom I met in their villages. They looked on me with fear, as if I had come to lay a new tax on them, and seemed utterly unable to comprehend me when I told them I was no Government official, but a servant of God, who came to them with good tidings from Him. The only school of which I heard was twelve miles distant, and I came to the conclusion that the establishment of primary schools would be very beneficial to the people, and highly favourable to my object. Though so illiterate that in well-sized villages I did not hear of a person who could read, a number expressed approval of my object. Some were forward with the promise to erect school-sheds, and to send their children, but the performance did not come up to the promise.

When we went to Ranee Khet there was not a single house at the place. The only Europeans were two Engineers and a sergeant, and they were living in their cook-houses, preparatory to building houses for themselves. I had arranged with a friend to have a wooden house erected, but when we went the work had only been commenced, and the first six weeks we lived in a tent. It was midsummer, and the tent was in the daytime intolerably hot. The trees around gave little shelter, they were chiefly pine; but we soon succeeded in putting up booths, and in them, except when storms came on, we were very comfortable during the heat of the day.

We were thankful when we exchanged our tent and booths for our rough wooden house. In it we remained two years and a half in tolerable comfort. There were two serious drawbacks. In the heavy rains the house leaked in such a degree that there was scarcely a dry spot in it; and, what was worse, the rats got into the open roof, and by their active movements, especially at night, were a great annoyance. Latterly the leakage was stopped, but the rats were too strong for us, and could not be dislodged. Notwithstanding these inconveniences, when we remembered the heat of the plains, during six months of the year, which we had endured, and our brethren were continuing to endure, and contrasted the climate there with the climate we were enjoying, we were never tempted to murmur. We felt deeply thankful for the Providence which had given us an abode in a country where summer heat was only a little greater than in our own, where there were no hot winds, where with windows open we could be always comfortable in the hottest weather, and where all around us was magnificent scenery.

I have mentioned rats. In their division of common rat and musk-rat, they are troublesome enough in the plains, but they are a plague in the hills. They abound in the fields, and are very hurtful to the crops. Not a house is erected into which they do not manage to make their way; but where a house is well built, and due care

THE SNOWY RANGE FROM RANEE KHET.

is taken, they find little shelter. They go into a rough wooden house as if they were entitled to full possession. These unwelcome intruders may be kept in check, but there is no hope of entire deliverance from them.

During our eight years in Ranee Khet we had to discharge the varied duties devolving on missionary pioneers. To one department, to which I knew much attention must be given, I looked forward with dismay—the erection of buildings. Remembering our experience in the plains we would gladly have shrunk from this work, but we knew it must be faced. Through the great kindness and efficient help of friends we succeeded in getting suitable buildings erected. The first building we put up was a place of worship. After considerable delay we succeeded in getting a suitable site for a mission-house on a knoll within a short distance of the native bazar. The servants' houses and the cook-house were first up, and leaving our hut we took up our abode in the cook-house, that we might be at hand to superintend the erection of the mission-house. Before its completion we got, close at hand, a site for a school-house, which, with its handsome hall and four side-rooms, furnishes more accommodation than has yet been required. To this building natives contributed liberally. As the stone and wood required had to be carried on men's heads and shoulders, every additional yard increased the expense, and we were obliged to use the wood and stone nearest, though at some distance better might have been procured. Our masons and carpenters were not of a superior order, and required to be constantly watched and directed. The buildings were not all we could wish, but they were suitable for the climate and for our purpose. Our house was commodious, was in the best position for mission work, had a magnificent view of the snowy range, and we would not have exchanged it for the finest house we had seen in the plains.

From the commencement of our residence in Ranee Khet, village schools received much of my attention. For a time I had nine under my charge, at distances of from six to fifteen miles. For the accommodation of three schools stone houses were erected, and for other schools sheds of grass and wood were put up. The attendance at these schools varied greatly at different seasons of the year: many came too short a time to get any benefit, the attendance of others was too irregular to admit of much progress; but a considerable number remained till they received a good primary education. On my visits I taught the pupils, and conversed with their parents and friends who gathered round. When the weather permitted I had my tent pitched for days near the school, and visited the adjoining villages. On these occasions I tried to sit down where or how I could, with the people around me, and entered into familiar conversation with them. The language was a great difficulty, as the dialect of Kumaon differs widely from the Hindee of the plains; but by dint of repetition, and putting what I had to say in different forms in the simplest fashion, I was often happy to find myself getting into the understanding of my hearers. Every second Saturday the teachers, often accompanied by senior pupils, came to my house to report what they had done, and to receive instruction.

I had reason to be thankful for having entered into this department of work. A large amount of Christian instruction was imparted; many of the boys showed remarkable aptitude in committing to memory portions of Scripture, such as the ten commandments and the parables of our Lord. Much general knowledge was acquired, a number of the pupils became better fitted for their secular calling, and the goodwill of the people was secured. Once, when thirty miles away from Ranee Khet, I met a lad whom I recognized as an old pupil. I asked him if he remembered what he had been taught. He said he did. He went to a house close at hand, brought a copy of St. Luke's Gospel, read at my request the fifteenth chapter, and explained its meaning with an accuracy which surprised me. At the same place I met a man of a different order. He told me he was going to a mela, to which I was also proceeding. I asked him what he was to do there. He said he was to bathe, to wash away his sins. I asked him what was the sin which oppressed him. He said, "I am a husbandman. In ploughing my fields I destroy much life, which is a great sin. This is the worst thing with which I am chargeable." The lad taught in the school knew something of what sin was, as the poor man did not. I can say nothing about the spiritual results of these school efforts. I can only hope that by God's blessing good has been done. The Government has now entered largely on primary education in the Province, and with its resources and prestige will, I trust, secure a large school attendance.

All through my residence at Ranee Khet I endeavoured to embrace the opportunities given to me of promoting the spiritual good of our own countrymen. A service was at once commenced with the few residents and visitors at the station. Towards the end of 1869 two companies of English soldiers were sent, and as soon as tolerable accommodation was provided a regiment was stationed at Ranee Khet. As for nearly three years I was the only resident Christian minister, I held two services every Lord's Day—one for Presbyterians, including all non-Episcopalian adherents, and the other for the Episcopalians, the Prayer-book being used at this latter service. I also visited the sick in hospital, and when at home conducted a weekday meeting. We first met in the open air, or verandah of our hut; afterwards in the hut used as a temporary canteen; for some time in the recreation-room; and during our later years in our place of worship, which we called Union Church. An effort was made to get up a girls' school, but it was unsuccessful, as the attendance of the few native girls in the Bazar could not be secured. So far as native women were concerned, all Mrs. Kennedy could do was to instruct the few living in the Mission compound. She found, however, an interesting sphere among the wives and children of the soldiers. The Sabbath school, commenced and carried on by her, assisted by others, was attended by all the children, Roman Catholic as well as Protestant; but no sooner was a Roman Catholic chaplain appointed than the order went forth for the withdrawal of the children of his Church, which was obeyed with manifest reluctance. We had much pleasure in these services with our own people, and had every reason to believe lasting good was done. Some of the boys of the Ranee Khet school expressed a desire to be taught English, and these came every second day to our house to be taught by Mrs. Kennedy.

While thankfully availing myself of the opportunities presented of preaching the Gospel to our own countrymen, such opportunities as I never had at any previous period of my Indian career, my chief attention was given to the work for which I had been sent to Ranee Khet. I have already mentioned missionary work done on visits to the schools. At Ranee Khet opportunities were found for conversation with shopkeepers and their customers. Thousands of work-people were employed on the buildings which were being erected, and these, when the work of the day was over, flocked to the Bazar to buy food. After the toil of the day, when eagerly anticipating their only cooked meal in the twenty-four hours, they were not inclined to listen to a stranger telling them of his strange religion. Occasionally I did succeed in getting for a time the attention of some not so eager as others to get their evening meal. Most heard quietly, but sometimes individuals replied with bitter words. Many of the work-people had come from a great distance. The most prominent of these was a band of Cashmeeree Mussulmans, who spoke against Christianity with a fierceness which showed what they would do if they had the power. From one of them I got a retort, which it was difficult to repel. I tried to put the party into good humour by asking them about their country, and I smilingly said, "Is there no food in your country, that you have come all this way for it?" To which I got the reply: "You, sir, have come much farther than we have done. Had you no food to eat in your country?" I must acknowledge I felt myself shut up under this rebuff.

During my residence at Ranee Khet I had much intercourse with two classes widely separated from each other—educated young men, and Doms.

I have mentioned that from the Almora Mission School a number of young men had gone into all parts of the Province. Several got situations in the public offices of

Ranee Khet, and to them in the course of time persons of the same class were added from Bengal. I visited these at their quarters, and did all in my power to maintain friendly intercourse with them. A room in the school-house, supplied, partly at their own expense and partly by the liberality of friends, with newspapers, periodicals, and books, was turned into a reading-room, which was always open in the evening. One evening in the week they met me in class, when we had as our text-book the Advanced Reader of the Christian Vernacular Education Society, which furnished full opportunity for conversation on the most useful and important subjects. The attendance was not so steady as could be desired. All were friendly in their bearing, and some seemed much interested in our study and talk. A few professed Brahmist views, but none were inclined to join the Brahmist community and break with their own people. There was no indication of the spiritual concern which compels the soul to earnest investigation, with a view to following truth wherever it may lead.

The other class with whom I had much to do at Ranee Khet were the Doms, to whom reference has already been made as in all probability the descendants of the aborigines of the country previous to the Hindu invasion. They are a most useful part of the community. As the artisans of the country, the people of every caste have much to do with them. They are largely engaged in agriculture. They do things by which the caste people would be defiled, such as carrying away the carcases of animals. In a high-caste village it is not uncommon to see, a little aside from it—if the ground permits, below it—a number of houses occupied by Doms. The pigs and fowls around the meaner dwellings, and the poorer looks of the inhabitants, tell what they are. As artisan work is now in great demand the circumstances of the Doms are much improved, and there is every prospect of their rising into a higher position. They bear, and for many a year they may be expected to bear, indubitable marks of having been for ages a servile, despised, downtrodden class, having no respect from others, and entertaining little respect for themselves. Their improved circumstances will do something towards raising them in the social scale, but we cannot look for high moral excellence and real manhood till they come under the power of the Gospel.

On account of the abundance of work which the formation of an English station was sure to afford, a colony of these people erected a village for themselves on the side of the Ranee Khet hill below the Bazar. I had when in Almora conversed frequently with Doms. At Ranee Khet I saw much of them, and had more encouragement among them than among any other class. To some who expressed regret they could neither read nor write, I said it was not too late; that I would take care that they be taught if they were willing to learn. To test them I opened a night-school, and a number availed themselves of it. It was a gratifying sight to see them, at ages varying from fifteen to thirty-five, conning their spelling-books at the door of the school-house as evening was coming on, or trying to form letters on their slates. A few became soon discouraged, but a number held on, night after night for two or three hours, with the greatest eagerness, till they could read, write, and count very fairly. One result of the school was that they began to attend, with great regularity, a service held every Sabbath afternoon in the hall of the school-house.

During the last year of our residence in Ranee Khet, the attendance at this service was larger than at any previous period, and it was mainly composed of Doms. Nothing could exceed the quietness and apparent interest with which they heard the simple addresses given. I cannot say I saw any evidence of spiritual awakening, but the torpor of their previous life was shaken in a way which inspired the hope of their being brought into the fold of Christ.

I have mentioned the fierceness of the Cashmeeree Mussulmans. This charge cannot be brought against them all. One of their number, a young lad, came to the school, and was in every respect one of the best pupils in it. With another, one so trusted by the rest that he was the go-between in the arrangements for work with the English engineer, I had much intercourse. Though the head of the party, and himself doing no manual work, he could neither read nor write, and was entirely dependent on accounts being kept by another. To my surprise he came to the night-school, and applied himself so diligently that he acquired a fair measure of elementary education, though his knowledge of the Hindee language was very imperfect. He regularly attended the Sabbath evening service, and seemed to listen most eagerly. One day he came to our house. I at once saw that he was greatly excited. He shut the door behind him, as if afraid of being seen, came close to me, got down on his knees, and said: "Sir, what am I to do? Last night Huzrut Isa" (the name given by Muhammadans to our Lord, which may be translated "His Honour," or "His Excellence Jesus") "appeared to me in a dream, and said, 'Follow me; follow me.' But how can I follow Him? My people will kill me, they will kill me!" I have seldom been more touched than when I looked on the anguish in the face of that poor man, and the tears coursing down his cheeks, as he uttered these words. I need not tell the Christian reader what I endeavoured to say. Shortly afterwards the Cashmeerees left Ranee Khet, and this man with them. I could not find out where they went, and I have lost all trace of my friend.

A considerable part, sometimes the greater part, of the cold weather was given to itineracy. Some winters we went down to the foot of the hills to prosecute mission work among the large population found there at that season. We moved from place to place, erecting our tent in central spots, from which within a radius of two or three miles we could visit populous villages, some built of rough stones, but most composed of grass sheds. I was generally accompanied by a catechist. We had many opportunities of speaking to the people on the highest subjects. Not infrequently we met persons whom we had met in the hills, and then we were sure of a special welcome. Once I came on a party of Doms, tailors, whom I had seen a short time previously, and I said to them: "As you have no cattle, and do not cultivate the ground, what has brought you down?" To which I got the reply: "We have come in search of the sun." This gave me an opportunity of speaking of that Sun in whose warmth and light their spirits might dwell at all times, in all places. I endeavoured to set up schools in the Bhabhur, but had not any encouraging measure of success.

There was much which was pleasant and exhilarating in this movement from place to place, and in camping under the trees: but it was at times very fatiguing, and in bad weather very unpleasant. More than once we were overtaken by severe storms, but happily the worst of these storms came on us in favoured places, where we could find shelter on escaping from our tent.

Hill ponies feel themselves strange when in what a friend used to call the "roomy plains." The pony I had for years was quiet enough in the hills, but I had to watch it narrowly in the plains, as it seemed to have always the sense of danger, and was ready to start in a fashion which more than once almost dismounted me.

Some winters were spent in itinerating in hill districts from which the people did not go to the Bhabhur. In these winters I had the opportunity of going to a mela held at Bageswur, about thirty-five miles from Ranee Khet, at the confluence of the Surjoo and the Kalee. This mela is the greatest held in the Province. To many it is the grand event of the year. The people from all parts flock to it for religious, commercial, and social purposes. In the motley crowd may be seen hill-men from all the districts of the Himalaya, natives from the plains, Tibetans from the other side of the snowy range, and Englishmen.

This mela is held in a low valley not far from one of the passes into Tibet. It is attended by many Tibetans, who succeed in bringing their ponies through the tremendous defiles which separate their country from Kumaon. These ponies bring high prices. They also bring sheep laden with salt and borax. These Mongolians are great stalwart men, with broad faces, clad in homespun woollen cloth of many folds, which is seldom taken off till it is worn off. They are accompanied by a few women and children. They take their religion with them in their praying-wheels, which they keep going. They are an intensely religious people, as Mr. Gilmour tells us, but it is in the most mechanical fashion which can be conceived.

If they were mere machines, wound up like their praying-wheels, they could not to all appearance be more devoid of thought, feeling, and conscience in the exercise of their religion. I marked their countenances, and could only wonder at their stolid look. Much that is absurd is found in man's religion, but the Tibetan form of it seemed to me the very *ne plus ultra* of irrationality. Some of these Mongolians are inveterate beggars, but it would not be fair to judge the people generally by these stragglers into India. There was more life in their dances than in their religion, though not much grace. It seemed to me that if elephants could dance, they would do it somewhat in that style.

In the town of Bageswur there are substantial houses belonging to the merchants of the Province, and these are occupied by themselves or their agents during the greater part of the cold weather. During the rest of the year it is deserted, as the valley is very hot and feverish. During the colder weeks of the year it is a very stirring place, but it is on the occasion of the melas, two of which are held within three months, that there is a large gathering. At the principal mela many thousands must be present. As in all Hindu gatherings, religion, business, and pleasure are eagerly prosecuted. A town of booths rises suddenly in the valley and on the sides of the hills. Whenever I have gone, I have for miles before reaching the place seen many carrying or trailing branches of trees, with which they were to erect their temporary abode. These answer well in good weather, but when rain or snow falls they give no shelter. The morning is given to bathing. One morning is peculiarly propitious, and then from the earliest dawn the people are in the stream, many of them, I suppose, getting well-nigh the only ablution they have in the course of the year. During the day selling and buying go on vigorously. As evening approaches the merry-go-rounds are patronized, and crowds gather round singing and dancing parties. The dancers are young men linked hand in hand, who move about in circles, shuffle their feet, and sing in a very monotonous fashion. Many set to the preparation of the evening meal, and the valley and the hill-sides are aglow with fires and lights. Amusement, however, has not come to an end. Singing is kept up till the small hours of the morning, to the no small disturbance of those who cannot sleep except when there is a measure of quiet. Between the singing of the people and the barking—rather the howling—of the Tibetan dogs, such barking as I have never heard in our own country, wearied though I have been by the work of the day I have for hours found sleep to be impossible.

Englishmen attending the mela find a temporary abode in tents, and in a staging bungalow erected for the accommodation of European travellers. They dine together in the hall of this house, and occupy their tents at night. Officials deputed by the Commissioner of the Province are present, for the double purpose of keeping order and of paying rewards to those who have killed wild beasts. The skins of the tigers, bears, and leopards, for the destruction of which rewards have been paid, are sold by auction under the direction of the officials. The heaps of skins exposed for sale give one a striking impression of the number of wild beasts in the country. There are many keen hunters, both native and European, and there is no likelihood of their occupation coming to an end for want of game. Tea-planters attend this mela to buy mats, which are made by the people in large quantities, and are required in the preparation of tea for the market. Military officers on leave and travellers from the plains are present from the double motive of seeing this strange gathering and of purchasing ponies.

For many years Mr. Budden, accompanied by native Christians, has been in the habit of going to this mela, and I have been happy to help him and his brethren when opportunity has been given to me. A colporteur has been present with his wares, and succeeds in selling at a small price portions of the Scriptures and tracts. An amusing instance of indecision occurred at the book-stall the last time I was present. A man had purchased a Gospel. He came back saying he was told by his people that he would certainly become a Christian if he took that book to his village, and he laid down the book on the stall and asked for his money. The colporteur refused to cancel the sale, and the man was sorely perplexed, reluctant to lose both his money and that for which the money was paid. At last he walked away with the book, the colporteur assuring him it would do him only good.

We took our stand at different parts of the mela, and spoke to all willing to hear. Many speedily passed on, but a number remained for some time, as if desirous to know what this new religion was. Now and then we encountered pundits, and if they were at all reasonable we were pleased with their presence and opposition, as a colloquy with them greatly quickened the interest of the people. On one occasion, after skirmishing with some pundits, it was arranged they were to meet us at a fixed hour for discussion. Our Christian party were present at the appointed place and hour, but our pundit friends did not put in an appearance. Our going, however, was not in vain, as we succeeded in getting hearers who listened patiently to what we had to say about the Saviour of mankind. One of our number was a converted pundit of Almora, who spoke to the people in a way I thought eminently fitted to make a favourable impression.

CHAPTER XXIII.

HABITS AND CONDITION OF THE PEOPLE. MISSION WORK AND RETIREMENT.

DURING our residence in Kumaon we had many opportunities of observing the condition and habits of the people. I have mentioned the new re sources opened up to them, and yet it must be acknow ledged that many are poor. The population is probably much larger than it has been at any previous period. The holdings are small, and by the division made on the occasion of the death of the head of the household they ever tend to become smaller. There are a number in theProvince who own no land, and are poorly remunerated for their labour by their countrymen. I have mentioned the new source of wealth opened up to the people by the canals and cultivation of the Bhabhur. Reference has also been made to the tea-gardens and public works, on which large sums of money have been spent, of which much has reached the people in the form of wages. Thus all classes, both those who have land and those who have not, have been benefited. Indeed, apart from income thus obtained it is difficult to conceive how the people could have been supported. If they do not make progress in material comfort the fault must lie in their want of energy.

Like their brethren in the plains, the people in the hills live chiefly on cereals—the cheaper cereals—and vegetables; but, like most below, including even many Brahmans and Rajpoots, they have no objection to animal food when they get it of the kind they approve, and prepared in the way caste rules require. As to Doms, nothing that is at all eatable comes amiss to them. They have no objection, indeed, to much we should deem uneatable. The Hindus eat the flesh of goats and kids offered in sacrifice. They also eat the flesh of short-tailed sheep, but long-tailed sheep are an abomination to them, as they regard them as a kind of dog. We saw once an amusing instance of the notion of uncleanness attached to this species of sheep. A few sheep were being chosen by a purchaser from a flock. The animals were scampering about, showing, according to their nature, their unwillingness to be caught. Three or four men were engaged in catching them, but one every now and then started back when about to lay his hand on a sheep, exclaiming, "*Wuh doomwala hai!*"—"It is a tailed one! it is a tailed one!"—as if he would be hopelessly defiled by touching it, while his less scrupulous companions of the same caste said, "You fool! what does it matter? It will do you no harm." They would not have eaten its flesh, but their caste spirit was sufficiently relaxed to allow them to touch it.

I have referred to sanitary regulations issued by the authorities to guard the people against epidemics caused by want of cleanliness. One of these regulations forbids the dwelling together of animals and human beings. On our first visit to the hills in 1847 I came unpleasantly into contact with this dual occupation of the same house. As night was setting in I came to the

LANDSLIP AT NYNEE TAL.

top of a hill, and from it I could see a few straggling houses at a short distance. I had with me two or three men, who proposed to put up a booth for the night. Unhappily for my comfort, a thunderstorm came on with heavy rain, and the booth was no protection. I was taken to a house a short way off, but on entering it the smell from the animals occupying it with their owners was so strong that it drove me out. I preferred to face the storm to bearing the effluvia of that highland abode. I was told of a little unoccupied grass-shed a mile down the hill. I found the grass so thick and well tied that the rain did not get through, and the entrance was on the lee side. Into this I crept, and slept soundly till the morning, for I was very tired with the long walk of the day.

The new sanitary orders have no doubt done good, but it is difficult to secure compliance with them, though fines are imposed on persons convicted of disobedience. If there had been a reward for informers I could have more than once won it by telling what I had seen.

A very pleasant break during our life at Ranee Khet was a yearly visit paid to Nynee Tal, about thirty miles distant, which had become the seat of Government for the North-West for half the year, and a place of great resort from the plains during the hot and wet months. It has many advantages as a Sanitarium. It is within sixteen miles of the Bhabhur, and has an elevation of from 6,300 to 8,000 feet above the level of the sea. There is a small, beautiful mountain lake, from one end of which one looks down on the plains over the intervening hills; while at the other end, beyond a piece of uneven ground, rises a lofty mountain. There are rather steep hills on either side, but hills with a gradient which admits of houses being built on them. Though so near the plains, this lakelet was till 1842 unknown, except to natives and a few English officials. In that year travellers with difficulty made their way to it, and drew attention to its attractions. We first saw it in 1847, and then it had very few houses. An old General, one of its first residents, told us that one day the preceding year he saw a tiger walking leisurely above his house, and looking down, as if wondering at the change which was coming over the place. Some of the first residents were startled by meeting bears in their walks. Since that time houses have been built on every side, and during the season there is a great population of both Europeans and natives. Four years ago there was a fearful landslip, which carried down a number of houses with it, and buried many under the falling mass.

At the beginning of 1857, the American Episcopal Methodist Church entered on mission work in Rohilkund. When the mutiny of that year broke out, the agents of this church in Rohilkund escaped to Nynee Tal, and from that time they continued to occupy it as a mission station, and also as a sanitarium for their brethren in the plains. The Mission has been efficiently conducted. English services have been maintained during the season. They have been well attended by all classes, and have done much good. Between native servants and shopkeepers from the plains, and natives of the hills, who flock into the place for service and work, there is a large sphere for mission work, and much has been done in the way of both preaching and schools. The Mission has been extended to other parts of the Province, to Gurhwal in the north, to Petorah in the east, and to other places, with manifest tokens of the Divine blessing.

With these American brethren we have been on the most friendly terms, and have co-operated with them in every way open to us. We formed an association with them for mutual counsel and help. One result of this association has been the holding of annual meetings in Nynee Tal in autumn, for the benefit of Europeans and natives, and conducted in both the English and native languages, ending with the celebration of the Lord's Supper. These meetings were largely attended, excited much interest, did, I believe, much good, and were very enjoyable.. On these annual visits to Nynee Tal we commonly remained a week or ten days, and had much pleasant intercourse with the missionaries and other friends. During several years Sir William Muir, as Lieutenant-Governor of the North-West, was resident for half the year at Nynee Tal, and our special thanks are due to him and Lady Muir for hospitable entertainment.

While, during our residence in the hills, time and strength were mainly given to effort for the spiritual good of our own countrymen and the native population, there were times, especially during the rainy season, when I was much at home; and I was glad to avail myself of the leisure afforded of writing for the press what I hoped might prove, and what I trust has proved, of spiritual benefit to natives and others. During our stay in the hills, in addition to articles for the "Indian Evangelical Review" and other periodicals, I wrote a Commentary on the Epistle to the Romans in Hindustanee, and Essays in English, which were published in book form under the title of "Christianity and the Religions of India." At an early period of my missionary career, at the request of my colleague Mr. Shurman, to whom the work of revising and in part translating the Bible into

Hindustanee was entrusted, I transferred the Pentateuch from the Persian into the Roman character, and translated the book of the Prophet Jeremiah, which, revised by Mr. Shurman and Dr. Mather, now forms part of the version. Before leaving India I did a little, at the request of the North India Bible Society, towards the revision of the Hindee translation of the New Testament. On this work a large and very able Committee is now engaged. During my Indian career I have written a good deal for the press—I must acknowledge in a very desultory manner.

Thus engaged in prosecuting our work, years passed on till the end of 1876, when we felt the time had arrived for retiring from the Indian Mission-field. In July of that year I had a severe illness, which laid me aside, and incapacitated me for carrying on mission work with any measure of efficiency. I might have continued at Ranee Khet, and done the work within my reach there, but by doing so the most important part of the work, the work in the district, would have remained undone; and I deemed it best to retire to make way for one who could fitly occupy the sphere. Medical men whom I consulted strongly advised my departure, and the Directors of the Society gave their prompt and kind sanction to our return to England.

I cannot end this account of our life in Kumaon without giving expression to our gratitude for the kind aid afforded us by friends in the prosecution of our work. Among these friends, one of the steadiest and kindest was the cantonment magistrate, Colonel, afterwards Major-General, Chamberlain, who identified himself with the Mission, and was ever ready to do all he could to promote its prosperity. During our lengthened absences from the station in the cold weather, and whenever I could not officiate, he conducted service with the English soldiers, and he was ready in every way within his power to render help. In addition to aid in carrying on the Mission, we received great personal kindness from him and his partner, of which we shall always retain a grateful recollection. He retired to England a short time after us, and within a little more than a year he was suddenly called away—to his own gain, we are sure, but to the grief of all his friends. It gives me a melancholy pleasure to render this tribute to his memory. For steady friendship and most valuable aid our best thanks are also due to Captain, now Lieut.-Colonel, Birney, R.E., the resident Chief Engineer; Robert Troup, Esq., a tea-planter in the neighbourhood; and Mr. Ashhurst, engineer. Among the friends not resident at Ranee Khet, to whom the Mission is largely indebted, are Sir Henry Ramsay and Sir William Muir. Besides the friends I have mentioned, many others contributed liberally to the Mission, without whose aid much which was done must have remained unaccomplished. By the liberal contributions received the operations of the Mission were carried on, and valuable property was created at very little expense to the Society.

We left Ranee Khet at the close of 1876. As we were leaving India with no prospect of returning, we spent two months in visiting different stations, seeing their Missions, and holding intercourse with friends and brethren. In the course of these months we visited Bareilly, Shahjehanpore, Agra, from which we went to see that wonderful deserted city, Futtypore Sikree, with its magnificent tombs, Jeypore, Lucknow, Cawnpore, Allahabad, Mirzapore, Benares, Jubbulpore, and Bombay. At Agra we attended the native service of the Church Mission. The minister who preached was a native who had been educated in our central school at Benares when I was superintendent, and was there led to the knowledge of Christ, though he was not baptized till his return to his native city, Agra. On this tour we saw and heard much which interested us greatly, as it showed the work of evangelization was being vigorously prosecuted with tokens of God's blessing resting on it. We embarked at Bombay in February, and arrived in England at the end of March.

We left India, where we had spent the greater and, I may say, the better part of our life, with feelings I will not attempt to describe. I can only say when we review our Indian life, that while deeply humbled at the recollection of many errors and defects, defects in wisdom, zeal, and love, we are deeply grateful for having been privileged to labour for so many years in the service of our adorable Redeemer, not, we trust, without proof that good was accomplished through our instrumentality; and so long as we breathe, our hearts will steadily turn towards India with ardent love, and with fervent prayer for the spiritual and temporal welfare of its inhabitants.

CHAPTER XXIV.

THE MISSIONARY IN INDIA.

ON reviewing these reminiscences I find there are several subjects of interest to which I have only casually alluded, and others on which I have made no remark. My readers will, I hope, bear with me while I detain them by stating facts and expressing views which will make the narrative more complete.

It is unnecessary to describe the office of missionary to the heathen. No one has rightly entered on the office without being deeply impressed by its greatness, arduousness, and responsibility. It is equally unnecessary to describe the qualifications required. No one can contemplate the demands the office makes on intellect, heart, and conscience, on love to the Lord Jesus Christ and love to souls, on wisdom, perseverance, and courage, without exclaiming with the great missionary Paul, "Who is sufficient for these things?" The idea that one unqualified for work at home would do for a missionary abroad is so preposterous that it is strange it should have ever been entertained by the most heedless.

There is, however, a great difference between an office and those who serve in an office. Because an office is great and honourable it does not follow that those who hold it have always the high character it demands. The question may, then, be fairly asked, Are missionaries worthy of their office? I, of course, use the word "worthy" in a relative sense, and I remember our limited acquaintance with the human heart. It must be acknowledged there have been a few, happily a *very* few, who have shown themselves utterly unworthy of the office, some by lack of intellectual fitness, and others by want of spiritual character and by indisposition to the work. There have been cases of the utter failure of character, but these have been extremely rare. Of missionaries generally it may be confidently affirmed they have been true men. I have a wide acquaintance with the missionaries of Northern India. During our long residence in Benares we saw many of all Societies, of all Churches, as they travelled up and down. Benares is one of the great halting-places between Bengal and the Upper Provinces, and residence there gives many opportunities for acquaintance with brethren. We have the most pleasing recollection of many we have met, and we have followed their course with deep interest.

I should be acting in opposition to my settled conviction if I were to speak of missionaries as more devoted to Christ's service, more self-denied, more ready to endure privation than home ministers. This glorification of missionaries, as missionaries, was much in vogue at one time, and is still sometimes heard. Our Master, the Lord Jesus Christ, gives to every one his work, and our devotedness is shown, not by our office, but by the way in which we do the work assigned us. Predilection to a certain sphere, supposed fitness for it, temperament and circumstances, have much to do in indicating to us the sphere our Lord would have us to occupy. Tried by the test of devotedness, as shown in daily life, I have never seen any reason for placing one class of Christ's servants above the other. Among ministers there is, as we all know, a great difference, not only in talent and attainment, but also in love, zeal, wisdom, and endurance —in every quality which their work demands. Similar is the variety among missionaries. There are many degrees of efficiency and, it must be acknowledged, of inefficiency. They, as well as their brethren at home, can go through the routine of their work in a very perfunctory and unsatisfactory manner; while they, too, can consecrate all their powers to the service of their Lord. It would be easy to select from the home field ministers who, in unwearied labour, self-denial, and privation for Christ's sake, greatly excel the ordinary run of missionaries; and it would be equally easy to select from the foreign field missionaries who greatly excel most of their home brethren.

In several respects there is a marked contrast in the position of ministers and missionaries. Ministers labour in their own language, among their own people, amidst home surroundings and associations; while missionaries have to part with loved relatives and to betake themselves to a foreign land, where they have to learn a foreign language, often languages, at the cost of much time and of wearying application, have for years, as in the greater part of India, to bear a severe climate, are called to prosecute their work among a strange, an unsympathetic, and sometimes a hostile people, and, what is felt by family people to be the greatest trial of all, they have to send their children to England, and to live separate from them for years. Some of these trials missionaries share with their fellow-countrymen, who fiom secular motives go to foreign lands, but others are peculiar to their vocation.

While I mention the trials of a missionary career I cannot forget the trials of ministerial life at home. We should require to shut our eyes to patent facts if we were to ignore the privations many excellent men are called to endure, and the varied difficulties they have to encounter from the character and circumstances of the people among whom they labour, from the peculiarities of our times, and from the abiding qualities of human nature, as it is now constituted. Missionaries are not rich, but they have adequate support, for good or evil are not dependent for it on the goodwill of those to whom they minister, and receive it as regularly as if it came from an endowment. With children sent home for education they have times of great pressure, but much has been done to aid them in meeting this additional expense. Viewed merely as to the comfort of living, and ease of mind as to support, the advantages are not all on the side of the home minister. To counteract the advantages of the missionary's position to which I have referred, it must be remembered the average career of service in India is short—some returning very soon, and others after a few years. Those who return after years spent abroad, and yet in the prime of life, are rightly expected to enter the list of the home ministry; but the work they have left and that on which they are entering are so different, that the mental habits acquired in the one are felt to be a poor preparation for, and often even an obstacle to, efficiency in the other.

In their duties, joys, and trials, ministers and missionaries have much in common. We have to deal with the same human nature, manifesting the same characteristics, though in different forms. We have the same message to deliver. We have the same great end in view, the salvation of those to whom we minister, their restoration to the character and joys of God's children. Whether we labour at home or abroad, we are required to endure hardness as good soldiers of Jesus Christ. If we have not entered on our work from love to Christ and love to souls, with an intense desire to spend and be spent in Christ's service, with a belief that He has called us to it, and given us a measure of fitness for it; if we are conscious of being dominated by inferior motives; if we have not delight in our work, even when there is great pressure on both mind and body; if we do not long for the success of our work, it is obvious we have missed our vocation, and it would be better for us to sweep the street, I would say it would be better to walk the treadmill than occupy our position for an hour. This I must say for myself, I am deeply thankful for having been privileged to labour in the foreign field, and consider it the highest honour which could have been conferred on me. With my brethren I have had many trials to endure, some privations to bear, some perils to encounter, but I have never for an hour regretted my early decision to give myself to Christ's work among the heathen. I am sure I here speak the feeling of my missionary brethren.

I have endeavoured in my reminiscences to give such a representation of a missionary's position and work in Northern India, that home ministers who may read my narrative can have no difficulty in comparing and contrasting ministerial and missionary spheres. It will be seen how varied are the duties devolving on the missionary, and how great are the demands on thought and effort for their proper discharge. They have, in many cases, to attend to harassing and perplexing secular work. A number give their time and strength to teaching, and

I know enough of this department to testify that those who give themselves to it in a climate like that of India lead very laborious lives. I have said little of the translation of the Scriptures, and the preparation of Christian books and tracts. This is a department in which there has been much exhausting effort of both body and mind, as all know well who have done even a little in it. In the prosecution of direct evangelistic work the missionary finds much to interest and encourage him, but also much to grieve and depress him, especially if he has a sensitive nature, and has no natural love for debate. Even to those who do not shrink from discussion there is often not a little which is very trying. I have a vivid recollection of times when I have returned from Benares to my home in the suburbs, so wearied in body and grieved in spirit by the opposition I had encountered and the blasphemies I had heard, that I have felt as if I could never enter the city again. But I went again, and perhaps the next time was much encouraged.

Missionaries at the same station are much more closely associated than ministers at the same place at home. The management of the mission, the policy to be adopted, and the respective places to be filled, are under common arrangement and control, subject to the district committee, and through them to the home directors. Many perplexing questions come before missionaries thus associated, and human nature in them must have parted with its usual infirmities, and put on peculiar excellence, if difference of judgment and consequent variance of feeling had never appeared. We cannot plead exemption from human imperfection. It cannot be denied that at times there has been strong diversity of judgment and painful alienation of feeling, when missionaries have too closely resembled Paul and Barnabas in their sharp dispute at Antioch; but it can at the same time be most truly affirmed that with very rare exceptions discord has soon come to an end, and those who have differed widely have become attached friends, as we know Paul and Barnabas did. The normal state of things is that of mutual love, respect, and helpfulness.

Missionaries have also had their differences with the Societies that have sent them out and supported them. The respective position of home committees and foreign missionaries are so different, that a difference of judgment is in some cases unavoidable; but confiding as they have done in the goodness of each other's motives, full harmony has been soon restored. I must be allowed to say of the London Missionary Society, whose agent I was for so many years in India, that my warmest acknowledgments are due to it for all the kindness and consideration shown to me and mine. If I were now to begin my career with my knowledge of the past, there is no Society with which I could so confidently connect myself.

All have heard of the friendly intercourse among missionaries of different churches. They, too, when near each other have had occasional differences; but with rare exceptions they have been on terms not only of courteous bearing, but of affectionate intimacy. There is nothing in our Indian life to which we look back with greater pleasure than our intercourse with Presbyterian, Baptist, Methodist, and Episcopalian brethren. With the Episcopalian and Baptist missionaries at Benares we were on as warm terms of friendship as if they had been members of our own Mission. For many years we were in the habit of meeting weekly with them for the study of the Scriptures, prayer, and Christian communion.

Most Europeans take no interest in missions, look on missionaries as good men engaged in a Quixotic enterprise, and know almost nothing about their work, but still they treat them with courtesy. There are, however, some of our own countrymen who take a deep interest in our work, visit our schools, occasionally attend our native services, and contribute liberally to our mission schemes. These do much to cheer our hearts and promote our success. Again and again my work would have been at a standstill but for the help given me by European Christians, and our intercourse with some has resulted in close and enduring friendship. If persons have a temperament preparing them for friendship, I cannot conceive any position more favourable to its formation and strength than that of a missionary in many of our Indian stations.

CHAPTER XXV.

THE MISSIONARY IN INDIA (Continued).

IT has been already stated that missionaries have an income, which enables them to live in a way conducive to the health of themselves and families. Things which would be luxuries at home are necessaries in India, and all they can do is to alleviate the suffering caused by the climate. As missionaries are often more stationary than European officials, both military and civil, and spend much less than they do on horses, establishments, and entertainments, their houses have an air of comfort which is surprising to those who know their income, and has led to much misrepresentation on the part of those who know not and do not care to know what it is.

Not infrequently young men have gone out to India as missionaries with the firm resolve to live to a large extent in the native fashion, and to eschew what they conceive the undue indulgence of those who had preceded them, but the experience of one hot season has generally brought them to another mind. Individuals have adhered to their resolution, and the result in one case I know was insanity, in other cases utter failure of health, and in others speedy death. A band of Germans determined to live, if not in the native style, at least in the simple style of the Fatherland, as to habitation, food, and service, and with scarcely an exception the plan was soon abandoned. The only successful case I have heard of in our day has been that of Mr. Bowen, a devoted American missionary in Bombay. We have had no William Burns, in Northern India at least. I can say for myself, that so far as the mere comfort of living is concerned I should greatly prefer a humble abode and simple fare in England, to the finest house and the most sumptuous fare in the plains of Northern India. It has been maintained by some that our only hope of success lies in our becoming ascetics, and outstripping by our austerities the Hindu saints. In other words, by acting as if we accepted Hindu principles of religion we are to overthrow Hinduism, and win the people to Christ. The proposal calls for no consideration.

Of late a good deal has been said about the substance of missionary teaching. Missionaries as a class maintain and teach the doctrinal views of the Churches whose messengers and agents they are. In these Churches a sifting process has been going on for a considerable time, which has led in some cases to a reversal of belief in matters of great moment, and in a greater number to the modification and softening of views hitherto entertained. Every one must decide for himself how far the sifting has been wisely done, how far chaff and only chaff has been given to the wind, and precious grain gathered into the garner. Missionaries have unquestionably been affected by doctrinal discussion, in a few instances, I believe a very few, to the reversal of some of their former views, in all, perhaps, though in different degrees, to a readjustment of their doctrinal position, to giving more prominence to some aspects of truth and less prominence to others, under the conviction that such is their relative position in the Word of God.

However much imbued missionaries have been with the views of their respective Churches, their position among the heathen has always led them to the constant and simple presentation of the great facts and doctrines of the Bible. These have been set forth in the manner deemed best fitted to commend them to the understanding, conscience, and heart of the people. Familiar illustrations have been largely used, and elaborate doctrinal discussion shunned. While the missionary finds much in the narratives and teachings of the Old Testament which is helpful to his object, he dwells chiefly on the life of Christ, His deeds, words, living, and holy example; death to redeem men; man's urgent need of such a Saviour, because guilty and depraved; the claims of Christ on His love, trust, and service; the blessedness of compliance with these claims on character and state; the misery and doom incurred by their persistent rejection. How often have I seen the heathen greatly moved by the parable of the Prodigal Son!

The missionary, like the home minister, has to guard against one-sidedness, if he would keep to the Book which he professes to be his standard. The many-sidedness of the Bible, its appeal to man's whole nature, is one of the most marked proofs of its superhuman origin. While it addresses itself continually to man's moral nature, to his sense of right and wrong, while it appeals to his intellect and heart, it also speaks to his fears and hopes. These appeals are made to all, whatever may be their diversity in character and condition. If we were to follow the course of many in our day who condemn appeals to fear, we should be ignoring a large part of Scripture, including many of our Lord's utterances, and at the same time ignoring that fear of hurtful consequences which the

Author of our nature has implanted in us as a great means of self-preservation. To hope as well as to fear much is addressed in the Bible, and the missionary who would approve himself to his Master is bound to appeal to both principles, while, like his Master, he makes his constant and main appeal to the higher part of man's nature.

While the missionary ought to strive to understand the people among whom he labours, and to discover the most promising avenue to their minds, while he ought to commend himself to every man's conscience as in the sight of God, he is not to seek acceptance for his message by accommodating it to the views of his hearers. He knows that between their views and his message there is not only a marked discrepancy, but on many points radical opposition, and the one must be displaced if the other is to be accepted. We have here for our guidance the example of our Lord and His apostles.

I have endeavoured to give a faithful description of the tenor of missionary teaching. It appears many are dissatisfied with it. We are told we must part with our narrow traditional views of doctrine, and become imbued with the larger and more liberal views of our times, if we are to hope for success. In the late Dr. Norman McLeod's "Life" we find him saying, "The chief difficulty in the way of advancing Christianity in India is unquestionably that almost all the missionaries represent a narrow one-sided Christianity." I cannot conceive what could have been his ground for this astounding statement, except his impression—it could not have been anything beyond an impression—that missionaries adhered to the doctrines of the Churches that had sent them out, his own among the rest, and had not followed him in his changes. Every one who comes out with new views, or modification of old views, assures us that success will speedily follow the acceptance and preaching of *his* phase of doctrine. Some tell us we must preach the moral aspect of the atonement, and part with what has been called the forensic aspect; we must only speak of the love it shows to man, and say nothing of its bearing on the Divine law and government; and then the great cause of so-called failure will be removed. So far as I know missionaries, they accept both aspects of the atonement; they believe both aspects are taught in Scripture, and they are convinced that instead of enfeebling they strengthen each other, while the doctrine thus presented meets man's deepest wants. Others, again, tell us we must preach what is called Life in Christ—the utter extinction of impenitent sinners, while others say this is a shocking doctrine, and we must preach universal restoration. This is no place for discussing the teaching of the Bible regarding the great Beyond, which is at present exercising so many minds. All I will say is that neither in the old views nor in the new is there anything which a Hindu or a Buddhist will accept, while he remains a Hindu or Buddhist. So far as I am aware, all students of Hinduism and Buddhism are agreed that eternal conscious existence, with identity of being firmly maintained, is alien from both systems. They do not hold the doctrine of either eternal happiness or eternal misery. To be extinguished, in the sense of being absorbed into Brahm and losing all conscious personality, is the reward of high virtue, while the wicked have to pass many miserable births before they reach this longed-for goal. With them salvation, liberation, is not deliverance from sin, but from conscious existence. They have both heavens and hells—heavens supernatural in their surroundings but intensely earthly in their character, doings, and strifes, and hells full of everything which is repulsive and painful; but both, after vast lapses of time, will be emptied into the great ocean of being, into the One without a Second. Cessation of conscious existence is not with them the punishment of wickedness, but the eagerly desired consummation of their being, the goal which is quickly reached by the eminently good.

Let missionaries by all means listen to what is said in favour of new views, let them modify or change their views if they think they see scriptural authority for the change, but I am profoundly convinced no shifting of our doctrinal position will secure success. Looking over the whole field of foreign missions since the end of last century, it is undeniable that God has done great things by them, for which we have abundant reason to be glad; and we know the teaching by which the desert has in many places blossomed as the rose. New phases of doctrine have yet to win their triumph. We must look in another direction for a greater degree of success—to more unreserved devotedness to Christ on the part of both missionaries and those who send them out; closer communion with Him; a higher degree of attainment in the mind which is in Him; a more persuasive deliverance of our message, and a larger effusion of God's Spirit.

The great obstruction at home and abroad to the acceptance of Christ as the Saviour is moral obtuseness, a dormant conscience. Our Lord's words throw a steady light on man's neglect of the great salvation, "*They that are whole need not a physician, but they that are sick.*" Till men know they are sick, and recognize the deadly nature of their sickness, there will be no application to the Great Physician. In addition to the indurating effects of sin everywhere, the people of India have been for ages so drugged, I may say, with pantheistic and polytheistic teaching, that if man's moral nature had been destructible it must have been destroyed ages ago. Happily it can not be destroyed. Perverted, stupefied, dormant, though it is, it still exists, and to it we can therefore address the message of Heaven, while we look up to God to make it effectual by the teaching of His Spirit. When man knows himself to be a sinner, when he knows what sin is, then, and only then, whether in India or in England, he casts himself with joy into the arms of the Saviour.

I am surprised when Christians speak as if only a modification or a new statement of doctrine was required in order to full and immediate success, as if they had never read such passages as "*The carnal mind is enmity against God;*" "*The natural man receiveth not the things of the Spirit of God;*" as if they were ignorant of the facts by which these statements are so amply and mournfully attested; as if they had never heard of One who appeared, as ancient sages longed to see, clothed with perfect virtue and dwelt among men, and was yet rejected and crucified by them; as if they knew nothing of His apostles, who spake as they were moved by the Holy Ghost, and yet had to lament over many hearers to whom their message was the savour of death unto death. Musing over the controversies of the day, the wish has often arisen in my mind: Would that the nature of sin was not kept so much in the background! Would that it was seen in its offensiveness to God and injuriousness to man—persistently daring high Heaven, while corrupting, degrading, disquieting, and ruining man! Would that the scriptural view of sin and sinfulness, which receives such ample confirmation from human experience and history, was more considered in the adjustment of doctrine! All readjustment in which the nature and effect of sin is not kept steadily in view must lead to serious error—error which misrepresents God's character and government, is inconsistent with facts meeting us on every side, and must prove most hurtful to man. I am convinced that while on some points there has been progress, and wise modification of doctrine, on the subject of sin the theology of former days was truer to Scripture and fact than the theology of our time.

I cannot conclude these remarks about the Indian missionary without mentioning—and I can do little more than mention—the names of loved fellow-labourers who rest from the toils of earth, and have entered into the joy of their Lord above. A feeling of sadness and yet of thankfulness comes over me, as I see before my mind's eye brethren of our own Mission with whom I was associated—Buyers, with his intimate acquaintance with the native languages, his large knowledge, and his kindly disposition; Shurman, the keen, impetuous, plodding German scholar, whose great monument is his translation of the Old Testament into Hindustanee; Mather, first of Benares and afterwards of Mirzapore, one of the most enterprising and devoted missionaries ever sent to India, whose peculiarity of temper and urgency with new plans led in his early years to unpleasantness, but who, when well known, was one of the truest and kindest of men, with whom for many years we had an intimate friendship, and whose memory and that of his excellent wife we shall always revere; and Sherring, one of the most amiable of men and most pleasant of colleagues, a man of marked attainments, and an indefatigable worker. The agents of other missions at Benares call for affectionate mention. I have in an early part of my reminiscences spoken of Smith, the founder and for many years the sole agent of the Baptist Mission at Benares, a quiet, diligent, Nathaniel-like man. This mission had for years George Parsons, a man of large linguistic attainments, of most amiable, meek, and devout character, than whom it would be difficult to find a more conscientious labourer. The Church Missionary Society was highly favoured in having had for a long period at Benares two men, Smith and Leupolt, who, in their respective departments, had, I believe, no superiors in India. For many years Smith, with resolute perseverance and great efficiency, often with severe strain on both body and mind, prosecuted evangelistic work in the city and the surrounding neighbourhood. No man was better known and more highly esteemed by the entire community. He had success to cheer him in the form of persons avowing themselves the followers of Christ, but the number was so small that he was often greatly depressed. I cannot doubt that by his ministry seed was sown in many minds which will yet bear fruit. During our later years in Benares, Fuchs was one of the agents of this Mission, an excellent biblical scholar, a diligent labourer, who required only to be known to be loved and esteemed, with whom we had much pleasant and profitable intercourse. He was suddenly called away in the midst of his usefulness, and in the prime of life. I have been confining my remarks to the departed; but I must mention two who survive—warm-hearted Heinig, of the Baptist Mission, now set aside by age and infirmity, after a long life of great toil in the service of Christ, and our greatly-loved friend Leupolt, of the Church Mission, who his still doing good service now in England, and was for many years the fellow-labourer of his friend Smith. His name and work at Benares will last for many a day.

Our departed brethren had their imperfections; who of us are without them? But I can truly say that in their general character, work, and bearing they were the messengers of the Churches to the Gentiles and the glory of Christ.

Looking beyound our Benares missions we remember a number of faithful labourers, whom we knew and loved, who have joined the majority, such as the learned and kindly Owen, the venerable Morrison, the apostolic Ziemann, and many others besides. I do not use these terms in a conventional sense, but as justly applicable to the men. Those I have named laboured, and others have entered into their labours, men worthy of all esteem, love, sympathy, and help.

CHAPTER XXVI.

NATIVE CHRISTIANS.

NATIVE Christians form so large and varied a community that right views of them can be obtained only by those who consider its component parts.

In Southern India there are thousands calling themselves Syrian Christians, still more frequently Christians of St. Thomas. Either the Apostle Thomas or some of his spiritual children went to India, and founded a Christian Church. Down through the ages the descendants of these first converts have clung to the profession of Christianity, and have kept up their connexion with their fellow Christians in Western Asia. They have the peculiarities of hereditary Christians exposed to a corrupting moral atmosphere, and possessing limited means of spiritual improvement. We are told that they have made great progress through their intercourse with European missionaries.

In Southern India and Ceylon there is a large body of native Christians, the descendants of the many baptized by Xavier and his companions. Every one who has read the life of Xavier knows how widely he opened the door of the Church; with what facility, to use his own favourite expression, he "made Christians." Many speedily relapsed into heathenism, but a sufficient number remained steadfast to form a large community, and their descendants are reckoned by tens, rather hundreds, of thousands. There is not—at least there was not a short time ago—any reliable census of their number. Protestant opinion of these native Christians is very unfavourable. It may be prejudiced, and yet it has been expressed by persons who have come into contact with them, who know them well, and who would shrink from doing injustice. Many facts have been stated in support of an unfavourable estimate. The Abbé Dubois condemned them as a scandal to the Christian name, and other Romanists have joined him in confirming the testimony of Protestants.

In Travancore and Tinnevelly, in the far south, there are large native churches, in connexion with the Propagation, Church, and London Missionary Societies, composed of Shanars, a people outside the Hindu pale and greatly despised by them, with a sprinkling of caste people. When whole villages come over to the profession of Christianity, we generally find a few who may be regarded as true believers in the Lord Jesus Christ, with limited knowledge but genuine faith, while the many, though favourably impressed, simply assent to the action of their friends and neighbours, and are little changed except in name. They are on the way to a happy change by having come under new and elevating influences.

All over Southern India there are native Christian churches, the work of conversion having proceeded in some cases gradually, individual by individual, while in other cases numbers have been admitted at the same time.

Among the non-Aryan tribes, the Kols and the Santhals, occupying the hills and forests of Central and Eastern India, a great work has been done during the last thirty years. Thousands have been brought into the fold of the Christian Church. In habits, character, and condition, these tribes bear a considerable resemblance to our rude Teutonic ancestors, and they have been brought to the profession of Christianity in a somewhat similar manner; with this difference, that they have not been headed by chiefs in the reception of baptism, and in many cases commanding it. The first converts were the direct fruit of mission labour; their number increased, inspired by zeal they told their countrymen the treasure they had found, and called on them to share it with them. Many listened to their words and accepted their message. The work thus spread from village to village, and from hamlet to hamlet, till it extended to parts of the country never visited by a missionary, and included many who had never seen a missionary's face, in some cases who had never seen a white face. A very dear friend and enterprising missionary, the late Rev. William Jones of Singrowlee, made his way through a wild roadless country to the border of the Kol region, and came to a hamlet where the people were startled by the appearance of a European, as they had never been visited by one before. Though from difference in language their intercourse was limited, they understood each other sufficiently to discover, to their mutual delight, that they had a common faith. The general character of a community formed of a rude people, emerging from fetish and demon worship, can be readily supposed. I suspect the converts made by the monk Augustine and his companions had not a little in their character and conduct to show the pit from which they had been taken; and yet that was the dawning of a day for the Anglian and Saxon race in our country for which we have abundant reason to be thankful. There is no doubt much imperfection in Kol and Santhal converts, but we may well anticipate for them a far less clouded day than that which dawned on our forefathers when Augustine went to them.

In Bengal there are two large native Christian communities, one in Krishnagurh in connexion with the Church Missionary Society, and the other in Backergunje connected with the Baptists. In both cases the conversion of individuals has led to numbers avowing themselves the followers of Christ. Where conversion is thus what may be called collective rather than individual, there may be in some a high degree of spiritual life, but the majority simply go with the stream. It will be observed that in the statistics of some missions so many are represented as baptized, so many members of the church, so many adherents, the last class often outnumbering the other two. These adherents openly declare their abandonment of idolatry, attend public worship with more or less regularity, call themselves Christians, and are called Christians by others. They may be described as in the outer court of the temple, from which not a few from time to time enter the inner.

In the great Presidency cities, Calcutta, Bombay, and Madras, and their immediate neighbourhood, the native churches connected with Protestant Missions are comparatively small. The members of these churches differ more widely in social position, mental culture, and I think I may add spiritual character, than any other native churches in India. Some of the members are highly educated, have acute and disciplined minds, and have an intimate acquaintance with our language and literature. Individuals among them have made sacrifices by becoming the followers of Christ, of which the only adequate explanation is that they have come under the power of an all-controlling faith, of the faith which gives the victory over self, the world, and the devil. Persons more established in the faith of Christ than some of these are, more thoroughly assured that He is the Son of God and the Saviour of the world, I have never met. In these churches there are degrees of culture and social standing, till we come to unlettered persons in the humblest rank of life, some of whom are, I doubt not, as genuine Christians and as devoted to the Saviour as their brethren of higher social standing and larger mental attainment.

I now proceed to speak of the native Christians of Northern India, with whom for many years I have been closely associated, and of whom I can speak with a measure of confidence.

In the North-Western Provinces, as in other parts of India, we have different classes that go under the name of native Christians. Most drummers of native regiments have been Christians, in the sense that they have been baptized persons. Many are descendants of Portuguese, who have gradually become mixed with the lower classes of natives, and cannot, except by dress, be distinguished from them, their hue being often darker than that of the people. These Portuguese descendants are numerous all over India, in the South very numerous, and hold very different positions in society, but those I have known in the North have been mainly of the drummer class. To these have been added a considerable number of natives, the waifs of native society, who have attached themselves to European regiments as camp-followers, not a few of whom have so separated themselves from their own people that they have found it convenient to profess the Christian faith. I have known individuals of this class who bore a good character, and were regular in their attendance on public worship. We had a number of them in our native Christian congregation at Benares, and we had for years a weekly meeting in their quarters. I cannot, however, speak highly of them as a class, either as to intelligence or goodness. Not a few went to a place of Christian worship only on Christmas Day, or on the occasion of a marriage or baptism, and their general conduct was no honour to the Christian name. Yet these people are proud of being ranked as Christians. We had a striking illustration of this at Benares. A person died, the son of an English colonel by a Muhammadan wife. I knew the man well. He often called on me, and was eager for discussion. He continually avowed himself a follower of Muhammad. He was never seen in a place of Christian worship, and was often seen in the mosque. When he died, the relatives of his mother made arrangements for the funeral; but the drummers and Christian camp-followers gathered in numbers, went to the magistrate, and claimed the body on the ground that the man had been baptized in infancy. As the result of inquiry it was found that at the father's instance he had been baptized, and on this account the body was made over to the Christians, who carried it to the grave in triumph, as if they had achieved a great victory for their faith, the chaplain of the station reading the funeral service. The native Christians connected with the different missions in Benares for the most part kept aloof.

I have already spoken of orphans and their descendants, and need say nothing more about their character. They form a considerable portion of the native Christian community in the North-West.

All our missions have had accessions from both Hindus and Muhammadans, but chiefly from Hindus. I heartily wish I could say all have joined us from right motives. This I cannot say. It is undeniable that persons have joined us from unworthy motives, some because they have broken with their brethren, others who are pressed by want in hope of support, and others again in anticipation of a life of less toil if they can get under the wing of a missionary. There have even been individuals who have made it a trade to be baptized, who have told most plausible stories, have hung on missionaries for a time, and have then set out in quest of new pasture. They remind us of the wild Saxons, who submitted to baptism again and again that they might obtain the white dress given on each occasion to the baptized. Some missionaries have been far more ready than others to administer baptism, but as a rule they have examined candidates closely, have made all possible inquiry, and have baptized them only on obtaining what appeared satisfactory evidence of sincerity. Some who proved most unworthy manifested the greatest apparent earnestness, possessed a considerable degree of knowledge, and were hailed by us as a valuable accession. I narrowly escaped baptizing a man who turned out the leader of a band of thieves. He came to me professing an ardent desire for baptism, paid frequent visits, made marked progress in knowledge, and was well spoken of by persons who said they knew him; but circumstances occurred to bring suspicion over him, and he suddenly disappeared. Long afterwards we found out that he was a leader of an infamous following.

To give one of many illustrations of the way in which persons try to connect themselves with us, I may mention that one day a well-dressed native, mounted on a good horse, rode up to my door. On coming to my room he told me he had come to be baptized, as he was convinced Christ was the Saviour of the world. He was urgent for immediate baptism. Life was uncertain, he might die at any hour, and how could he know he was safe if he did not come under the wing of Christ? I told him if he believed in the Lord Jesus Christ it would be well with him, whether baptized or not, and that I could not baptize him till I should make inquiry and know more about him. It occured to me that he had a motive for such urgency which I could not discover. I sent for one of the most judicious of our native Christians, and begged him to find out what the object of the man was. He took him away, and soon returned to tell me he had got it all out—that the man had had a violent quarrel with his relatives, and had vowed to bring disgrace on the family by becoming a *Kristan*—a Christian. I recalled the man, and told him he must come to me from another motive and in another temper, if I were to baptize him. He rode away, and I never saw him afterwards.

CHAPTER XXVII.

NATIVE CHRISTIANS (Continued).

I SUPPOSE there is no community of any extent that has not unworthy members, persons that may be called its excrescence and blots, who have increased its size, as a tumour increases the size of the body, but are actually its weakness and disgrace. Such were the unworthy persons of whom I have been speaking. Very different is the general character of the native Christians connected with the various missions in Northern India. Some of our converts have made sacrifices, by avowing themselves the followers of Christ, to which persons in our country are never called. They have literally left father and mother, houses and lands, wife and children, for the sake of the Lord Jesus Christ. Whatever may have been the position of our converts, they have, as a rule, parted with much which is highly valued by their people. Caste standing, even when the caste is not considered high, secures many advantages, and is greatly prized. Its loss is deemed a dire calamity, and this loss our converts are called to endure. They join a despised and hated community, are called vile apostates, and are charged with the most sordid motives. I have heard the charge advanced against converts who, to my knowledge, had left their place in native society under the power of the profound conviction that Christ was entitled to their hearts and lives, though the conviction required of them the most painful sacrifices, and exposed them to the bitterest reproach. During my first years at Benares, one of the catechists of our Mission was a Brahman, who had been baptized by Mr. Ward of Serampore. He was stripped of the property to which he was the heir, of which the annual rental, according to an official document, was 5,000 rupees (£500), because he could not perform the funeral rites of his father. His income as catechist was small, but I often heard him charged with the lowest mercenary motives by those who knew not, and did not wish to know, anything about his antecedents. He bore the charge patiently, deeming it an honour to be reproached for his Master. He was far from being a perfect character, but no cloud ever seemed to come over his belief that Jesus was the Saviour of the world. When he was on his death-bed I asked him if he regretted the life of comparative poverty and of great reproach he had led because he had become a Christian. He tried to raise himself on his pillow, and said with an energy that startled me, "If I had a thousand lives, I would give them for Him who died for me." In reference to him and others, the remark was often made by our hearers, "We are willing to listen to you—you are a good man and have kept to your religion; but we do not wish to hear these, for they are apostates."

In all communities there are so many varieties, that the most successful attempt at characterization on the part of those who know them well can only claim an approach to correctness, and must be received with deductions. Those who look at a community from a distance, who know only a few individuals, perhaps know none at all, but judge from what they hear from others, and these deeply prejudiced, are sure to form a very false estimate. When speaking of our native Christians, I have the advantage of long and intimate acquaintance not only with those of our own Mission, but with those of other missions in Northern India, and I think I should understand them better than many who have the most superficial and partial knowledge of them, perhaps do not know them at all, and yet speak of them in depreciating terms.

I cannot speak of our native Christians, even of those who have made great sacrifices, as possessing a lofty character, as marked by signal excellence. We learn from the Epistles of the Apostle Paul he found much which was faulty in his converts, and we need not wonder at the faults which are too manifest in ours. Is there any home minister who is not tried by the conduct of some of his people? Is there any minister or missionary who has not frequent reason to be dissatisfied with himself? Indian missionaries are sometimes sorely tried by their converts. All around is a low moral tone. Slight, inadequate views of sin prevail. Truthfulness is praised, but little practised. Our people breathe a tainted atmosphere, and by becoming Christians they do not escape its deleterious effects. While these defects are frankly acknowledged, truth enables me to state, without any misgiving, there is much in our people which is very estimable. Observe their daily life, go with them to their respective businesses, and you will find them with few exceptions diligently pursuing their vocation, and honourably supporting their families. See them at their homes; you will be gladly welcomed, and you will generally find them striving to have everything clean and tidy, and as comfortable as their means permit. You will find the

Bible and a few Christian books on their shelves, and you will learn that family worship is largely observed. When conversing with them you are often impressed with their manifest sincerity, with their gratitude for having been brought into the fold of Christ, with the honour conferred on them by bearing His name, much reproached as they are on account of it, and with their desire to walk worthy of their profession. See them in the house of God, cleanly clad, and as they engage in the different parts of the service you are struck with their devout appearance. Observe them in their intercourse with each other, and you will find much of mutual kindness and helpfulness. Observe them in their intercourse with Hindus and Muhammadans, and you will find that instead of hiding their Christian profession, and being ashamed of it, they glory in it. I have said that missionaries are tried by their converts. I ought in candour to add that converts are sometimes tried by missionaries. Their training has been so different from ours, their position is so different from ours, that it is very difficult for us to understand them thoroughly; and so far as we fail to understand them, we fail in sympathy and in right action towards them.

The native churches passed through a fiery ordeal in the Mutiny of 1857, and came out of it in a way which reflected great honour on their Christian constancy. Even those who had the most favourable opinion were not prepared for the readiness shown by them to part with all, to part with life itself, rather than part with their Lord. I cannot say how many were put to death, but we know that thirty-four were killed on the Parade-ground of Furruckabad by order of the Nawab, and seven or eight perished at Cawnpore. In Foxe's "Book of Martyrs" there is not a more striking instance of witnessing to the death for the Lord Jesus than was manifested by Vilayat Ali, in the Chandnee Chauk of Delhi, when, surrounded by infuriated Muhammadans calling on him to recant or die, he declared Christ to be his Saviour and Lord, and when falling under the swords of his enemies uttered with his last breath the prayer of Stephen, "*Lord Jesus, receive my spirit.*" The account is furnished by a witness of the scene. There were defections, but if our view be confined to Christians connected with the different missions they were remarkably few, fewer, it is affirmed, than those of Europeans and East Indians. One whom I knew well, though he was not of our Mission, apostatized to save his life, and died most miserably, abandoned by his new fellow-religionists, and tenderly watched by those whom he had left. Full details of the conduct of the native Christians in that terrible crisis are given by Mr. Sherring in his book, "The Indian Church during the Great Rebellion." This book had, I believe, a considerable circulation when it was published, but like many other good books it has passed into oblivion. The information it contains was furnished by persons intimately acquainted with the facts, and is very valuable as proving the genuineness and constancy of native Christian piety. It gives more insight into the real character of the native Christian community than can be obtained by perusal of large volumes full of ordinary mission details. The friends of missions would do good service by seeking its republication.

The loyalty of the native Christians to the British Government, as well as the constancy of their Christian faith, was strikingly shown throughout the Mutiny. This loyalty was maintained amidst much fitted to discourage it in the conduct towards them of Europeans, both official and non-official.

We have seen native Christians in joy and sorrow, in trial and temptation. We have been present at their death-bed, and have heard their words of hope and trust when entering the dark valley. We have had abundant reason to regard them with esteem and love. With many we have had pleasant intercourse, and from our intercourse with some we have received intellectual and spiritual profit. At one time there was a small band of highly-educated native Christians at Benares connected with the different missions. It gave us great pleasure to have them now and then spending an evening with us. They were always ready to start some important subject, and their remarks were stimulating and instructive. I remember more than once our remarking, when they went away, Could we have had a more pleasant and profitable evening if our European brethren had been with us? At the great Missionary Conferences which have been held in recent years the native Christian brethren have taken a prominent part, and both intellectually and spiritually they have been found worthy of standing abreast of their brethren from Europe and America. It must be acknowledged there has been a difficulty at times in adjusting the exact relationship of these highly-educated native brethren to their missionary friends, and there has been in consequence unpleasant jarring; but amidst differences Christian principle has asserted its uniting power, and their ordinary bearing is that of mutual esteem and love.

It may be said, "If native Christians as a community deserve the character you have given them, how is it that people from India speak so much against them?" The explanation can be easily given.

There is no part of the mission-field, the South Seas, Africa, the West Indies, China, as well as India, from which persons have not come affirming that the so-called converts are changed in name only; that they are no better than they were, and in many cases worse. Do we not find analogous cases nearer home? It is often said of professors of religion—very truly of individuals, very untruly of the class—that they are less worthy of trust than avowedly worldly persons. Large communities remarkable for religious zeal, like the people of Wales, are condemned in the face of favourable evidence which seems well authenticated. Persons have even stoutly maintained that Christianity itself has been a failure in its moral influence on the nations. Want of sympathy and antipathy blind the mind to facts, and lead to most erroneous judgments. The great majority of Europeans in heathen countries have no sympathy with missions, and have neither the knowledge nor the spirit indispensable to the formation of a correct judgment. They hear a loose report of converts from persons who in turn have been told by others what they say, and the report is at once believed and circulated. They have, perhaps, met an unworthy native bearing the Christian name, and he is regarded as a fit representative of the entire community.

It is a common opinion among many of our countrymen in India that Hinduism is as good for Hindus as Christianity is for us, and they cannot conceive why a person should leave the one for the other except from sinister motives. When speaking on one occasion with a lady who regularly attended church, and no doubt deemed herself an excellent Christian, about a native gentleman of high rank, whose kindly temper and courteous demeanour we were both praising, I said,

"Would that he were a follower of our Saviour!" She looked surprised, and said, "Do you think so? He is, I think, a better man by remaining as he is." So strong is this feeling with some English people, that a native who calls himself a Christian is regarded by them as on that account a suspicious character. I know a well-educated native Christian who applied for a Government situation. He had good certificates; they were sent in, and when the official to whom he applied came to know he was a Christian—he knew nothing more about him—he threw them aside with the word "*namunzoor*," "not accepted" —the technical term for "rejected." One result of this English dislike to native Christians is that natives have told me that none but missionaries and a few associated with them wished them to become Christians; that English people generally wished them to remain Hindus. It can be conceived how great is the stumbling-block thus put in our way. A Church of England missionary of great experience once said to me, "Would that there were no Europeans near us! We might then hope for progress." I am not to vindicate the remark. I mention it to show the effect on the mind of a devoted missionary by English hostility to the conversion of natives. On every side, from European as well as from native society, there is every worldly obstacle to their embracing the Gospel.

At one time there were obstacles to the profession of Christianity which do not now exist. When India was being brought under the sway of England, our rulers regarded the Gospel as a disturbing and threatening element, which ought to be carefully excluded. Long after the Christian feeling at home had forced open the door, the Gospel was treated as an intruder to be in every possible way thwarted and disgraced. In illustration of the opposition the Gospel had to encounter, I quote a few sentences from a recently-published volume, "Asiatic Studies, Religious and Social," by Sir Alfred C. Lyall, K.C.B., the present Lieutenant-Governor of the North-West Provinces :—"We disbursed impartially to Hindus, Mussulmans, and Parsees, to heterodox and orthodox, to Juggarnath's Car, and to the shrine of a Muhammadan who had died fighting against infidels, perhaps against ourselves." "The chief officers of the Company in India were so cautious to disown any political connexion with Christianity that they were occasionally reported to have no religion at all." "Up to the year 1831 native Christians had been placed under the strongest civil disabilities by our regulations . . . Converts were liable to be deprived not only of property, but of their wives and children; and they seem to have been generally treated as unlucky outcasts, with whom no one need be at any trouble of using any sort of consideration." We are told that they were even forced by Government order to pull the car of Juggarnaut, and severely punished if they refused. According to a parliamentary paper of 1832, "our interference extended over every detail of management: we regulated funds, repaired buildings, kept in order cars and images, appointed servants, and purveyed the various commodities required for use of the pagodas." Under home pressure this state of things has gradually given place to neutrality, which, if impartially maintained, is I suppose the only policy open to us in the peculiar circumstances of India.

I have already said there are very unworthy persons bearing the name of native Christians. To judge our Indian churches by these is as unfair as to judge English Christians in India by Englishmen, of whom, alas! there are many, soldiers and others, who are notorious for drunkenness and licentiousness. We have even English beggars in India, wretched men, who have drifted out of the army, railway, or other department, and who disgrace our name. Strong men have come whimpering to my door, to whom I have given help, and I have seen them a few hours afterwards—I remember one case well—rolling in the bazaar in beastly drunkenness. It would be as fair to take these men as a specimen of English Christians, as to judge native Christians by persons bearing the name while they disgrace it.

The very acknowledgment of missionaries about the imperfections of their communities, about the utter hollowness of some individuals, has been turned into adverse testimony. In the recent meeting at Exeter Hall to welcome the Madagascar missionaries, Messrs. Cousin and Shaw, Mr. Cousin, in the course of his very interesting address, said that much of the Christianity of the Malagash was "purely nominal and utterly worthless." I should not at all wonder if some day I found this brought forward as a missionary's acknowledgment that the Christianity of the Malagash is purely nominal and utterly worthless, and that missions in Madagascar, as elsewhere, had been a failure.

The support of native Christians has sorely tried and perplexed missionaries. They have been desirous, on the one hand, of holding out no inducement to persons to join them from unworthy motives; and on the other they have felt that persons thrust out of their caste and employment, and not infrequently from their family, had claims on help, with which every Christian feeling bound them to comply. Persons able to work have never been allowed to live in idleness, but the difficulty has been to find suitable work. In some missions, when persons have shown an aptness for domestic service they have been trained to it. In a number of missions trades have been started, and have been carried on for a longer or shorter period, with more or less success; but, as a rule, the relation of employer and employed does not accord well with the relation of pastor and people. The difficulty continues, and will no doubt continue, but it is decreasing every year. When travelling down through Northern India in 1877 we found Christians in every place at which we stopped, and we learned they were supporting themselves in various modes, in printing offices, bookbinding establishments, railways, and public offices. A number were in domestic service. I wish fewer were thus employed. When anything goes wrong in a house the Hindu and Muhammadan servants are sure to blame the Christians; masters and mistresses look for more from them than can be reasonably expected, and they no doubt are apt to fall into the well-known and objectionable habits of the class. The more capable of the native Christians, the higher in character and education, are for the most part employed as teachers, catechists, and native preachers. A few have risen to responsible and lucrative positions in civil life. A native Christian from Bengal held for some years, to the great satisfaction of both Europeans and natives, the office of Postmaster of Benares. He and his wife were members of our native church. Another member of our church for a time was the Inspector of Post-offices in the Benares district.

I believe in every mission in the North-West native Christians contribute regularly to the support and diffusion of the Gospel, and, considering their means, their contributions are liberal. I remember hearing years ago of a native church in Calcutta agreeing, without a dissentient voice, to give a month's salary for the erection of their new church building—an act of liberality which has been seldom equalled in our country.

Much has been said about the compound system, as it has been called—Christians living together apart from the heathen, and in most cases in the immediate neighbourhood of the missionary's residence. Much has been said, I think unjustly, in condemnation of this arrangement. It is not the hot-bed, which it has been called, in which robust Christian character cannot be produced. Native Christians, thus living together, hold constant intercourse with the heathen in the business of life, and are at the same time saved from the peculiar trials and temptations incident to living among Hindus and Muhammadans. So far as native Christians make their light to shine, it will be well seen by the heathen though their dwellings be apart. One great advantage of living in a mission compound, near the place of worship and the missionary's residence, is that wives and children can regularly attend public worship, and can come under the teaching of the missionary, and especially the missionary's wife, as otherwise they could not have come. For a time we had quite a number of native Christians in our compound at Benares, who paid a small rent for their houses, and went out every day to attend to their respective callings. If they had lived in the city I cannot conceive how mothers and children could have attended worship as they did, or how my wife could have taught the children and held constant intercourse with the women. Because living in the compound, it does not follow that they are dependent on the mission for support. There is nothing more desired by missionaries than that their people should maintain themselves by their own exertions. Living among the heathen is often indispensable—it is so increasingly with our native Christians; but where circumstances admit, I think great advantages result from Christians living near each other and near the mission church. In our own country, are not favourable surroundings sought for the young and the inexperienced?

When I look back to the beginning of 1839, when I landed in Calcutta, and compare the native Christian community of that day with what it is now, I am struck with the great change which has taken place. If we confine the term to those connected with missions, they were then a mere handful. Now they are considerable in number, and they have become a recognized and appreciable portion of native society. They are increasing in number, though not so rapidly in the North as in the South, and are becoming rooted in the land. The largest native Christian community in the North-West is, I suppose, that connected with the missions of the American Episcopal Methodist Church in Rohilkund and Oude. It is largely composed of Muzbee Sikhs, a people much despised by both Muhammadans and Hindus. Of late the Salvation Army has entered on the campaign against Hinduism and Muhammadanism. Its organ boasts largely of success, but its statements have been strongly questioned by persons acquainted with the facts, on whose warm attachment to the cause of Christ full dependence can be placed. A well-known missionary of the Episcopal Methodist Church in Oude has been lately pursuing the tactics of the Salvation Army. Accompanied by a band of native Christians, he has been entering villages and towns with song and drum and tambourine. The people in crowds have gathered round him. He and his brethren have preached Christ to them, have urged them to accept Him as their Saviour, and have given on the spot baptism, *chin*—the mark of the Christian Church, to any avowing their readiness to become Christ's disciples. Time will show how far the work is genuine. Perhaps we old missionaries have been too slow in administering baptism. Of this I am sure, that nothing is more fallacious as the test of success than the number of persons baptized—so different is the opinion held by missionaries regarding the qualifications required in order to baptize. Native Christians are more self-dependent than they were, and are receiving a healthy impulse from feeling that they must push out for themselves. They have to contend against much which is adverse and hurtful, but without indulging too sanguine hopes we may firmly anticipate for them a brighter and better future than their past has been.

CHAPTER XXVIII.

THE PEOPLE AMONG WHOM WE LABOUR.

MUHAMMADANS.

ALL over Northern India—I may say all over India—we find the followers of Muhammad. They are very unequally distributed. In some districts they form the majority, in others their number is very small, while in the cities they abound. There is among them all the variety of station which might be expected in a community composed of millions, ranging from princes, wealthy landholders, and great merchants, down to labourers and beggars. There is among them all variety of culture, from profound learning in a narrower or wider groove, down to utter illiteracy and gross ignorance. There is also variety of character, many leading notoriously wicked lives, while others are noted for goodness, and are honourable and useful members of society.

Looking at the Quran and the Bible, one might suppose there is a close accord between them, as both assert the unity and sovereignty of God, both condemn idolatry, and in both the same names continually meet us, such as Abraham, Jacob, Joseph, David, Solomon, and our Lord Jesus Christ. In fact, however, in India, as elsewhere, Muhammadanism has shown itself intensely hostile to the Gospel. The reason is apparent. I think it is difficult for any one to read with candour the Quran on the one hand, and the Bible, especially the New Testament, on the other, without perceiving the marked contrariety between them, notwithstanding their agreement on some points.

A true follower of Jesus Christ, one imbued with the spirit of His teaching and bent on the imitation of His example, cannot fail to cultivate holiness of heart and life, to cherish a humble, lowly temper, to look on all with love, however unworthy of love their character and conduct may be, and to promote their good in every way within his power. A follower of Muhammad, so far as he is imbued with his teaching, regards God with profound reverence as the Sovereign of the universe, deems homage to Him most due, looks with indignation on the worship of idols, attaches immense importance to outward rites and services, glories in Islam, pays comparatively little attention to inward excellence, and sees no need for a change of heart. As a worshipper and servant of Allah, following the precepts of the Prophet of the later age, he deems himself the spiritual aristocrat of the race, and looks down with scorn on all outside the pale of his community, whom he is in some cases bound to put to death, and in all cases to subject to degrading conditions, so far as he has the power. However wicked his conduct may be, as a worshipper of Allah he is sure of more tender treatment in another world than that which awaits Christians and idolaters. Thus the typical Muhammadan is one who scrupulously observes the laws of Islam, goes through his devotions with all the regularity of a soldier on drill, fasts at the appointed season, gives alms to the poor, attends to all prescribed rites, and at least once in his life goes on pilgrimage to Mecca and Medina. Outward religiousness, pride and self-righteousness, are his distinguishing characteristics.

Much has been said about the sensuality of Muhammadans. The sanction given by Muhammad to polygamy and extreme facility of divorce has borne bitter fruit. His own example has had a depraving influence. He alleged, indeed, a special Divine sanction for the dissoluteness of his later life, but this has not deterred his followers from thinking they could not go far wrong in imitating him. In addition to these facilities for a life of sensual enjoyment, the teaching of the Prophet in reference to female slaves has had a most depraving effect on family life. The Hindustanee expression for *libertine*, *profligate*—*luchcha*—is, I think, more frequently applied to Muhammadans in Northern India than to any other class of the community. It must be confessed, however, there is so much licentiousness among other classes—not only among Hindus, but I am grieved to say among many from our own land, soldiers and others—that I can scarcely join in declaring Muhammadans sinners in this respect above all others. There is this difference between the licentiousness of so-called Christians and Muhammadans, that in the teachings of the Gospel, while no unnatural restraint is laid on those who accept it, the strongest motives are brought to bear on them in favour of purity of heart and in opposition to licentiousness of life; while in the teachings of the Quran, amidst severe condemnation of the gratification of unlawful desire in some forms, there is much, if not to encourage, at least to give every facility for a life fatal to personal and domestic purity, a facility of which the adherents of Islam have largely availed themselves.

While agreeing with the views generally held by Christians regarding the teaching of the Quran and its influence in the formation of character, I cannot join in the sweeping condemnation of the Muhammadans which I have sometimes heard, as if they were one mass of corruption. In the middle and lower classes in Northern India we are told, by those whose testimony can be trusted, monogamy is the rule. Many lead a quiet, orderly life, with the domestic affections in full play which beautify and gladden the home. A Muhammadan writer, who may be supposed to know his own people, tells us that polygamy is getting out of favour, and that a strong feeling has set in in favour of a man having only one woman to wife. Among them there are undoubtedly persons of high character, whose bearing would do honour to the adherents of a far higher creed. I have conversed with some who seemed to me set on knowing and doing the will of God, who showed, so far as I could obtain an insight into their character, a reverent, earnest, humble temper, as if they had come under the power of the few passages, occurring here and there in the Quran, which inculcate spirituality of mind and love to all men, and as if they had in a measure escaped from the externalism so prominent in that book, and from its hard, fierce, bitter tone towards all who refuse to receive it as a revelation from heaven. With two Muhammadans I was for years on as friendly terms as I could be with any whose belief and practice differed so widely from my own. As to courteous, kindly demeanour, they were all that could be desired. I had many an earnest talk with them on the highest subjects, and I was struck with the apparent candour with which they listened to all I had to say. They read with evident interest books I gave them, and in the case of one such an impression was made that I hoped he was coming to the acknowledgment of Christ as his Lord and Saviour; but after going to his Moulvies he kept to Muhammad, though with manifest misgiving.

While I cannot join in the sweeping condemnation of Muhammadans, I must acknowledge my experience accords with that of my missionary brethren regarding those with whom I have come ordinarily into contact. When I have been speaking to a company of Hindus, and have apparently secured their attention, I have been sorry to see a Mussulman coming up, as past experience had prepared me for the immediate introduction of such questions as the Trinity, the Sonship of Christ, His propitiatory sacrifice, and not infrequently the eating of pork. I have done my best to stave off such untimely discussion, and to keep to the subject I was teaching, but in not a few instances my audience has been broken up by the new-comer insisting on being heard. During my long missionary career I have had many discussions with Muhammadans in public and in private, in some cases conducted with a calmness and fairness which promised good results; but in still more numerous cases with a readiness on their part to resort to the veriest sophistry, and fly from one point to another, and with a love of disputation which led to wrangling, and could accomplish no good. The controversy between Christianity and Muhammadanism has been carried on by the press as well as by oral discussion. In this department the late Dr. Pffander, Sir William Muir, and Mr. Hughes of Peshawur, have done excellent service.

It might be supposed that as Muhammadanism is so near to Christianity that it may almost be called a

Christian heresy, and as we have in consequence much common ground, we might expect to find its adherents more accessible than Hindus to the Christian missionary. The opposite is the case, furnishing another illustration of the fact that no religionists are so antagonistic to each other as those who most nearly approximate. At the present time all over the world, Popery, under the conduct of the Jesuits, is far more hostile to Protestant missions than any form of heathenism.

It ought to be mentioned to the credit of Muhammadanism that it arose as a protest against polytheism and the worship of idols. This protest it has maintained down to our day. Not even a religious symbol is allowed to appear in their places of worship, and hence the marked contrast mosques present not only to Hindu temples, but to Christian churches.

Muhammadanism is a proselytizing religion as well as Christianity. During my Indian career I have heard of a convert now and then from Hinduism in the North-West, and very occasionally one from Christianity; but these accessions have been very few. In Bengal, on the other hand, it appears that during the last thirty or forty years a great number of low-caste people have been drawn into the Muhammadan ranks, many of them small farmers, who think that by belonging to a large and influential community they can the better contend with the landlords. It is said that the change is simply one of name and ritual.

The accessions from Muhammadanism to Christianity have been very few; but some of the best converts in the North-West belong to this class.

For centuries Hindus and Muhammadans have been near neighbours in India. In the ordinary course of life they have had much intercourse with each other, and have exerted a strong mutual influence, the Muhammadans, especially of the lower class, having become in a measure Hinduized, while the Hindus of the lower class have become, if I may use such a word, in some degree Muhammadanized. I believe the stricter Muhammadans are of pure Mogul and Pathan descent, while the more lax are the many who at different times have been drawn or forced into Islam. Our Muhammadan servants speak continually of their caste, have many Hindu notions, and follow many Hindu practices. Low-caste Hindus, on the other hand, are prominent in some Muhammadan processions. Both Muhammadans and Hindus, as a rule, are satisfied with their respective position, as assigned to them by Allah or Fate, have no repugnance to each other, and no wish to disturb each other.

So far, however, as Muhammadans and Hindus are imbued with their respective systems they must be antagonistic; and their antagonism, though generally latent, every now and then breaks out into fierce strife, which but for the interposition of Government would lead to civil war. Early in this century there was in Benares a pitched battle between them, when they assailed each other with the utmost fury, and were separated by military force. All have heard of a recent conflict in Southern India, where blood was shed and property destroyed. About thirty years ago Oude was threatened with the outbreak of a war between the parties. There have been recently conflicts in Rohilkund on the occasion of processions, which but for prompt interference would have led to disastrous results.

Of late years a reforming party has arisen among the Muhammadans with both political and religious ends in view. This party painfully realizes the loss incurred by their fellow-religionists on account of their neglect of the English language, and their failure to accommodate themselves to their new masters, thus allowing the Hindus to get in advance of them. They consequently discourage exclusive attention to Arabic and Persian literature, and advocate the cultivation of English. A few of this class have come to England to prosecute their studies, but for the many who must remain in their own land an institution has been opened at Allygurh, in the North-West, in which provision is made for imparting a liberal education. It cannot be expected that Indian Muhammadans can have a strong liking to the English Government, but this reforming party wishes to reconcile itself to the new order of things, and to identify itself with our rule so far as the Quran permits. In religious belief these reformers range from strict orthodoxy to rank rationalism. Their leader is an able and ardent advocate of Islam, though he has thrown off what he deems unauthorized and hurtful accretions, and many of his followers no doubt agree with him. A Bengalee Muhammadan, a graduate of Cambridge, has published a book entitled "The Life of Muhammad," which is saturated with rationalistic views. I cannot suppose he stands alone in his rationalism, but I have no means of knowing to what extent his views are shared by others. The whole party is the antipodes to the Wahabees, the extreme Puritans of Islam, who aim at following strictly the instructions of the Quran and the Traditions, and wage war to the knife against Christians and idolaters. Between the Wahabees and the reformers there is a very numerous party—it is supposed the great majority of Muhammadans—who have little sympathy with the strictness of the former, but as little with the looseness of the latter, who in their opinion are sacrificing Islam to their ambitious and selfish views. Between the reformers and those who cannot advance with them there has been sharp controversy, and there is no prospect of its coming to an end.

CHAPTER XXIX.

THE PEOPLE AMONG WHOM WE LABOUR (Continued).

HINDUS.

I HAVE endeavoured in my account of Benares to describe the Hindu idolatry there practised, and in my account of our missionary preaching I have stated the arguments by which that idolatry is defended. The Hindu system, it is well known, is at once pantheistic and polytheistic. The universe, we are told, is God expanded. *Brahm*—he alone is the Existent One; but there are several persons and objects in which he is more manifest than in others, and as owing to *Maya* (illusion) we believe in our separate existence, it is fitting that to these objects special honour should be paid. I have mentioned the hideous aspect of the images worshipped at Benares, and their hideous aspect well accords with the character attributed to the gods worshipped under these forms.

We are all familiar with the maxim, Like priest, like people. May we say, Like God, like worshipper? If so, we must regard the Hindus as in the very mire of moral debasement. Just think of a whole people acting like Shiva, Doorga, and Krishna! I think it cannot be doubted by any one who looks at the nature of the human mind, and the power exercised over it by its belief, that the worship of these and similar gods, along with the prevalent pantheistic and fatalistic views, which strike at the very root of moral distinctions, have done much to deprave the Hindu mind. The people, indeed, often assert "to the powerful there is no fault." The gods had the power and the opportunity to do what they did, and therefore no fault attached to their conduct; but ordinary persons have neither the one nor the other, and for them it would be very culpable to pursue the same course. Can a people fail to occupy a low place on the plane of morals to whom the maxim I have quoted would be tolerable? I believe they do as a people occupy a low place, and yet not nearly so low as might have been anticipated.

There is much to counteract the influence exerted on the Hindus by the evil example of their gods, by their excessive trust in outward rites apart from all mental working, and by the pantheistic teaching of their philosophers. They retain a moral nature, and acknowledge the distinction between right and wrong as readily as we do, though the distinction be inconsistent with the views they often express. The requirements of society and of daily life exert a powerful and salutary restraint by the obstacle which they present to a vicious career. The family constitution has conferred immense benefit on the Hindus, as on other nations.

It must be acknowledged that however long we may reside in India, our knowledge of the inner life of the people is very limited. We may be for years on the best terms with them; we may meet them frequently, and converse with them freely on all subjects; there may be not only acquaintance, but to all appearance friendship: and yet we have no entrance into the family circle, we cannot join them in the family meal, we can scarcely get a glimpse into their home life. If they be of the poorer class they would be shocked at our entering their houses, and conversing with their women and children. If of a higher class, they visit us and we visit them. They have a room of audience in which they welcome us. On occasions they prepare sumptuous feasts for Europeans, of which they themselves do not partake. However friendly we may be with natives of rank in Northern India, it is difficult, often impossible, to secure an interview between our wives and the female members of their families. As to English gentlemen, they never see the face of a native lady. Still, notwithstanding our being kept so far outside Hindu family life, we know enough about it to be sure there is often strong family affection. We have many proofs that parents regard their children with the most tender love; and we know that in the lower classes, at least, children often requite this love by sending a large portion of their wages to their aged parents. I myself have often been the channel of communication. It cannot be doubted that this family affection is widely extended, and has a very happy influence on the character and life of the people.

Professor Max Muller, in his recently-published book, "India, what can it teach us?" discusses at length the character of the Hindus. He quotes the views entertained by persons of large Indian experience, who had mixed freely with all classes, and yet differ widely in their testimony, showing that in forming an estimate of the character of a community we are greatly influenced by our temperament and by the standard we employ. Sir Thomas Munro, the famous Governor of Madras, speaks of the character and attainments of the Hindus in the most laudatory terms. He says, "If civilization is to become an article of trade between England and India, I am convinced that England will gain by the import cargo." Sir Charles Trevelyan, on the other hand, speaks of them as a morally depraved people, to whom "the phenomenon is truly astonishing" "of a race of men on whose word perfect confidence may be placed." "The natives require to be taught rectitude of conduct much more than literature and science."

The Professor is evidently inclined to take the favourable view. He thinks the ordinary view of their falsehood and dishonesty is applicable only to the rabble of the cities and the frequenters of our courts, but is most unjust to the unsophisticated people of the country, whose truthfulness he extols. After the laudation of these honest and truthful people, I must say I was amused with the *naïveté* of the learned Professor, when he goes on to show that the excellence of his *protegés* is not sufficiently strong to be maintained in the face of temptation. He says, "A man out of his village community is out of his element and under temptation. What would be called theft or robbery at home, is called a raid or conquest if directed against distant villages; and what would be falsehood or trickery in private life, is honoured by the name of policy and diplomacy if successful against strangers." The lauded truthfulness and honesty are so delicate that they cannot stand the breath of the nipping cold which has to be encountered when they leave their sheltered enclosure. The excellence is, according to the Professor, though he does not say so in words, merely conventional, as it rests on the principle of mutual insurance among those who form a closely-knitted community, bound together by common interests and associations. Even then excellence needs to be guarded by an oath, which is viewed with superstitious awe. I do not think the Professor's friends will thank him for this defence of the morality of their countrymen.

When I think of the wickedness rampant among large classes in a country like our own, notwithstanding our great privileges, I shrink from applying to the Hindus the strong terms of condemnation which I have often heard. There is among them, as I have already said, much family affection; they are, in ordinary circumstances, very courteous; they often manifest a kindly disposition; almsgiving is reckoned a high virtue; many lead quiet, orderly, industrious lives; and, as Max Muller tells us, from the earliest age *satya*, "truth," in its widest sense, has been represented by them as the very pillar on which goodness rests, though it must be allowed it has been much more praised than practised.

Am I then to say, as many have done, that Hinduism has done its adherents no harm, and that Christianity has done its adherents no good—that the Hindus as a people stand as high morally as we do? With every desire to speak of them as favourably as I can, with a pleasing recollection of many acts of kindness and courtesy, and with every desire to rid myself of prejudice, I must dissent strongly from this view. I cannot forget the lurid light cast on the native character during the Mutiny; the treachery, ingratitude, falsehood, and cruelty shown by many who gloried in their caste purity—relieved, however, it is only right to acknowledge, by notable instances of faithfulness and kindness. I cannot but remember the impression often made on my mind of their low standard of character, the absence of high motive, even when full expression has been given to the distinction between right and wrong. Happily, in our land there are many, in every class of society, who, as the result of faith in the Lord Jesus Christ, hate sin in every form, and strive after excellence, an excellence springing from supreme love to God, and prompting to sustained effort for the good of man, for which we look in vain among the best of Hindus, though among them we discern the workings of conscience and the desire to do what is right. The standard of character is undoubtedly far higher among us than it is among Hindus, and this standard, protesting as it does against wickedness, and calling us to aspire after goodness, is in itself an incalculable benefit to a community. For many a day it has been my settled conviction that Hindus are vastly better than, looking at their religion, we could expect to find them, and that we on the other hand fall far below the excellence to which our religion summons us. If Hinduism was allowed full sway over its adherents society would go to pieces, while we should rise to the excellence of angels if we were to come under the full sway of the Gospel.

All have heard of the caste system of India, but only those who have lived among the people can understand its innumerable ramifications and its remarkable effects. Every caste, down to the lowest, is endlessly sub-divided. There are Brahmans who would as soon eat, drink, and intermarry with people of low caste, as with many who like themselves boast of Brahmanical blood. In books the Sudras are described as the fourth, the low, servile caste; but in fact a vast number in Northern India, who are loosely reckoned Hindus, are far below the Sudras, and thus the Sudras acquire a relatively high place.

These low-caste people, on whom the people above them look down with contempt, are in their own fashion as tenacious of caste as their superiors, and they, too, multiply their divisions, one class maintaining its superiority to others. We have a large community called *Chumars,* "leather-people" as the word means, though many of them have nothing to do with leather. One of them once told me there were twelve divisions in their caste. We had near us at Ranee Khet a little colony of Dhobees, washermen, whom I visited now and then. I observed some huts were built separate from the rest, and I asked the reason. The man to whom I was speaking, for his class an intelligent man, expressed his surprise I did not know the reason. He said, with an air of dignity, "These are of an inferior order, and it is requisite their huts should be built apart."

It has been often shown that this caste system is most baleful. It narrows the sympathies of the people, keeps them in the same groove, fetters their minds, represses individuality, and is a bar to progress. It would be unfair, however, to say that all its consequences are pernicious. It so far benefits those bound by it that it restrains them from some forms of evil, and secures mutual helpfulness, just as the close trade guilds of our own country did, of which we have happily got rid. When the clan system was in full force among the Scotch Highlanders, there were broken men, men who had left the clan or were expelled from it, and these were notorious for their crimes. In like manner there are persons who break away from caste, and are the worst members of the community.

The patriarchal system, the system so prevalent in India, by which the people, instead of forming separate families in their separate dwellings, all form one household, to a large extent with a common purse and under a common rule, is perhaps still more fitted to fetter the mind and to obstruct progress than even caste itself. Those who have embraced Christ as their Saviour have often suffered more from their own kindred, dwelling together, than from their caste brethren.

Many things tend to the disintegration of caste, such as education, the subjection of all to the same laws, the growing demands of commerce, and travelling together in railway-carriages. The attractions of the railway, notwithstanding its disregard of class distinctions, are irresistible. Thousands of pilgrims thus make their way to distant shrines, though by travelling in this easy fashion they lose the merit which suffering would bring. When railways were constructed, a proposal was made by leading Hindus to have separate carriages for separate castes, but compliance with the proposal was of course out of the question; and now high Brahmans and low Chumars—who are never seen in the same temple even though they worship the same gods, as the presence of a Chumar there would be deemed a profanation—may be seen packed in the same carriage in as close contact as two human beings can be. When they separate the Brahmans have recourse to lustrations, and satisfy themselves the impurity has been washed away.

In the great Presidency cities caste is no doubt greatly weakened. Many openly violate its rules, and are never called to account, but these very persons take care to maintain their caste position for certain domestic and social purposes. Leaving these cities and a small class scattered over the country, the mass of the people seem as much bound by caste as they ever were, so far as its outward requirements are concerned, though, as I have said, there are no doubt influences widely spread which tend to its relaxation. This is the case in Northern India, at any rate.

Much has been said about the Brahmist movement. The number of its professed adherents is very small, but many of the educated class are imbued with its spirit. Years ago branches of the Brahmist Sumaj were formed in the great cities of the North-West by young Bengalees employed in the public offices. For a time their services were kept up zealously, but soon they declined. The last time I heard about these communities most had ceased to exist, and only two or three had any sign of vitality. So far as I have learned, the Brahmists have had very few adherents from the Hindus of the North-West. At first sight Brahmism seems an advance towards the Gospel, and a preparation for its reception, but the best of our native Christians in Calcutta look on it as furnishing a welcome abode to those who cannot remain Hindus, and yet for various reasons refuse to embrace Christ as their Lord and Saviour. Its avowed hostility to definite doctrine, to what is denounced as dogma, the dreamy sentimentalism characteristic of the system, the ignoring to a great extent of the terrible facts of man's depravity and guilt, and the coquetting with Vedism, do little towards bringing its adherents to the feet of Jesus. The Brahmists used at one time to taunt us with our divisions, but for a long time they have had two separate Sumajes, composed respectively of Conservatives and Liberals. In consequence of Chunder Sen's Hindu proclivities in his later years, the Liberals became divided among themselves, the majority having seceded, while a few remained his devoted followers, who are likely to settle down into a Hindu sect, tinged with Christian thought and feeling.

From time to time reformers have appeared among the Hindus. Gautam, the Sakya Saint, was one of the earliest and greatest of the class. Successive reformers have had a great following, but the stream has not risen above its source. From Gautam downward some fundamental principles of Hinduism have been retained, and in the end these principles have asserted much of their former sway. This threatens to be the case with Brahmism. Notwithstanding its assertion of the Divine Unity, it has a strong pantheistic tinge, and already we see its effect. As it has arisen in a measure as the result of Christian teaching, and among a people to whom the Gospel is made known, it may be hoped that many, influenced by it, may travel upward to the light, instead of turning to the darkness from which they have emerged.

Increasing effort has been put forth in late years for the mental and spiritual improvement of the female portion of the population. From the commencement of missions, the wives of missionaries have bestowed much labour on the women and girls to whom they could find access. These have been well-nigh exclusively either Christians, or of the lower class of society. Very occasionally individuals of a higher class come under Christian teaching. A daughter of the late Rajah of Coorg, a state prisoner at Benares, was for a time under the tuition of Mrs. Kennedy. She was brought daily to our house, sat with us at table, and was taught with our children. The Rajah wished her to be brought up as a Christian and an English lady, in the hope that he might thus be helped in getting back his kingdom. Eventually she was brought to England, was baptized by the Archbishop of Canterbury, the Queen standing sponsor, and was married to an English officer. She survived her marriage a very short time. This was altogether an exceptional case. It has been most difficult for the wives of missionaries to obtain even an occasional interview with native ladies, as I have already intimated, though their husbands have been our frequent and friendly visitors. From the Reports of Zenana Missions we learn that of late years access has been obtained to many native families which had till recently been excluded from all Christian, and, indeed, from all European influence. The lady physician is often welcome where the ordinary teacher can find no entrance. In a city like Benares—and I suppose it is the same elsewhere—except for the lady physician in her professional capacity, and only rarely even in that capacity, the door of the Zenanas in the houses of the great magnates continues shut against all who would seek to awake and guide the dormant minds there.

Nothing can be conceived more deplorable than the condition of the ladies of India, living, as the phrase is, behind the curtain. They are, as a rule, utterly uneducated, know nothing of books, are shut out from the world, and have no refuge from *ennui* in such employments as needlework, knitting, and embroidery, for which the nimble fingers of the sisterhood are so well adapted. They have no society beyond the women of the household, their husbands and their children. An occasional glimpse has been got by our ladies into their state, and, as might have been expected, their minds have been found utterly childish and dwarfed. Happily for themselves the vast majority of the women of the country are under no such bondage. Their husbands cannot afford to curtain them. They move about freely as they do in our country, only with the hood ready to come down over the face. They are seen in the streets of Benares as they are seen in the streets of our own towns.

All have heard of the low view of woman entertained in India, and of the humiliating customs to which she is subjected; but nature asserts itself there as elsewhere, and notwithstanding all the inferiority with which she is charged, she exercises a profound influence on the male portion of the community. This is recognized by the people always saying, *Ma*, *Bap*—Mother, Father—not *Father and Mother*, as we say. It is well known that in the large households of which I have spoken the dowager lady is the supreme ruler, often the tyrant—not the less a tyrant because in her youth she had been treated as a slave. The state of widows, many of them mere children, is sad indeed.

Shut out though we be to a large extent from native families, we have many proofs presented to us of the power of female influence, a power often most perniciously exerted, as it is the power of ignorance and superstition, a power opposed to all intellectual and spiritual progress. The devout women of India are often our most formidable enemies, as they were of Paul in Antioch in Pisidia, and no doubt in other places. Some of our converts have known from painful experience what their opposition to the Gospel is, and it cannot be doubted that many have been prevented from joining us by the pressure brought to bear on them by their mothers, wives, and sisters. Well may every friend of India pray earnestly that Zenana Missions may be crowned with success.

A returned missionary is often asked what are the prospects of missions. From careful and trustworthy statistics we learn the number of Christians is increasing rapidly. It is right to observe that this increase has come mainly from the non-Aryan tribes, and people of low caste. We have valuable converts from the higher castes, but they are few. When we leave statistics we have recourse to impression, and that impression depends greatly on circumstances, and still more, perhaps, on the temperament of the observer. It is very difficult to gauge public opinion. When we think of all the influences at work, such as education, both primary and more advanced, Christian literature, missionary effort in many forms, railway travelling, commerce, and a Government bent on doing justice, we look forward with hope to an awaking of the Hindu mind, under which it will seek and embrace the highest good.

The obstacles to success are most formidable, so formidable that, notwithstanding promising appearances, we should despair if we were not assured that the work is of God. The literature of our own country is strengthening the opposition to us. The unbelief of many educated natives, an unbelief springing both from repugnance to the Gospel and from dread of the sacrifices to which its acceptance would subject them, is fortified by the perusal of sceptical books and periodicals. Years ago I met a Bengalee far up in the mountains, who told me I need not speak to him about Christianity, for all reasonable people in England were abandoning it. In proof he put into my hands a letter from Professor Newman in answer to a letter he had sent to him. The Professor counselled his correspondent to worship God as his conscience and reason directed him, and to keep apart from the Christian Church.

Notwithstanding these obstacles to the reception of the Gospel, there are persons to whom it has come with a Divine sanction, but who are so bound by family and social ties that they do not avow their faith. Striking instances of this failure to act in accordance with conviction have come under my observation. I mention only one. I once had an interview with a dying young Hindu, who had been taught in a mission school and was well acquainted with the Gospel. With tears in his eyes he said all his trust for salvation was in the Lord Jesus Christ, and that he knew it was his duty to avow his faith, but he could not, for if he did his relatives would one and all abandon him. He seemed to dread any one but myself hearing the confession of his faith. I have known others who have had a strong drawing to the Saviour, but they have stifled their convictions, and have become, as I remember with sadness, bitter foes of the truth. Let only the tide set in in favour of Christianity, and many, I doubt not, will be ready to flow with it.

It ought ever to be remembered that in India we have a vast population. In the North-Western Provinces and Punjab alone there is a population twice as large as that of Great Britain and Ireland. Those of this population who may be said to be educated in a high degree are the merest handful. You travel hundreds of miles through regions full of towns, villages, and hamlets, where you find that the partially educated are very few compared with the wholly uneducated many. Even most of the shopkeepers who can keep accounts well are unable to read a book with ease, as the written and printed characters are very different. All know that their English rulers are called Christians; those who live near the great lines of road hear an occasional address from a passing missionary, many frequenters of melas have come under the sound of the Gospel, but the vast majority have not the slightest conception of its meaning. When Christianity had spread to a considerable extent in the Roman Empire, country districts were so little affected by it that *pagani* (villagers) became soon synonymous with "heathen," the only meaning which attaches to the word as it is now used by us. A vast work has to be done before the villagers of Northern India cease to be pagans in our sense of the word. The work of evangelization is only in its initial stage. It is yet with us the day of small things—but it is the day, not the night. The morning has dawned; over a great part of Northern India we can only see the faint streaks of the coming day, but the light will spread, the darkness will vanish, and the millions of that great country will yet be gladdened by the beams of the Sun of Righteousness.

I mention, and merely mention, help which India gives for the solution of some great questions:—

(1) *The immobility of the Eastern mind.* In manner of life, in salutations, in offerings of inferiors to superiors, in many customs, the far East, like the nearer East, continually reminds us of the East as presented in the records of antiquity—above all as presented to us in the Bible. He must be a very careless observer who has not been struck with the resemblance. The restless changing West furnishes in this respect a striking contrast to the staid, unchanging East. There has been no such immobility as to religious opinion and practice. There, as elsewhere, it holds true that man's mind never remains in one stay. The Hindus of the present day speak of their Vedic ancestors with profound reverence, but if they were to rise from their graves and act as they

did when denizens of earth—kill cows, disregard caste, drink largely of the intoxicating juice of the som plant, and worship in an entirely different manner—their reverence would turn into horror and detestation. We cannot say that the modern Puranas do not rest in any degree on the Vedas; some Vedic principles are manifest in them: but in the gods they set forth for worship and in the practices they enjoin, there is between them and the Vedas a marked diversity. The numerous sects which have arisen from time to time among the Hindus show that they too have had that measure of mental activity which has led to new forms of thought and practice.

(2) *The genesis and evolution of religion.* In the dim remote past to which the Vedas introduce us, we find the Hindus a religious, a very religious, people. There is no indication of any period when they could be called secularists. Their religious views and practices have changed, there has been an evolving process; the connection may be traced, and we see the result in the Puranic system of our day. Has this movement been forward, or backward? Has the fittest survived and the weak and useless perished? The Vedic system little deserves the praise often lavished on it, but surely it is preferable to that which has taken its place. There has been deterioration, not improvement. Has not this ever been the case in reference to religion, so far as the working of the human mind is concerned? Is not modern Buddhism a falling off from ancient Buddhism? Does not Rabbinical Judaism belittle and dwarf Old Testament Judaism? Does not Roman Catholic Christianity materialize New Testament Christianity? The facts of man's religious history prove incontestably

that his constant tendency is towards retrogression, not towards advancement.

(3) *Comparative religion.* On this subject elaborate treatises have been written with the object of proving that all religions have had their origin in the human mind, and have been evolved under purely human conditions. Some of the writers, prompted, we may hope, by a devout feeling, allow in vague terms an influence exerted on the evolution by Providential arrangements. Still, in the result we are not to see in any case the effect of a supernatural revelation, but in all cases an approximation in different degrees to truth, secured by the unaided working of the human mind. Does a comparison between the sacred books of the Hindus and the Bible support this view? Listen to a Sanscrit specialist like Professor Max Müller, who has spent years in the study of the Veda, and who has every conceivable motive to say everything he can on its behalf: "That the Veda is full of childish, silly, even to our mind monstrous conceptions, who would deny? But even these monstrosities are interesting and instructive. I could not even answer the question, if you were to ask it, whether the religion of the Veda was polytheistic or monotheistic. Monotheistic in the usual sense of the word it is decidedly not." The dreamy, vague teaching of the Veda has hardened into the unmistakable polytheism and pantheism of modern Hinduism. In no country in the world has mind been more active than in India; in no country have the learned had such abundant leisure, such full opportunity for quiet, sustained thought—and you see the result. We follow with deep interest and sympathy the straining of these minds to understand themselves and the world around; as they grope after God we find they

occasionally obtain a glimpse of the highest truth, but the darkness, though for the moment relieved, is not dispelled. The truth has continued to elude them. They have not arrived at the knowledge of even the first principles of a theology worthy of God, and fitted to direct, purify, and guide man. Excellent, high-toned sentiments are no doubt found in Hindu writings, but these do not alter their general character. The Bible, by its teaching regarding God and man, above all by its record of the peerless excellence of our Lord Jesus Christ, and of the provision made through Him for the supply of man's deepest wants, presents a marvellous contrast to the Veda, to the great epic poems of the Hindus, to their philosophical treatises and their Puranas. I know a good deal of what has been said to show that the characteristics of the Bible may be accounted for on merely human principles, but the certain facts of the case refute, to my mind, the arguments adduced. Max Müller says in one of his writings—I cannot quote his exact words—that we are not to look in the songs of the Veda for anything so advanced as we find in the Psalter. Why not? Had not the Pundits of India far more cultured minds than David and the hymnists of Israel? Their works are different, for their teaching came from different sources. One benefit I have got from my residence in India, a conviction deepened by every successive glimpse into Hindu teaching and practice: that in the Bible we have a supernatural revelation of God's will, and that in building on it we are building on a rock which cannot be shaken.

(4) *The migration of nations.* Few things in the history of the world are more surprising to us than whole nations making their way to new and remote countries. I have

thought I have got a little help towards understanding these movements when I have observed large bands of people—men, women, and children—pursuing their journey, carrying with them all they deemed necessary, and lying out at night on the bare ground, with a blanket, which they had carried over their shoulder, as their only covering. They took food with them when they knew that at their halting-place it could not be procured. Very differently do our native regiments travel. They are attended by a host of camp-followers, and have a formidable amount of baggage. I once saw a party of woodmen in the hills sleeping under a tree when there was frost on the ground; and on the remark being made it was a wonder they could live, a hillman remarked, "Has not each got his blanket? What hardship is there?" When nations migrated they no doubt sent out scouring parties, who seized all the food on which they could lay their hands. When travelling alone in the hills I had commonly with me a tent so small that a man carried it on his head, but I must acknowledge I could not approach the simplicity of the native traveller's arrangements.

CHAPTER XXX.

EUROPEANS IN INDIA.

THE climate of India precludes the possibility of its being a sphere for European colonization. With the exception of the hill districts, the intense heat during the greater part of the year makes out-door occupation trying even to the native, and well-nigh unendurable for Europeans—a heat uncompensated by the coolness of the night, for in the North-West, at least, the stifling closeness of the night is more trying than the heat of the day. If this heat lasted for only a few days, as in Southern Australia, it might be borne, though a hindrance to work; but in India it lasts for months, and it is succeeded by months of drenching rain, during a great part of which the moisture and mugginess are as unpleasant as the previous dry heat had been.

Apart from climate, there is no room for us as colonists. In India we have not to do with rude tribes, as in America, New Zealand, and Australia, and in a measure in Southern Africa, that cannot be said to possess the land over which they and their fathers have long roamed, or of which they have cultivated a very small part. We have to do with ancient nations that have taken full possession of the land by cultivation of the soil, and by pursuit of the arts of civilized life. We find in India no tribes wasting away before the white stranger, but a people growing in number under the security of our government. There are districts in the North-West more densely peopled than any districts in Europe occupied by an agricultural population. The emigration of coolies to the Mauritius, to Bourbon, to the coast of South America, and to the West Indian Islands, has done little to relieve the pressure. Migration to unoccupied parts of Central India and Assam has been carried out to a small extent, and it is very desirable this migration should increase. Non-Aryan tribes occupy a large part of the mountains and forests of Central and Eastern India. They have no wish for accession from the people of the plains, and still less do they wish for the entrance of Europeans. I can say nothing about the mountains of the South, but so far as I have travelled over the sub-Himalayan range in the North there is no place for Europeans in it, except for officials or employers and managers of native labour, such as tea-planters.

While India presents no sphere for European colonization, it presents an increasingly wide field for European agency in the civil and military services, in the departments of education, commerce, manufacture—for instance, of cotton goods, railways, indigo, and tea. In these different departments Europeans are in constant intercourse with natives of every class from the highest to the lowest. There is often much pleasant and courteous intercourse between them ; but in language, habits, religion, in almost everything in which human beings can be separated from their fellows, they are so different that they remain to a great degree strangers to each other, however kindly may be their mutual feeling. English people never call India "home," though they may have lived in it the greater part of their life. This name is always reserved for our fatherland. (I had better say that the term English, as used in India, includes all from Great Britain and Ireland, and to them also the term European is mainly, though not exclusively, applied.) I have heard persons of pure English descent, who had never been out of India, speak of England as "home." The reservation of the word to the land from which we have gone, indicates the fact that in India we are strangers, and cannot cease to be strangers. Colonists in America and other lands may make a similar reservation; but living as they do among their own people, in a country which they expect to be the home of their descendants, the term as applied to England is deprived of much of its endearing force.

In the great Presidency cities, and in a less degree in other cities throughout the country, we have a large educated class of natives, who are well acquainted with our language and literature. They have pursued their studies in the hope of securing good situations, and this hope is in a large measure realized. They are found all over Northern India occupying responsible and well-paid positions. Many persons of this class come daily into close intercourse with Europeans in the discharge of their duties, and have means of knowing them which no other class possesses. The intercourse is generally courteous, in not a few cases friendly, and they talk freely with each other on a great variety of subjects. There is, however, not infrequently an underfeeling with educated natives that they are not sufficiently appreciated—that they do not get the place due to them—that they are treated as an inferior race; and there is consequently a suspiciousness fatal to cordiality. I am far from thinking that Europeans always treat educated natives with the courtesy due to them. I have known instances of marked discourtesy; but I am sure many of our people are bent on treating them with all justice and kindness, and sometimes, at least, this friendly feeling has not been reciprocated. Human nature being what it is, however much we may regret, we need not wonder at the grating between parties that have so much in common, and yet owing to that very circumstance have clashing feelings and interests.

Many native gentlemen, some of the highest rank, cultivate European society, and every European who has anything of the gentleman in him treats them with the courtesy due to their position. Natives of this class are, as a rule, most gentlemanly in their demeanour, and intercourse with them is very pleasant.

Between Europeans and most natives with whom they have to do, there is such a difference of station there is no room for jealousy. To some Europeans they stand in the relation of agents, clerks, and labourers; to a greater number in the relation of servants. In India, as in our own country, there is a great variety in the character of both masters and servants. There, as here, there are hard, selfish, unreasonable masters and mistresses, and there are undoubtedly bad, false, dishonest servants; but I have no hesitation in giving my impression—I may say stating my belief—that native servants are generally well treated, and that this treatment draws forth no small degree of gratitude and attachment. This was strikingly shown in the Mutiny period. Servants often remain for years with the same masters, render most useful and faithful service; their wages are continued in whole or in part during the temporary absence of their masters from India; on their return they are found waiting for them at the port of debarkation, and on final departure for Europe it is not unusual for old Indians to pension those who have been faithful to them. When I speak of faithfulness, I do not mean that, with the exception of very rare cases, full dependence can be placed on their truthfulness, or even on their honesty in the strict sense of the term. It is very difficult for them to resist the temptation to tell a lie, when a fault is to be screened or benefit to be obtained, and there are certain understood perquisites of which they are inclined to avail themselves in too liberal a degree; but they are at the same time very careful to guard the property of their master against all others, and are deeply concerned for the honour of his name. As a rule natives, both servants and others, are treated with less justice and kindness by the lower class of Europeans than by persons better educated and of a higher position. There are indeed soldiers and others who look on "niggers," as they call all natives, with contempt, and are inclined to abuse them, so far as they are permitted, to the full bent of their rude nature. The term "nigger" is used by some who call themselves gentlemen. All I can say of such gentlemen is that I wish they would speak in a manner worthy of the name.

Of late years the position of Englishmen in India has greatly changed. By the overland route, and by the weekly postal communication, England and India are brought near to each other in a degree which could not have been deemed possible in former days. Persons on leave for three months can now spend a month or five weeks with their friends in England, and at the end of their leave be ready to resume their duties. Every week a stream of literature, in the shape of newspapers, periodicals, and books, is poured over every part of India, reaching the European in the most remote part of the land. Hill stations have become very accessible by rail, and to these Europeans betake themselves in great numbers for the hot months. All these things give greater force than ever to the home feeling, by strengthening home sympathies and ties. The result is our people in India are birds of passage as they never were before, ready to return to their own land as soon as circumstances will allow them.

There are some advantages from this altered state of things. Many of the early residents became, to their own deep injury, too intimate with the people of the land. They learned their ways, and became like them in character. It was often said, when the Mutiny broke out, that the officers of native regiments had in former days maintained friendly intercourse with the Sepoys, and thus secured their attachment, and that the cessation, or at least the lessening, of this intercourse was one great cause of the outbreak. If good resulted from it in the weakening of national antipathy, in many cases evil resulted from it in the deterioration of character. Many of our countrymen at an early period formed native connections, and by doing so brought themselves down to the level of their new friends. Some became so entangled that they gave up all thought of returning to their own country. It must not be supposed that all who settled down in India for life were of this character. Some who had kept themselves aloof from all improper connection with natives became so attached to India and to the mode of living there, that they made it their permanent abode. A few of this class remain, but their number is rapidly decreasing, and none are taking their place. The persons who have thus made India their home have often had a large circle of attached native friends.

The constant communication of Englishmen with their native land, frequent visits to it, and the anticipation of getting away from India at the earliest possible period, tends to lessen their interest in Indian affairs, and weaken their sympathy with the native population. The closer connexion with England is, however, attended with some advantages. It can be confidently affirmed that many of our countrymen in India are bent on promoting the good of the people with whom they come into contact, and strive to perform their duties faithfully. We may hope that home influence may strengthen them for the more efficient discharge of their work, and may thus prove a benefit to the people.

In many respects there has been a marked improvement in European society. The small house near the large one, significantly called the Zenana, is never seen near the houses of recent erection. Even in the smaller stations there are places for Christian worship, where Europeans meet on the Lord's Day, when some official reads the prayers of the Church of England, and, if he be a zealous man, a sermon. A chaplain pays occasional visits to these places. The attendance on public worship is far from being what it ought to be, and we have much reason to fear it is often very formal; but it furnishes a pleasing contrast to the neglect which formerly prevailed. Along with this church-going there is, no doubt, a great deal of unbelief in India. I have already said we have in India Christians who are earnest for the honour of their Lord, and do all they can to promote His cause; but the greater number of our people are not, and have never been, friendly to the propagation of the Gospel. I am afraid the unfriendliness has been increased by the sceptical tone of much of the literature of the day. I have known gentlemen giving to their native subordinates for perusal periodicals and books which could only lead them to the conclusion that Christianity was dying out in England.

There are, happily, counteracting influences. Christian as well as sceptical literature makes its way to India, and is telling on many minds. And then, at our larger stations, where Europeans and Eurasians are in the greatest number, more is done for their spiritual benefit than at any previous period. Well may every Christian heartily desire success to all such effort, for nothing would do more to bring the people of the land to the feet of Jesus than the prevalence of living godliness among our own countrymen.

CHAPTER XXXI.

THE GOVERNMENT OF INDIA.

THE first question which comes before us when considering the government of India is, What right have we to govern it? For an answer to this question we must betake ourselves to the history of our connexion with India. This history cannot have for us the interest and fascination of the history of our own country; but it has strong claims on us as the subjects of the British Crown, contains much that deserves and repays perusal, and must be known by us in order to the right understanding of the position we have obtained.

My reading of Indian history leads me to the conclusion that in all likelihood we should never have been rulers in India had we not been grievously injured as traders, in violation of rights accorded to us by the native powers. All know the story of the black hole of Calcutta, which led to our waging war on the Nawab. We had previously fought with the French and French allies in the south, we had contended with other European rivals, but our rule began with the victory of Plassey. After that victory our only alternative was either to leave the country altogether, or to go on conquering till we should become the supreme power over the whole of the continent. If we had retired from the land we had conquered, and had sought to remain as traders, our retirement would have been attributed to weakness, and demands would have been made on us which would have made trading impossible. If we had determined not to advance, but simply to retain what we had acquired, and had satisfied ourselves with repelling attacks, these attacks would have been continued till we had either gone forward, or resigned our conquest altogether

We can understand the course pursued by the founders of the British Empire in India only when we look on them as placed between the alternative mentioned. The Directors of the East India Company did not seek the government of India. They deprecated it. By it commerce was disorganized and dividends lowered. Some of their servants in India made enormous fortunes by the new state of things, but this was no comfort to them. Order after order was sent out against the extension of territory. Governor after governor was commissioned to carry out the peaceful views of the home authorities, but still conquest went on under the direction of these very governors.

I am far from vindicating all that was done; deeds were committed which deserve severe condemnation; but it would be a travesty of history to say that the governors, who set out with peaceful intentions, succumbed to the lust of conquest. They were often forced to adopt war measures. Many instances might be adduced. I give only one. The Marquess of Hastings had denounced the conquering career of the Marquess of Wellesley. He was selected for the very purpose of reversing his policy, so far as it could be reversed. If any person could be trusted for giving peace to India he was the man. Shortly after his arrival our connexion with the Ghoorkhas, the ruling body in Nepal, became strained. They made raids into our territory beneath the hills, and murdered and robbed our subjects. The Marquess was extremely desirous to avoid a rupture with them. Remonstrances were addressed to them, and proposals made to settle differences by the better defining of the boundaries between their country and ours. These proposals were regarded as a proof of weakness, and the bold demand was made we should give up to them the great fertile region north of the Ganges. There was no further hesitation. To yield to this demand, for which there was not the pretext of right, would have been to announce to all the potentates of India that we were unable to defend ourselves, and would have led them to assail us. War was declared, which, after two campaigns and a severe struggle, ended in the discomfiture of the Ghoorkhas, and in their cession to us of the large territory they had conquered a few years previously. Ought the Governor-General to have yielded to the Ghoorkha demand? Yes, if we were prepared to leave the country altogether, but otherwise not.

No sooner had the Marquess of Hastings landed in India than he began to doubt the policy he had formerly advocated, and events soon compelled him to abandon it. The policy on which he acted was declared by him in unmistakable terms: "Our object in India ought to be to render the British Government paramount in effect, if not declaredly so . . . and to oblige the other states to perform the two great feudal duties of supporting our rule with all their forces, and submitting their mutual differences to our arbitration."

Till we became confessedly supreme we were not for

any length of time allowed to remain at peace. There were two main reasons for the unrest, which prepared the way for war. One reason was that the native powers hated and dreaded us, and were eager for our overthrow even when they professed the greatest friendliness. When we were involved in difficulties they were ready to rise against us. Every indication of our desire to avoid hostilities was interpreted as a sign of weakness, and thus became an incentive to the renewal of the struggle. Another reason for the fresh outbreak of war was the treachery of the native princes. I cannot say that in the matter of treaty keeping we had clean hands. The gross deceit played on Omichund, as described by Macaulay in his Essay on Lord Clive, stands nearly alone in our public conduct in India, but other transactions have been unworthy of our character for high-minded integrity. It may, however, be confidently affirmed, that looking at our governing conduct as a whole, it presents by its faithfulness to engagements a marked contrast to the conduct of those who had entered into treaty with us. Many of our Indian wars would have been prevented had there not been on their part the violation of engagements in a manner which showed they never intended to keep them an hour longer than they were compelled by circumstances.

If a review of the course pursued by our people in India shows how we became the governing power, and indicates the ground on which our rule rests, a review of the history of India for ages previous to our advent, and of the condition in which we found it, will help us greatly in answering the question—Has India been benefited or injured by our having seized the sceptre?

For centuries Muhammadans were the rulers of India.

They entered, not to avenge wrongs done to them, but as the servants of Allah, called to put down idolatry, and entitled to rule over the nations they subdued. Centuries elapsed before the extension of their rule beyond the North-West region. Gradually it extended to other parts of India. The seventeenth century was well advanced before the greater part of Southern India came under the rule of the Emperor of Delhi—the Shah-un-shah, King of kings, as he was called. His suzerainty was generally acknowledged in those lands which continued under Hindu rulers.

As we turn over page after page of the Muhammadan rule in India, what scenes of strife, of bloody war, of treachery, of desolated countries, continually meet our view! No sooner did an emperor die than the struggle commenced for the vacant throne between his many sons, brother fighting with brother till one became the victor, and then woe to the vanquished! The governors of Provinces, as soon as they thought they had sufficient power, rebelled against the sovereign, and struggled—not infrequently with success—to secure an independent throne. In the course of these civil wars countries were overrun, towns and villages levelled with the ground, their inhabitants massacred, and their property pillaged. We read of rival dynasties which contended with each other for empire. We are told of terrible invasions like those of Timour and Nadir Shah. There were no doubt great emperors, such as the illustrious Akbar, during whose rule India suffered comparatively little from war, and enjoyed great prosperity. Governors were now and then firm and just rulers. Looking at the whole period of Muhammadan rule, during no part of which India was free from the scourge of war, and during a great part of which war on a large scale was carried on, untold misery must have been endured by many of its inhabitants, and there was little security for life and property. The aristocracy of the emperors' courts was mainly that of office, and only to a limited degree that of blood and ancient possession. We find persons of mean birth rising to greatness, and persons on the very pinnacle of honour cast down to the ground. There was a succession of emperors called Slave Emperors, as they had originally been slaves in the court, whence they rose to supreme power. When we consider the teaching of the Quran respecting those who do not submit to Islam, we may suppose what the condition of the Hindus was under Muhammadan rulers, so far as they acted out their principles. Happily during this period, though constantly exposed to terrible disasters, the people in their villages were often left to manage their own affairs.

When our nation commenced its conquering career in the middle of the eighteenth century, the Muhammadan Empire was in a state of collapse. Within thirteen years of Aurungzeb's death, in 1706, six sovereigns were seated on the imperial throne. Shah Alum was nominal emperor from 1759 to 1806, and all the time he was a wanderer, a prisoner, or a pensioner of the Mahrattas, the Rohillas, or the English. He was as melancholy an example of fallen greatness as can well be conceived, a greatness which retained its title while its bearer was subjected to every indignity. He had been for some time in the hands of the Mahrattas, who used his seal freely, and at the same time treated him with the utmost cruelty. The food supplied was so insufficient that he and his household were almost starved. When Lord Lake took Delhi from the Mahrattas in 1803 he found the poor old blind emperor under a tattered canopy, trembling at what might now befall him. Some years previously his eyes had been gouged out by one of his Rohilla keepers. At once he was treated by us with the highest consideration. Power was not given, but a handsome pension was assigned, and he was personally treated with all the honour due to a reigning sovereign. When these facts are remembered, it is strange we should be charged with overthrowing the Muhammadan Empire in India. Whoever was injured by our conquest, Shah Alum and his family were assuredly benefited.

Our contention was with those whose only claim to rule rested on the sword. Bold adventurers had risen everywhere, and were snatching at the fallen sceptre. There were still emperors, as we have mentioned, and their prestige gave value to documents bearing their seal, but they did not retain a shred of power. Daring Europeans, helped by native allies, had set to carving out principalities for themselves. The viziers and nawabs that ruled in the name of the emperors rendered them neither obedience nor tribute. Our first great battle was fought with Suraj ud Dowla, the Nawab of Bengal, the grandson of Aliverdi Khan, an Afghan adventurer, who had acquired the government of the country. In the South we fought with Hyder Ali, a trooper who gathered under him a marauding band, and by courage and craft rose to being a sovereign, and with his son Tippoo Sahib. Our longest and most severe contests were with the Mahrattas, a warlike tribe of Hindus in Western India, who came first into prominence in the seventeenth century under Sivajee, a petty chieftain, and gradually advanced under various leaders till they became for a time the paramount power. Their hordes of horsemen scoured the country in all directions, north and south, east and west, demanding the *chauth*, the fourth part of the revenue, and returning to their capitals laden with spoil. The leaders with whom we had most to do, sometimes in the way of friendship, far more frequently in the way of warfare, were the Peshwa, the head of the Mahratta confederacy, the heir of Sivajee; Ranojee Bhonsla, a private horseman, who became Prince of Nagpore; Pilajee Gaikwar, a cowherd, who ruled in Baroda; Ranojee Scindia, a menial servant of the Peshwa, who made Gwalior his capital; and Mulhar Rao Holkar, a shepherd, who became Maharajah of Indore. Not one of their number professed to belong to the ancient ruling families of India.

As we glance at India as it was under Muhammadan rule, and consider its state when our conquering career began, we find there were no elements of stable government: the Imperial power had become a shadow; ambitious leaders were everywhere striving for the mastery, ready to beat down all opposition within their own immediate sphere, and then prepared to wrest power from neighbouring chiefs. India had at that time a very dark prospect before it.

This review of the past history of India may seem an unduly long introduction to a brief statement regarding its condition under our rule, but it is only by looking to the past a right answer can be given to the questions: What right have we to govern India? From what evils has our government delivered it? What benefits have we conferred on its population? Inattention to the past has led many to give in some cases an utterly wrong, in other cases a very inadequate, answer to these questions. It is clear that India has been brought under our rule by what may be rightly called aggressive war only to a very limited extent. It is also clear that the hostile forces we encountered were not those of the ancient princes of the land, but of adventurers who were struggling to rise on the ruins of the disorganized empire. At the present time, on the mere ground of the length of possession, our rule has a stronger claim than that of the potentates whom we overthrew.

A review of the past prepares us to see some of the advantages our rule has conferred. No longer are armies marching over India, supplying their wants by the plunder of its people, and leaving ruin in their track. No longer has the husbandman, when he sees at a distance the dust raised by the tramp of the Mahratta cavalry, to flee to his walled village, if he has one to flee to, or to his hamlet if he cannot do better, leaving his field, perhaps ready for the sickle, to be trodden down by the unwelcome stranger. No longer are hosts of marauders like the Pindarees, who scarcely professed to be anything else than marauders, allowed to roam over fertile and populous regions in their robbing and murdering expeditions. No longer are professional robbers called Dacoits allowed to set out on excursions, and make their way under various disguises to towns, to rise at an arranged signal, attack the houses of the rich, and force them, often under torture, to reveal their treasures. No longer are Thugs, professional murderers, left to arrange their plans for insinuating themselves into the goodwill of travellers, with a view, when the opportunity came, to throttling their victims, robbing them, and then burying them, that all mark of their deeds might be effaced. From Dacoity and Thuggery Europeans had nothing to fear, but natives suffered frightfully; and special departments were formed for their suppression. In Northern India, at least, these bands of robbers and murderers have been broken up. No longer are the lives and property of the people at the disposal of their rulers, as was to a large extent the case previous to the British era. They are now under the ægis of law.

If any one think that the advantages thus conferred by the establishment of a stable government are of little value, all we can say is they have no conception of the misery brought on thousands from generation to generation, when these advantages were unknown.

Never was a comparatively small nation entrusted with so vast a work as that committed to us by our undertaking to administer the government of a continent thousands of miles from our shores, inhabited by two hundred and fifty-four millions, who differ widely from us in language, religion, habits, history, associations—in almost everything in which one nation can differ from another. Two hundred millions are under our direct rule, and the rest are under native rulers who acknowledge our Queen as suzerain. It would have been a miracle had we not in the course of our government, during more than a hundred years, done many unwise, many wrong, even many cruel things. He would be a bold man who would stand forth and maintain we had done good, and only good, to the nations of India. We take no such optimist position. You can adduce many things in our dealings with the people which the best of the officials have themselves condemned, and you can mention evils which have followed our rule for which we can scarcely be said to be responsible. This, however, we say with the fullest conviction, as the result of long residence in India and of extensive observation: that considering our position as Western strangers, and the difficulties with which we have had to contend, our Government has had a success far greater than could have been anticipated, and has conferred vast advantages on the country.

It would be difficult to find in the history of the world a more remarkable class of men than those who have been engaged in the administration of India. There have been inefficient, selfish, idle, unprincipled men among them. In former years we used to hear of John Company's bad bargains; and now that India has come directly under the rule of Queen Victoria we now and then hear of John Bull's bad bargains. These have been the exception, not the rule. There has been in succession a band of men who have earnestly sought the good of the people, and have shown a capacity for administration which I have no doubt surprised themselves, as it has those who have watched their progress. Sir John Kaye has given interesting sketches of some Indian worthies, but it would require a series of volumes to record the deeds of the many who have taken a warm interest in the people, have toiled for their good, and have been trusted, and in some instances literally adored, by them. I have had a considerable acquaintance with the *personnel* of the Government of the North-West Provinces, from some occupying the highest position down to assistant magistrates. I cannot say I admired all, but I can say that I have been surprised at the number who did their duty faithfully, were thoroughly interested in their work, and rejoiced when they had achieved any measure of success.

With a few exceptions the Governor-General has been an English nobleman who has filled some important office at home; but Lieutenant-Governors, and not infrequently Governors, have been persons of large Indian experience, who have passed with honour through all the grades of the Civil Service. These, assisted by the Commissioners of Provinces, exercise a strict supervision over the entire administration. Officials have continually to report their doings, and irregularities are quickly discovered. We know of no class who have more onerous duties to discharge than magistrates of districts and their subordinates. They have long hours in crowded courts in an exhausting climate, decide many intricate cases, maintain order within the bounds of their jurisdiction, receive reports of what is being done and give directions, prepare reports for the Government, and they are expected to give a courteous reception to native gentlemen when they call, however long these gentlemen may be inclined to prolong their visit. We have been at times in a position to see the daily life of some of these men, and have been struck with the amount of work devolving on them, and the patience they have shown where there was strong temptation to impatience.

As strangers, it is difficult for us to understand the people, and the result is that with the best intentions we have at times adopted measures utterly unsuited to them. Our very attempt to secure the rights of all classes by the careful drawing up of civil and criminal codes, and by the institution of courts where they are administered, has fostered the litigiousness of the people, and has led to a fearful amount of perjury. Litigiousness got no play where courts did not exist, and perjury could not show itself where witnesses were not examined. It is said that in one of our most recent acquisitions, the Punjab, the people have deteriorated under our rule. Runjeet Singh had no prisons. Thieves caught in the act were maimed and allowed to go their way. Murderers and other great offenders were at once put to death. We can scarcely adopt this primitive mode of maintaining order, and by our codes, courts, judges, and witnesses we have no doubt opened the door to evils of which the Punjab knew nothing in Runjeet Singh's time. If the early colonists of New York and Boston had retained their primitive simplicity, those cities would not now be disgraced by the slums, with their vice, crime, and misery, which make them too closely resemble the cities of the old continent. When society makes progress, new, social, and political, arrangements are indispensable, the countervailing good being much greater than the incidental evils which come in their train.

In India there are Regulation and Non-Regulation Provinces, the Regulation Provinces being those which have been long under our rule, and are subject to all our laws; and the Non-Regulation Provinces being those to which our codes are only partially applied, and where much is left to the discretion of the administrator. In the former the chief offices belong to the regular Civil Service, while in the latter military men as well as civilians are employed. Both classes have furnished most able and capable men.

Considering the resources of India its taxation is heavy. Our Government pays its servants of every description, high and low, civil and military, with a regularity utterly unknown under native rule, and the income must in regularity keep pace with the outlay. When we read of seventy millions as the expenditure, it must be remembered that what is called the land-tax is really rent, for in India the land has always been considered the property of the state. This is kept before the mind of the people of Madras by the yearly assessment of the tenants, and before the people of the North-Western Provinces by the new assessment made every thirtieth year. By the perpetual settlement of Bengal, the tax-collectors were at once raised to the position of land-holders, of which they have often taken undue advantage. It must also be remembered that a considerable sum is expended on remunerative works, such as canals and railways. The expenditure on the army is great. I cannot conceive why our Government keeps up so large a native army. It would appear to those who are outside the Government circle, that its reduction would conduce to safety as well as to economy. The European part of the army is comparatively very small, and it would be most perilous to lessen it. Years before the Mutiny, Sir Henry Lawrence said it was the backbone of our strength, and events proved how true his remark was. Yet it is, and must continue to be, very expensive, like every other form of European agency. The Mutiny among its other results left behind it heavy pecuniary responsibilities, which have added to the debt and led to increased taxation. Many are of opinion that the amalgamation of the Royal and Indian armies was an unwise measure, and has caused much unnecessary expense. Often complaints have been made that successive home Governments, from their unchallenged control over the affairs of India, have imposed an unjust burden on its resources by keeping at home too large a force at its expense, and by undue charges for stores sent out, as well as by making it pay sums which were more properly due by the imperial exchequer.

"The net land revenue has risen in the ten years beginning 1870–71 from £20,335,678, or nearly half the total net revenue of £42,780,417, by about two millions sterling, to £22,125,807, with a total net revenue of £49,801,664. The gross revenue of the latter year, 1879–80, was £68,484,666, the difference being derived from sources other than taxation, such as the opium monopoly. The revenue of 1880–81 was £72,920,000, and the gross expenditure £71,259,000. Including the land revenue as land-tax, the 200 millions in the twelve Provinces of British India pay about 4s. a head of imperial taxation, besides municipal or local and provincial cesses, which purchase such local advantages as roads, schools, police, and sanitary appliances. This incidence of taxation varies from 5s. 6d. per head of the land-owning classes to 3s. 3d. for traders, 2s. for artisans, and 1s. 6d. for agricultural labourers. The fiscal policy of the Government has of late been to reduce the burden of the salt monopoly, which is a poll-tax, and to abolish import duties. The 54½ millions in the Native States pay only to their own chiefs, who enjoy a net annual revenue of fourteen millions sterling, and pay £700,000 as tribute, or less than the cost of the military and political establishments maintained on their account" (Dr. George Smith's "Geography of British India"). Deducting land-tax, opium, railways, irrigations, post-office, and suchlike remunerative services, the taxation is reduced to 2s. per head of population.

If the European army in India be the backbone of our military sway, European administrators are, I believe, the backbone of our government. During the terrible years 1857 and 1858, the services rendered by those who were engaged in civil employment were of the highest value in restoring peace to the distracted country, and in re-establishing our government. European officials of every grade showed equal zeal and determination. There were many native officials in these Provinces, some of them highly paid and greatly trusted. A few remained faithful and did good service, though the help rendered, when summed up, cannot be reckoned great. Many proved unfaithful, and some became our bitter enemies. If instead of Englishmen as judges, magistrates, and collectors, we had had at that time highly educated natives of Bengal holding these offices, the men who receive for themselves the best hearing in England, can we suppose that, however well inclined, they could have borne the brunt of the contest, and aided largely in securing the victory? It would ill become me to speak against these men. I know some of the class for whom I have not only a high esteem but warm affection. Among them there are not a few who are great in attainment, keen in intellect, and strong in purpose to do the right. Still I do not think they themselves would maintain they have the physical courage, the firm mental calibre, the moral strength, and the high place in the confidence of the community, which would qualify any of their number to occupy the position of Governor-General, Governor, Lieutenant-Governor, and Chief Commissioner, or would make it desirable they should form the leading body of the administrative staff. The successful candidates for the Civil Service have come, we believe, exclusively from the highly-educated youth of the Presidency cities, between whom and the millions of their own Provinces there is no such bond as unites the so-called leaders of the Irish with the majority of their countrymen. In the other countries of India they are little known, and are regarded with no special interest.

Many mistakes would be prevented if English people would remember that we have in India nations differing widely from each other. We have a striking illustration of this fact in the part of India in which we have lived. Bengalees abound in the public offices in the North-West Provinces and in the Punjab. They are deemed sharper in intellect, and are better educated, than the Hindustanees, and on account of their superior education they have got situations which would have been filled by natives of the country, had their educational acquirements been equal. These Bengalees are not strangers in these Provinces to the same extent as Englishmen, but they are strangers, and are looked upon as such by the people. Where they are numerous they keep mainly to themselves, and however friendly they may be with Hindustanees they are regarded as belonging to another country. When you meet them you know them at once by their look, dress, language, and habits. A part of Benares, called Bengalee Tola—Bengalee district—is inhabited almost wholly by Bengalees, and when you enter it you feel you have come among another people, who speak a different language and present a different appearance. During the Mutiny they were regarded in the North-West with suspicion, as half-English, and many were happy to seek shelter where we were able to keep our footing. If the question was put in Hindustan Proper to any large body of people—Would you have Bengalees or Englishmen for your magistrates and judges? I think in most places the well-nigh unanimous response would be, The Englishman.

If my opinion is to rest on my own observation, I would confidently say that notwithstanding the injustice and unkindness charged against some English officials, the people generally have profound trust in our justice—in our *insaf*—and as a rule, except when they think the native partial to themselves, they prefer to have their cases tried where an Englishman presides. When on a journey I once came up to two men engaged in eager talk. I heard them use frequently the words, *Ungrez* and *Insaf*—*Englishmen* and *Justice*—and on stopping I heard the one telling the other of the bribes taken by native officials in a case he had, and of the justice done when the Englishman took it up. He ended with the words, " What a wonderful people for *insaf* these English are ! " to which remark the other man assented. I thanked them for their good opinion, and held on my way.

If the administration of India in its present state must, in its chief offices, remain in the hands of Europeans, it must be expensive. The great officers of state, considering the dignity they have to maintain and the establishments they have to keep, must he highly paid. When we think of the qualifications required by those who are charged with the ordinary administration, the great expense to which they are put, the years they spend in laborious work in an exhausting climate, and their unfitness as a rule for work in England on their retirement, I do not think their income or pension can be to any large extent safely or justly reduced. The era of nabobs, returning with vast wealth to astonish the English people, has long since passed away. These men had small pay, but great perquisites. The pay has been greatly increased, but the perquisites are gone, and India has benefited vastly by the change.

Indian magistrates have much to tell of the litigiousness of the people, their constant attempts to overreach each other, the carefully woven lies which they have daily to unravel, the trust put in bribes to influence decisions, and the deeply ingrained notion in the minds of native officials that they should get more for their services to the public than the bare pay, the *sookha tulub—dry wages*—as it is contemptuously called.

The people of Northern India are mainly agricultural, and they are unquestionably poor. Our very success has in one aspect tended to their impoverishment. With very few exceptions they marry young, and during the many years of peace which have passed over them, with the exception of the short sharp crisis of the Mutiny, the population has greatly increased. Whenever an epidemic breaks out, means are at once employed to check it. There is a vaccination department for the purpose of preventing the ravages of small-pox. Female infanticide, which had prevailed to a frightful extent among certain castes, has been diminished, though not, it is feared, wholly suppressed. It is well known that famines have been sadly destructive of life, but there is evidence that previous to our rule, when there were few roads and little communication between one part of India and another, famines were still more so. Among so vast a population directly dependent on the soil, in a country where rain is so indispensable, and is now and then a failure, we have too much reason to fear famines may yet recur; but such provision is now made against their ravages, that it is hoped the catastrophes of the past will be escaped.

It is believed that, as the result of the new order of things, India at the present time has by many millions a larger population than it ever had previously. Mention has been made of the improvement effected in the Province of Kumaon; and other parts of India present instances of equally successful administration, but the area of new cultivation has not kept pace with the increase of population. It is sad that so many of the people should be underfed. In our own country and in Ireland this question of sufficient food for the entire population is one of the pressing difficulties of the day. Much is within the power of people themselves to improve their condition. We know it is so at home, and it is so in India. There, there is a vast body of sturdy beggars, under the guise of religious devotees, who feed on the people. Lending and borrowing go on at a most hurtful rate. If a person finds himself possessed of some twenty or thirty rupees, he either puts it into jewels for the female members of his family, or lends it at an exorbitant rate of interest. It has sometimes seemed as if creditors and debtors included the entire population. Debt, not by law but by custom, is hereditary, and a man is expected to pay the debts of his grand-parents. Marriage expenses are so heavy, that very often a debt settles down on a man on his marriage day under which he lies till the day of his death. Government has done much to induce leading men to bind themselves to a moderate expenditure on the occasion of marriages, in the hope that the example might prevent the unreasonable and pernicious profusion of the marriage season. If the habits of the people were changed the pressure of poverty would be greatly lightened.

There is much room for improvement in the incidence of taxation. The land-tax, we may say the land-rent, is the main source of revenue, but it is alarming to think of dependence on the opium monopoly for the millions it contributes. Intoxicating drugs are largely used in India, and among them opium holds the favourite place. Permission to the people to grow and manufacture opium for themselves would be as hurtful as permission to distil whiskey and gin would be to our country. It is devoutly to be wished the present system may come to an end, and that in its place a fiscal system be adopted similar to that of England in reference to alcoholic drinks. In reference to spirits, every effort should be made to discourage their sale, however much the revenue may suffer in consequence. The salt-tax has been so productive that it has been kept up in a manner which has borne heavily on the people. It has been reduced, and it is hoped that it will be reduced still further.

Regarding some of the questions at present much discussed, I can only say that every friend of India, I may say every friend of justice, must desire that the people be largely entrusted with the management of their own affairs, that local government be encouraged, and every facility given to the admission of natives, so far as they are qualified, into the rank of administrators. Much is being done in this direction, and still more will be done in the future. The police has been improved, but it stands much in need of further improvement.

Happy changes were expected from the assumption by the Queen of the direct government of India. Progress has been made since that time, but I do not think it is in any large measure owing to the change. For some time previously increased attention was given to the sanitation of towns, the improvement of roads, the laying out of market-places, the planting of public gardens, the building of hospitals, dispensaries, and town houses. Many wealthy natives, stirred up by magistrates, have contributed liberally to these improvements. Of late years these works have been carried on with increasing zeal. In 1877 we saw some of the principal towns in Northern India, and were struck with the contrast they presented to their condition during the early years of our residence. The filthiest place in Benares, which almost sickened me every time I came near it, is now a beautiful garden, with a fine town-house attached to it. The very bulls of Benares have been got rid of. No longer are these brutes encountered in the streets.

My readers will observe that I am far from agreeing with those who describe our rule in India as an unmixed blessing to its inhabitants. It is undeniable that our rule, because foreign, lies under great disadvantages. I am still farther removed from agreement with the extremely pessimist views which are sometimes advanced. The history of India rebuts the assertion that we have acquired our sovereignty mainly by fraud; and whatever may be said of other parts of India, no one acquainted with Bengal and the North-Western Provinces can say that he has there seen "the awful spectacle of a country inhabited only by officials and peasants." When one thinks of the atrocious crimes, upheld by religious sanctions, such as suttee and infanticide, which we have put down in the face of determined opposition and even threats of rebellion from the most honoured classes of the community, it is strange to be told that "before we went the people were religious, chaste, sober, compassionate towards the helpless, and patient under suffering," and that we have corrupted them. We are told that "while we have conferred considerable advantages, the balance is wofully against us." As the result of long residence in India, and of reading about India, I have come to the conclusion the balance is immensely in our favour.

All friends of India desire the improvement of its government, and the increasing welfare of its people. Whence is the improvement to come? We are told "nothing is to be hoped for from the Indian official class." From whom is anything to be hoped for? From the Home Government? The leaders of our political parties have passed measures beneficial to India, but they have again and again taken advantage of its helplessness to impose on it burdens to which it ought not to have been subjected. Are we to look to the people at home for relief? How difficult is it to secure attention to the subject, or to make them understand it when their attention is gained! Are we to look to the non-official class in India? I have nothing to say about the Ilbert Jurisdiction Bill, except that while officials have been divided about it, many of the most eminent being in its favour, non-officials almost to a man have been bitterly opposed to it. Where I have spent the greater part of my life, nothing has been more common than complaints by Europeans of injustice done to them by partiality shown to natives at their expense. Are we to look to the great landholders, bankers, merchants, shopkeepers, and well-to-do classes in the cities of Bengal and the North-West, who have benefited most by our rule? What may be expected from them is illustrated by the fact that when the finances were thrown by the Mutiny into confusion, many protested against an income tax, and some of high position proposed that the finances should be rectified by an increase of the salt-tax! In these influential classes there are high-minded and benevolent individuals, but if we look at them in their collective capacity we shall be disappointed. When we look at the long roll of distinguished Indian officials, mark their achievements, hear their protests against what they deemed hurtful measures, and their advocacy of beneficial changes, I think we find in them India's warmest friends, who have done it the most signal service, and from whom more can be expected than from any other class.

There are ample materials for arriving at correct views regarding the condition of India and the way in which it is governed. No Parliamentary Committee, no Royal Commission, is required to elicit the facts. The recently completed "Gazeteer" of India, in which Dr. Hunter and his assistants had been engaged for years, furnishes full and reliable information. The state of India is described in that imperial work with a frankness and fulness which leave nothing to be desired. If one of our great writers, who has secured the ears of our country, would set to the drawing up of a volume of moderate size, founded on the "Gazeteer," showing in a readable interesting form what has been done and what has been left undone, what has been done well and what has been done ill, and if the intelligent people of our country could be induced to give it a careful perusal, untold good would be done both to England and to India. Nothing would please Indian officials more than the eye of England being thus fixed on their doings and misdoings, that the whole truth might be known, and praise and censure be justly distributed, and still more that the changes most beneficial to the people might be effected.

It is undeniable, as already said, that our rule because foreign lies under great disadvantages. When the ancestors of the present Hindus crossed the Indus and gradually made their way into the Continent before them, they subdued and to a great degree enslaved its inhabitants. For many a day their rule was foreign. This was also the case with the successive Muhammadan conquerors. Rule founded on the suffrages of the people remains to the present day unknown. There is, however, this difference between the previous rulers of India and the English, that they remained in the country, and gradually became amalgamated with its inhabitants, while we show no disposition to make India our home. As we do not, it would be far better if Hindustanees were the rulers of Hindustan, Bengalees of Bengal, the members of other Indian nations of their respective nations, provided they were qualified by character, attainments, and the estimate entertained of them by the ruled, with a strong central power to secure order throughout the Continent, while leaving unfettered the general administration. Towards this ideal strenuous efforts should be directed; but when we look at India as it is now, with its divergent and antagonistic elements, with the weakness induced by ages of superstition and despotism, what a long road has it to travel before it can reach this goal! The question, then, is not what is absolutely best, but what is practicable. Thus regarded, we are shut up to the continuance of our rule. Every friend of India must desire that it may be improved in every possible way, so that it may be in an increasing degree a blessing to its teeming population.

No one can predict the future of India. Within its borders there are many who for various reasons would be delighted with our overthrow, while I believe the vast majority in the parts of India I know best would deprecate our departure as a dire calamity. It is a notable fact that when our own native soldiers, sworn to uphold our rule, rose fiercely against us, and rebellion in many districts followed in the wake of mutiny, not a single native prince of the highest rank availed himself of the opportunity to throw off the suzerainty of our Queen. The army of the Prince of Gwalior rose against us, but by doing so they rebelled against their own sovereign. When in 1877 we were in a native state in Rajputana, a gentleman, who knew well the temper of the people, said that if our control was withdrawn the Rajputs and Mahrattas would be at each other's throats in a month. Our army has something better to do than to uphold an alien government. It has to prevent the outbreak of war which would desolate India from one end to the other. Happily its prestige is sufficient to avert this terrible evil, but the prestige can only continue while the army exists. By the suppression of the Mutiny our prowess was shown in a manner which has made an indelible impression. It is scarcely conceivable we can again have to encounter a similar outbreak, though trouble may come from unanticipated quarters. Our immensely improved means of communication contribute largely to our security. Good government, the conferring of manifest benefits on the people, will do more to establish our rule than all other things combined. It is obvious to all who have any just conception of our position in India, that never was a nation charged with greater responsibilities, never was such a tremendous task committed to a people, and never was there a more urgent call for the highest qualities, if the duties devolving on us are to be worthily discharged. Our Government cannot, and ought not, to undertake its evangelization, but if the work of government be rightly done, it will indirectly, but very effectually, help the Christian Church in giving the Gospel to the millions of India, which, when accepted by them, will purify and elevate their character, improve their condition, and fit them for true, healthy, national life, while securing their spiritual and eternal good.

STATISTICS.

Area of India and British Burma, 1,495,574 sq. miles.
Population in 1881, 254,899,516.

Under British rule		197,815,508
Under Native rule		57,084,008
Hindus		187,931,450
Muhammadans		50,127,585
Buddhists—almost entirely in British Burma		3,418,884
Sikhs		853,426
Aborigines—mainly Demon worshippers		6,426,511
Christians—		
Europeans [1]	142,000	
Eurasians	62,000	
Protestant Native Christians [2] ...	492,882	
Roman Catholics	865,643	
Syrians—about	300,000	
		1,862,525
Other Creeds not specified		4,479,135

The increase of the Native Christian community connected with Protestant Missions from 1851 to 1861 was 53 per cent.; from 1861 to 1871, 61 per cent.; and

[1] Including 65,000 British soldiers.

[2] Including 75,510 in British Burma, but not the 35,708 in Ceylon.

from 1871 to 1881, 86 per cent. The number of communicants rose from 14,000 in 1851 to 113,000 in 1881. Within the last decade the number of native ordained agents has risen from 225 to 461; of native lay preachers from 1,900 to 2,400; of native Christian teachers from 1,900 to 3,400; of native Christian female agents from 800 to 1,600. The number of male pupils in Mission schools in 1851 was 50,000; in 1881, 129,000. The female pupils increased within that period from 11,000 to 56,000. The increase in Zenana pupils was from 1,900 in 1871 to 9,100 in 1881.

UNWIN BROTHERS, THE GRESHAM PRESS, CHILWORTH AND LONDON.